MENLO SCHOOL
· MENLO COLLEGE ·
founded 1915

Gift of

Mr. David H. Osborne

Also by David G. Green

Power and Party in an English City
Mutual Aid or Welfare State
Working-Class Patients and the Medical Establishment

The New Conservatism

The Counter-Revolution in Political, Economic and Social Thought

David G. Green

St. Martin's Press
New York

David G. Green, 1987

First published in the United States of America in 1987

Printed in Great Britain

ISBN 0–312–00477–X

Library of Congress Cataloging-in-Publication Data

Green, David G.
  The New Conservatism.
  Bibliography: p.
  Includes Index.
  1. Liberalism—United States. 2. Libertarianism—
United States. 3. Laissez-faire. 4. United States—
Politics and Government—1981–   . 1. Title.
JC599.U5G69 1987   320.5'12'0973   86–27878
ISBN 0–312–00477–X

Dedicated to
My Mother

Contents

Tables

Preface

Thanks are due to a number of colleagues who read and commented on the book. I am very grateful to Lord (Ralph) Harris and Arthur Seldon for their helpful comments, and particular thanks are due to John Burton for helping me to avoid error in the discussion of monetarism. I am especially grateful to Ray Robinson. Reading other people's manuscripts is a pretty terrible chore at the best of times, but to do it for an adversary was well beyond the call of duty. Special thanks are equally due to Peter Saunders, who also commented on the book from the standpoint of someone not wholly convinced by the new liberal case. I have considerable sympathy for a good deal of the new liberalism, and I was therefore particularly grateful to Peter Saunders and Ray Robinson for drawing my attention to occasional passages which seemed too supportive. I must also thank Norman Dennis; John Gray for characteristically valuable comments on Chapter 5; Norman Barry for equally useful criticisms of Chapters 5 and 1; and Chris Tame, particularly for his comments on anarcho-capitalism.

I apologise to them all for not having always had the good sense to take their advice. I need hardly add that they share no blame for remaining inadequacies.

Finally, thanks are due to Ken Smith, the IEA's librarian, Miss Shila Shah, who typed the manuscript, Kathy Smith, who typed the bibliography, my wife, Catherine, who helped with proof reading and the preparation of the index, and my daughter, Elizabeth, who also helped to prepare the index.

St Neots, May 1986

Introduction

The radical right, libertarianism, supply-side economics, the taxpayers' revolt, monetarism, Thatcherism, Reaganomics, the new right, the new conservatism—these are some of the labels given to the body of argument offered in recent years as a challenge to the post-war consensus. Keynesian demand management has been challenged by monetarism and supply-side economics; egalitarian redistribution has been questioned by an alternative individualist view in which property is the right of everyone who is prepared to work, not the privilege of a few; the assumption that radicals should automatically look to the state as the chief instrument of reform has been challenged by a new-found faith in self-help and the power of the voluntary association; belief in the competence and unselfish motivation of public servants has been brought into doubt by the public choice school; the deterioration of modern democracies into elective dictatorships exposing the state machine to sectional abuse and sharpening social divisions has been attacked; constitutional reform to maintain democracy without granting unlimited power to the majority of the moment has been forcefully advocated; and the value of competition as a device for discovering hitherto unknown ways of meeting human needs and tending to encourage the sovereignty of the consumer has been asserted.

The challenge of the 'new conservatism' has been issued, not only to public policy makers, but across the social sciences: economics, sociology and political science.

There is no unified new conservative view, although new conservative thinkers lie in the common tradition of western classical liberalism.

This revival of interest in the liberal tradition began to attract critical attention from the mid 1960s onwards and gathered pace throughout the 1970s. In America the term 'new right' was applied to the ideas on which Ronald Reagan contested the California governorship in 1966. In Britain David Collard, in a Fabian Society pamphlet published in 1968, was among the first to label the new liberals the 'new right'. And in Britain the term 'new right' has become the established label. In America adherents of the new thinking often call themselves libertarians to indicate that they lie in the classical liberal tradition without inviting confusion with the 'liberal' politics of Edward Kennedy. At least since the New Deal, a liberal in America is a collectivist who wants to extend the power of the state into ever more corners of national life. Others in the new tradition prefer the label 'conservative' because 'libertarian' implies some sympathy with the full-blooded hostility to all state power which characterises the anarcho-capitalists. Still others, not wanting to relinquish their rightful links with the classical liberal tradition, prefer the label 'Adam Smith liberal'. There is, therefore, no automatically obvious term of convenience by which to refer to the revival of interest in classical liberal thought. In Britain the 'new right' is the best approximation, but in America the 'new conservatism' is probably the better choice. Hence it forms the title of this book. However, because it is not wholly suitable and because what we are witnessing is a revival of classical liberalism, from Chapter 2 onwards I shall try to avoid using the term 'new conservatism'. For the most part, I shall speak of the 'new liberalism', or the 'liberal tradition'.

This book introduces the non-specialist reader to the thinking of the 'new conservatives'. Part I explains the historical roots of the new philosophy and describes the central themes of each school within it. Six main schools are distinguished. Chapter 2 considers three traditions which, beginning from a natural rights standpoint, arrive at different conclusions. The first is anarcho-libertarianism, which denies that there is any legitimate role for government, even in the maintenance of law and order. The second is the minimal statism of Robert Nozick, the only libertarian philosopher to receive wide attention from the academic community. He holds that the government may maintain a framework of laws, but no more. The third tradition is Ayn Rand's 'objectivism'. Chapter 3 describes the classical economics tradition, represented today by Milton Friedman and the Chicago School. Economics is seen largely as the science of wealth creation, and 'capitalism' is viewed as a vital bulwark of personal freedom, though Chicago economists allow a much wider role for the state than do natural rights theorists. Chapter 4 considers the public choice school, which is noted for its application of classical liberal insights to the study of the behaviour of governments. Chapter 5 discusses the work of Friedrich Hayek. Each chapter in Part I concludes with a 'guide to reading' which directs the reader to the secondary literature, with particular emphasis on critical sources.

Part II considers the political agenda of the new liberalism and its impact on public policy.

At first sight it might seem that two other traditions of thought ought to have been included. The first is conservatism, in the British sense of that term. Its dislike of socialism implies a close affinity with the classical liberal tradition, but this is misleading, for conservatives often dislike liberalism as much as socialism. Conservatism, writes Roger Scruton, one of the leaders of modern conservative thought, 'arises directly from the sense that one belongs to some continuing, and pre-existing social order, and that this fact is all important in determining what to do' (1984, p. 21). Conservatives do not oppose all change: 'The desire to conserve is compatible with all manner of change, provided only that change is also continuity' (ibid., p. 22). No society should be made to fit some preordained pattern or set of purposes: 'The subjection of politics to determining purposes, however "good in themselves" those purposes seem, is, on the conservative view, irrational' (ibid., pp. 23–4).

The conservative rejects the appeal to 'social justice' favoured by socialists and to 'freedom' made by liberals: 'The conservative, unable as he is to appeal to a utopian future, or to any future that is not, as it were, already contained in the present and the past, must avail himself of conceptions which are both directly applicable to things as they are and at the same time indicative of a motivating force in men.' This force must be as great as the desire for freedom and social justice offered by the conservative's opponents. In place of freedom and social justice he offers three alternative values: authority, allegiance and tradition (ibid., p. 27).

Tradition embodies the wisdom of past generations, and by allegiance he means a bond that is 'transcendent not contractual', like the family or a sense of patriotism (ibid., p. 45). But it is the conservative view of authority which most fundamentally differs from the liberal standpoint. For the conservative, 'the value of liberty is not absolute, but stands subject to another and higher value, the authority of established government.' It is 'through an ideal of authority that the conservative experiences the political world': 'The state has the authority, the responsibility, and the despotism of parenthood' (ibid., pp. 19, 111). Its power should be enforced in the face of every influence that opposes it. But, he adds, it should not be arbitrary. It should be constitutional and civilised. The conservative does not support the 'minimal state'. It is 'possible for the conservative as it is for a socialist to be, should the need arise, "totalitarian"' (ibid., p. 33).

There is, according to Scruton, no 'logical identity' between conservatism and capitalism, but the right to private property should be upheld (ibid., p. 94). This is not because the conservative is concerned with the creation of wealth, but because property is 'necessarily a part of the process whereby man frees himself from the power of things, transforming resistant nature into compliant things. Through property man imbues his world with will, and begins therein to discover himself as a social being' (ibid., p. 99). Scruton explicitly rejects the classical liberal view that economic affairs are self-regulating. On the contrary, the 'posture of the state is all-important, and that without the state's surveillance, destitution and unemployment could result at any timc' (p. 113).

The character of the conservative standpoint reveals how misleading it is to view politics as a left-right continuum. If any simplification is permissible it would be more accurate to view political disputation as a conflict between three distinct perspectives: conservative, liberal and socialist. At any given moment the particular allegiances of party and faction are likely to draw on more than one of these standpoints, but the three positions remain no less distinct for that.

Put at the simplest level possible, each philosophy is based on a single principle governing how we should act. Conservatism, as the term is understood in Britain, dislikes abstract ideas, preferring to remain firmly rooted in the concrete traditions of nation, locality and family. For this reason it can with some justice be said that there is no general *theory* of conservatism, only particular conservatisms. The liberalism of Adam Smith by contrast, tends to mistrust tradition and prefers to judge any given social order against the yardstick of universal ideas, and in particular against one central idea—individual freedom. It is, more than anything else, a theory about the proper scope of government. Socialism centres on social class. It is a doctrine which, above all, takes sides by championing that group seen as the underdog in the concrete circumstances of the time—the working class, the poor, the disabled, ethnic minorities. Socialism is often articulated as a general search for a universal ideal—social justice—but this ideal is always interpreted as the pursuit of the interests of some identifiable group at the expense of some other group.

Among these three philosophies it is liberalism that lies at the heart of the thinking of those academics who have become collectively known as the 'new right'. Traditional conservatism, therefore, lies properly outside the scope of this volume.

The second school of thought which might have been discussed in this book is American 'neo-conservatism'.

This is the name given to the group of scholars organised around the journal *The Public Interest*. Its leaders are Nathan Glazer, Irving Kristol, Robert Nisbet, Seymour Martin Lipset, Daniel P. Moynihan, Daniel Bell and James Q. Wilson. These neo-conservatives are excluded from this book because most of them began as collectivists and despite modifying their views remain collectivistic. Seymour Martin Lipset has described the neo-conservatives as 'a group of people who were once actively involved in liberal or radical left politics and who, while not abandoning their concerns for equality, feel that the current political scene has interposed other threats to freedom and equality.... A neo-conservative believes that the experiences of the past four decades indicate that the standard liberal [i.e. collectivist in the American sense of the term] solutions to problems—increasing government involvement, regulation, and expenditures—have frequently created more problems than they've solved.' They differ from 'plain' or 'old-fashioned' conservatives in that most neo-conservatives continue to believe in the left's welfare values and in greater enforced equality (Horowitz and Lipset, 1978, pp. 45–6).

In *Reflections of a Neo-Conservative* (1983) Irving Kristol identifies the chief features of neo-conservatism. It is, he says, anti-romantic, looking upon romanticism as 'one of the chief plagues of our age'. Neo-conservatives do not think that liberal-democratic capitalism is the 'best of all imaginable worlds', but they do believe it is the 'best, under the circumstances, of all possible worlds'. This, Kristol believes, distinguishes them from both the 'old right' and the 'new right'.

Neo-conservatives value economic growth for its contribution to economic and political stability, but they are not libertarian in the sense that Friedman and Hayek are: 'A conservative welfare state—what was once called a social-insurance state—is perfectly consistent with the neo-conservative perspective. So is a state that takes a degree of responsibility for helping to shape the preferences that people exercise in a free market—to "elevate" them, if you will.' People, believes Kristol, want their preference to be 'elevated'. The political movement which 'prescribes massive government intervention in the marketplace but an absolute *laissez-faire* attitude towards manners and morals, strikes neo-conservatives as representing a bizarre inversion of priorities'. Family and religion are 'indispensable pillars of a decent society' (1983, pp. 75–7).

As this brief account shows, the American neo-conservatives have been at pains to distinguish between their ideas and the thinking of Friedman and Hayek, which lies at the heart of the new liberal tradition. I have therefore excluded the neo-conservatives from this account of the modern liberal revival.

Part I
THE NEW LIBERALISM IN THEORY

1 The Liberal Tradition

How did western liberalism originate? It has its roots in the religious, political and economic reaction to the 'old order'—the medieval communalism dominant in the sixteenth and early seventeenth centuries.

SEVENTEENTH-CENTURY ROOTS

During the Middle Ages most aspects of life were regulated by communal bodies: agriculture by the village courts, industry by the craft guilds, commerce by merchant guilds at home and trading companies in foreign dealings.

The Village: The village community of the late Middle Ages was a partnership. The occupiers of the soil each had strips spread throughout the open fields combined with rights to use the waste land or common meadow land. Particular practices varied. If there was a single lord of the manor, customary practice was enforced through manorial courts and the lord's officials; or if there was no single lord, affairs were conducted much in the manner of the villages of Wymeswold and Wigston in Leicestershire. Key decisions about the rotation of crops, timing of ploughing, sowing and reaping, allocation of meadows, management of the common waste land, rights of way, rules for hedging, and the maintenance of roads and paths, were taken by a meeting of the whole village. Infringements of village decisions were punished by the imposition of fines payable to the parish church (Hoskins, 1965, p. 97). Thus in many villages individuals were denied complete individual control of their land, although they might have had a say in reaching the common decision.

The Town: The town was also corporate in character. Each branch of trade or industry was governed by a guild of merchants or craftsmen. This was partly the product of royal policy. The Crown had granted charters to boroughs conferring monopolies and other privileges in return for taxes. Townsmen tended to confine participation in their privileges to those who shared in the fiscal burden, and therefore strongly resented attempts by non-taxpaying outsiders to compete with them. Guilds regulated all aspects of the artisan's life. They not only controlled wages, hours, output and prices, but also had religious functions, an educational role, and assisted in the settlement of disputes.

Economic Individualism
During the sixteenth and seventeenth centuries conflict between the forces of tradition and the forces of change was intensifying, and by 1550 the communalism of both the villages and towns was beginning to break down. In the villages there was conflict between supporters of the field system and those who wanted to consolidate landholdings in order to turn from arable farming to sheep production. In the towns the restrictions on competition imposed by the guilds led many traders and artisans to move outside the historic boroughs to set up business in outlying villages and hamlets where the guilds had no power.

These changes might have proceeded in a piecemeal manner had it not been for the policy of the Tudor and Stuart monarchs. In agriculture, industry and commerce they set themselves, in the name of tradition, firmly against the rising individualism. They resisted, albeit rather weakly, the demands for rural enclosure. Most legislation affecting the commerce of the period from the 1550s until the Puritan revolution of the 1640s sought to put fetters on the rising individualism, usually by turning local customs or the practices of the municipal boroughs into national laws. Wages were controlled by law. The Statute of Apprentices (or Artificers) of 1563 empowered JPs to fix maximum wages calculated to 'yield unto the hired person both in the time of scarcity and in the time of plenty a convenient proportion of wages'. Later James I laid down a minimum wage law.

The 1563 Act also required that no one could be employed for less than a year at a time and employers were prevented from laying off men in times of depression. In the serious downturn in the wool trade between 1620 and 1624, the Privy Council, for instance, ordered employers to keep men on. The Statute of Artificers also required employers to hire only men who had served an apprenticeship, thus restricting entry to many trades.

The government laid down rules prescribing which materials could be used and which mechanical appliances were appropriate for many industries, but especially for the most important of all industries at the time, wool. Prices were fixed from time to time for cloth, silks, ales, wines, tea and especially bread and coal. Royal monopolies were granted across a wide range of industries: in 1621 there were around 700 (Hill, 1978, p. 38).

Religious Individualism
In religion, as well as in economics, there was a rising tide of individualism. The Reformation in Europe followed Luther's protest against the sale of indulgences in 1517. In England it began in the reign of Henry VIII when papal authority was renounced in 1534. Our interest focuses on the individualist religious sects which grew in importance during the sixteenth century. These sects, which came to be called Independents, asserted that individual believers did not need intermediaries between them and God. Priests were unnecessary; the individual had the prime responsibility for his or her own spiritual destiny.

Religious individualism stood in sharp contrast to the Catholic tradition in which sacraments were central. Sacraments—such as baptism, confirmation, the eucharist, penance, extreme unction, orders and matrimony—were ceremonies regarded as outward signs of inner grace or merit. For the Catholic, this was how piety was demonstrated. But this was anathema to the Protestant Independents. For them every individual must find their own salvation by rigorous self-examination and the performance of good deeds here and now.

Church authority was equally repugnant to them: all persons were held equal in the sight of God. Some of the Elizabethan Individualist sects rejected any sort of Church role, whether by bishops or elders. For groups like the Brownists and Barrowists each person should have direct contact with God; all authority and ceremonial was an outrage. Such groups were persecuted and their leaders executed by Elizabeth, but during the early seventeenth century their numbers multiplied. Most numerous were the Congregationalists and the Baptists. They rejected both episcopacy and presbyterianism, insisting that each congregation should be autonomous. Preachers were elected by a general meeting of members.

The religious sects also adopted an individualist moral code. In sixteenth- and seventeenth-century Britain marriage customs varied a good deal. In Leicester in 1598, for instance, marriage involved no church ceremony. The man and woman made a public agreement, more like a modern engagement, and this could be followed by living together (Laslett, 1965, pp. 141–2). Such contracts were abolished within the Catholic Church by a Papal Bull of 1564 which laid down that a priest must officiate at a marriage ceremony and that it was a grave sin to have sexual relations before the religious service. In many Puritan sects marriage consisted of a public promise which could be followed by consummation. Church ceremonial was seen as irrelevant. What counted was the sincerity of the promise of lifelong commitment the two individuals made to each other. Some Puritans went even further: in 1680 a Scottish Presbyterian, William Lawrence, described ecclesiastical matrimony as an 'unnatural outrage' (Laslett, 1965, p. 144).

These sects were islands of self-rule in an environment otherwise devoid of democracy for the common citizen.

Church members elected their priests and shared in the work of organising their own affairs and assisting each other in hard times through mutual aid.

Under James I (1603–25) the Independents (who favoured the election of priests) and Presbyterians (who favoured church rule by elders), collectively known as. Puritans, were persecuted. Many left for America (the *Mayflower* sailed in 1620) carrying their self-reliance and their commitment to self-government and mutual aid with them. Persecution continued under Charles I and intensified while William Laud was Archbishop of Canterbury from 1633–45. Uniformity of worship was enforced, discipline and ceremonial insisted upon and Puritan pamphleteering suppressed through the royal prerogative courts, the Court of Star Chamber and its equivalent in the northern counties, the Council of the North. The Church at this time further condemned itself in the eyes of reformers by supporting the doctrine of the divine right of kings which asserted that the king was answerable only to God.

Hand in hand with the doctrine of the divine right of kings went the notion that the social order was an organism, like the human body, with each part having a function for the sake of the whole. It was controlled, like the human body, by the head: the king or pope. This analogy was used by Paul in his Letter to the Corinthians (I Corinthians, 12, 12) and by both Elizabeth I and James I. Elizabeth warned the House of Commons in 1566 against interfering in the succession: 'As to liberties, who is so simple that doubts whether a Prince that is head of all the body may not command the feet not to stray when they would slip' (Neale, 1953, p. 175).

The Rise of Science
The individualism asserting itself in economics, religious life and political behaviour, also found expression in intellectual life. Modern science, distinguished, as Whitehead has shown, by its passionate interest not only in general abstract principles but also in 'irreducible and stubborn facts', emerged during this period. Copernicus, whose main work was not published until after his death in 1543,

may justly be regarded as the originator of the modern scientific tradition. But on the Continent the Church was able to stifle the influence of science until the middle of the next century. Giordano Bruno was burnt at the stake for his belief in the Copernican system of astronomy in 1600 and Galileo was forced to recant his views in the 1630s.

In England the Catholic Church proved less of an obstacle. In 1605 Francis Bacon published his *The Advancement of Learning* which set out the modern approach to science. His views were more fully expounded in *Novum Organum Scientiarum* in 1620. In about 1645 the Royal Society began to hold meetings. They were, in the view of one contemporary, a band of thinkers 'who had begun a free way of reasoning'. Newton formulated his universal theory of gravitation in 1685.

Revolution
In the early seventeenth century the government and the established church stood in the path of the rising individualism. These tensions came to a head in the 1640s. After the Eleven Years Tyranny (when Charles I had ruled without Parliament through Laud and Strafford) Parliament was finally recalled in 1640. But the Short Parliament was soon dissolved, and civil war broke out in 1642. Parliament was victorious and soon began to dismantle royal power. Both Laud and Strafford were impeached and, along with Charles I, eventually beheaded. The Court of Star Chamber and the Council of the North were abolished along with the King's right to grant trade monopolies. The levying of all taxes was prohibited without parliamentary consent and the King was forbidden to dissolve Parliament without its agreement. Greater freedom of opinion was demanded within the Church of England, and when Cromwell assumed power in 1649 religious toleration was granted to Puritans (though not to Catholics).

Once Cromwell established himself, however, further abuses followed. To win the civil war a powerful army had been established. The New Model Army comprised largely Independents whilst the Presbyterian wing of the parliamentary army had relatively less military power. Consequently, in Pride's Purge, Cromwell was able to remove around 100 MPs in order to create a majority of Independents in Parliament. Britain had fallen into the hands of a military dictatorship.

The Restoration of the monarchy in 1660 saw the loss of many of the reforms introduced after the civil war, but for the most part Charles II ruled as a constitutional monarch. He agreed to raise taxes only with Parliament's consent, although he connived with Louis XIV to defy Parliament by accepting French subsidies. Arbitrary arrests, common under the earlier Stuarts and during the Commonwealth, were curtailed and towards the end of his reign, in 1679, Charles II consented to the Habeas Corpus Act.

Generally, and often against his will, Charles II toed the parliamentary line, but James II, who succeeded him in 1685, was a bigoted Catholic who engaged in further treacherous connivances to turn England into a Catholic country, subservient to France. This led to the Glorious Revolution of 1688 when the defeat of arbitrary royal power at the hands of parliamentary democracy was consolidated. James II was expelled and William and Mary placed on the throne on the conditions enshrined in the Bill of Rights of 1689. Religious tolerance was finally granted to Non-Conformists and Catholics, though both remained under certain disabilities.

The Puritan Revolution of the 1640s and the Glorious Revolution of 1688 set the character of English liberalism. The tone of the Glorious Revolution, in particular, was cool in temper, and respectful of the past. If there was outrage it was because the Stuart monarchs were held to have betrayed a long tradition by conniving (with foreigners) at the overthrow of liberties bequeathed to Englishmen by their forbears. This appeal to ancient rights was the tone of the Bill of Rights of 1689 as much as of the Petition of Right of 1628 and of Magna Carta in 1215. No monarch could rule as he pleased. He was subject to the law, which was higher than the will of any man. No man, wrote John Locke to justify the Glorious Revolution, was entitled to rule another without his consent:

'The liberty of man, in society, is to be under no other legislative power but that established, by consent ...' (1963 edn., II, 22).

The experience of royal oppression at the hands of the early Stuart monarchs, followed by the excesses of the Commonwealth, only to be followed by the counter-revolution from 1660 to 1688, also imparted another distinctive element to the British liberal tradition.

During the seventeenth century both those on the side of individualism and those who opposed it were on the receiving end of overmighty central power. Notwithstanding the excesses of the Cromwellian Major-Generals, individualists were generally inclined to mistrust state power. But it was peculiar to England at this time that those who opposed the rising individualism in the name of stability, hierarchy, and kingly and episcopal authority—and who were not usually slow to resort to the use of armies to get their way—became at least as hostile to a strong state. This group was soon to be known as the Tory Party and was distinguished, Macaulay writes, by its 'peculiar zeal for monarchy and for the Anglican Church'. It was also vigorously opposed to the formation of a standing army:

One such army had held dominion in England; and under that dominion the King had been murdered, the nobility degraded, the landed gentry plundered, the Church persecuted. There was scarcely a rural grandee who could not tell a story of wrongs and insults suffered by himself, or by his father, at the hands of the parliamentary soldiers.... The consequence was that those very Royalists, who were most ready to fight for the King themselves, were the last persons whom he could venture to ask for the means of hiring regular troops (Macaulay, 1967 edn, vol. 1, pp. 229–30).

Thus, all parties, including those otherwise inclined to resort to force to achieve their ends, were wary of granting the state too much power.

The Emerging Liberal Ethos
Thus we can trace the origins of the liberal tradition to the sixteenth and seventeenth centuries. In the seventeenth

century the power of the centre in the form of the government and the established church was seen as an obstacle to the self-directing, self-developing person. Liberalism— as this body of thought was later called—originated as a reaction to this state of affairs. All round were fetters, in economic life, in religion, in politics and in intellectual life. Liberals sought release from serfdom, government monopolies, the arbitrary power of kings, bishops and popes, and from the stultifying weight of tradition in village life and municipal guilds.

Liberals wanted free examination in religion, no interpreter between man and the Scriptures and no intermediary between man and God. They desired freedom of conscience, thought and expression. They sought security against oppression at the hands of private individuals and organisations and looked to the state to provide it. But because they were keenly aware that the state's protective role could be abused, its powers were to be severely circumscribed. They wanted freedom of movement from place to place and job to job, since otherwise individuals might fall prey to some dominant personality or organised power in a particular locality. They sought the freedom to exchange products and services at mutually agreed prices, to accumulate capital, and to lend and borrow without undue hindrance. They wanted everyone to enjoy the right to own and use property as each thought best. They sought equality before the law, and the independence of the judicial tribunals from the legislative and executive arms of government.

If Acton is correct, the desire for freedom of worship was the dominant factor in the emergence of liberalism. It was, he says, the 'deepest current' in 1641 and the 'strongest motive' in 1688. Men learnt that it was only by abridging the power of governments that the liberty of churches could be assured. That great political idea, wrote Acton:

sanctifying freedom and consecrating it to God, teaching men to treasure the liberties of others as their own, and to defend them for love of justice and charity more than as a claim of right, has been the soul of what is great and good in the progress of the last two hundred years (1907, p. 52).

EIGHTEENTH-CENTURY MATURITY

From its seventeenth-century origins we can follow a long line of adherents down to the modern 'new right'. But first it is important to understand how the individualist reaction to the old order took two quite distinct, indeed opposite, forms.

The Two Individualisms

The first tradition was, according to Bertrand Russell, 'individualist in intellectual matters, and also in economic, but was not emotionally or ethically self-assertive'. Locke and Hume, who were its spokesmen, were both tentative in the conclusions they drew for political action:

Since ... it is unavoidable to the greatest part of men, if not all, to have several *opinions*, without certain and indubitable proofs of their truths; it would, methinks, become all men to maintain peace and the common offices of humanity and friendship in the diversity of opinions. We should do well to commiserate our mutual ignorance, and endeavour to remove it in all the gentle and fair ways of information; and not instantly treat others ill, as obstinate and perverse, because they will not renounce their own, and receive our opinions (Locke, 1924, edn, pp. 337–8).

The second tradition was rooted in the philosophy of Descartes (p. 115 below) and Rousseau's social contract theory and gradually developed into the antithesis of liberalism. According to Russell, it extended individualism 'from the intellectual sphere to that of the passions'. Later adherents, like Carlyle and Nietzsche, worshipped heroic leadership along with nationalism and war in pursuit of 'liberty'. But, writes Russell, 'since we cannot all have the career of heroic leaders, and cannot all make our individual will prevail, this philosophy, like all other forms of anarchism, inevitably leads, when adopted, to the despotic government of the most successful "hero"'. And, he continues, 'when his tyranny is established, he will suppress in others the self-assertive ethic by which he has risen to power' (1979, p. 580).

Thus, for Russell the continental tradition encouraged a particular type of personality—the individual certain of his rectitude, impatient with critics, and quick to assert himself by force. For this reason I shall call it egoistic liberalism. The tradition of Locke and Hume (pp. 22–3 below) appealed to an entirely different type—the person who was tolerant of differences, and tentative in his approach to practical affairs, prepared to act with vigour where necessary but always entertaining a healthy doubt. I shall call this tradition, critical liberalism.

The continental tradition of egoistic liberalism, in its outright opposition to the dead weight of tradition, tended to overestimate human capacity to remake institutions from scratch. The critical tradition entails an evolutionary view of human action and progress; and the notion of government as a protector and facilitator of individual self-direction. It rejects straightforward servility to tradition and favours corrective social reform but asserts that projects intended to remake the whole fabric of the social order should be entered into with caution. As Burke later put it, it combined conservation with correction. Its adherents believed we should not lightly throw away our institutions, nor assume that we understood everything about them. The purpose of any particular custom or institution might not seem apparent, but this did not necessarily mean it had no function.

A more recent representative of the critical liberal tradition is Sir Karl Popper. In his classic discussion of the principles which underlie an 'open society' he opposes 'utopian' or 'holistic' social engineering in favour of 'piecemeal' social engineering, a tradition which stands opposed, not to change as such, but to efforts at change which fail to be aware of the limits of human knowledge and which consequently allow inadequate room for the correction of errors.

The dualism in the liberal tradition came into the open during the French Revolution. There are two contradictory elements in the French Declaration of the Rights of Man and Citizen of 1789. The individual was granted certain rights against the state, as critical liberalism required. But at the same time the unlimited popular sovereignty favoured by egoistic liberalism was assumed. In the critical tradition freedom is the liberty to do whatever does not harm others. But in the tradition which speaks of the 'general will' and of self-rule, freedom is seen as popular sovereignty. Resistance to the state, it could therefore plausibly be argued, was resistance to oneself. As the French revolutionaries learnt to their cost, this provides a rationale for rule by any faction which can grasp the reigns of power.

This book focuses on that tradition of liberalism that does not contradict itself, the critical tradition which reached its mature expression in the works of Adam Smith, David Hume and Edmund Burke.

Locke, Hume and the Rule of Law
The state must of necessity be a compulsory association if it is to protect the liberty of all. But once it has been accepted that the state is vital to protect the liberty of each citizen the question remains, who can be trusted to rule impartially? The liberal answer was that no one could be trusted and that, therefore, no one should rule: that a government of *laws* was preferable to a government of men.

Locke first clearly formulated this idea. In the state of nature men were inclined to be biased in their own interest. Thus it was vital that there should be: *'established*, settled, known *Law*, received and allowed by common consent to be the standard of right and wrong, and the common measure to decide all controversies' (1963 edn, II, 124). In the state of nature passion and revenge were apt to carry men too far, and so a 'known and indifferent judge' was vital, with the authority to settle differences according to 'established law' (1963, II, 125). More important, the power of government to make laws should also be limited. Its power must not be 'absolutely arbitrary'. Legislative power ought to be 'limited to the public good of the society' (135). If men consented to government to avoid the inconveniences of the state of nature only to find they had lost their right of self-defence to an arbitrary government they would be worse-off than before. It therefore followed that the ruling power 'ought to govern by *declared* and *received* Laws, and not be extemporary Dictates and undetermined resolutions' (137): 'They are to govern by promulgated established Laws, not to be varied in particular cases, but to have one rule for rich and poor, for the favourite at court, and the country man at plough' (142). In this manner rulers would be 'kept within their due bounds' (137).

The value of rules is that everyone can know where they stand, and have confidence that in the event of a dispute there will be fair play according to *known* rules. It is possible for people with disparate interests to agree upon a clear, settled rule. But it is very difficult to maintain the peace if justice is believed to be arbitrary. Without settled law 'justice' becomes a matter of power and individuals organise themselves to advance their own interests. But it is impossible to guarantee that every particular judicial outcome will suit every person at every time. To imagine that this is so is to misunderstand the nature of the problem. The tradition of a rule of law is the liberal answer to the question, 'how can we eliminate the *main* sources of conflict between individuals with widely divergent interests?' It is not an answer to the question, 'how can we make everyone happy?'; nor the question 'how can we eliminate *all* conflict?'

Hume explains the value of justice so conceived by distinguishing it from benevolence. Benevolence has a direct result and its wider consequences are not considered. A benevolent act is performed, gladly, for itself—to aid a particular person with their interests in mind. Justice is different. Its usefulness flows from the fact that particular interests are *not* considered, and that instead a rule is followed. Justice, writes Hume, is 'absolutely necessary to the well-being of mankind', but the benefit resulting from it 'is not the consequence of every single individual act; but arises from the whole scheme or system, concurred in by the whole, or the greater part of society' (1906, p. 490). It is the agreement, or rather the acceptance— whether by conscious process or by habit—that is central. For it is this that eliminates a whole array of possible sources of conflict and disorder. In this respect justice is like some other phenomena, namely those that are 'advantageous to two or more persons if all perform their part', but which lose all advantage if only one person conforms. The acceptance of money as a medium of exchange is one such case, and the acceptance of language as a means of communication is another (1906, pp. 491–2). The necessities people face require them to combine their efforts. Without concurrence, or acquiescence, in rules this is impossible. If some people disregard human life, or the justly acquired possessions of others, or break agreements with impunity, the stability necessary for us to be able to make the most of our lives would be impossible. Without a 'stable rule in all controversies' people organise to secure their own ends.

In much of the West the importance of removing some matters from the realm of arbitrary power may not seem as apparent as it does elsewhere in the world. In the Philippines, Argentina, Indonesia and El Salvador there are, or have been, semi-official murder squads in place of law. In Indonesia, for instance, officially sanctioned murder squads have responded to the rise in crime by eliminating racketeers, thieves, pick-pockets and extortion gangs. A survey conducted in 1983 found that two-thirds of the population approved. But soon the squads began adopting a more 'flexible' definition of crime and innocent people began to suffer. In one notorious case a devout church-going 17-year-old was gunned down. Many more live in fear of mistaken identity. Tattoos are worn by many criminals, and consequently many frightened non-criminals who happen to have tattoos are queueing up to have them removed by plastic surgery (*Sunday Times*, 21 August 1983). A rule of law can produce absurd outcomes. It is, for instance, respect for settled law that permits the convicted train robber and escaped prisoner Ronald Biggs to go on avoiding extradition from Latin America. But, all things considered, the rule of law is preferable to both the lynch mob and the government killer squad.

American Constitutionalism
Developments in America made a vital contribution to the emerging liberal ethos. The American Revolution against

rule from Britain was undertaken with reluctance and in a most conservative manner. Moreover, the mother country was itself divided in its attitude to the war, with some of England's finest political leaders supporting the American cause, not least Chatham and Burke. The temper of the American Revolution was that of the Petition of Right of 1628 and the Bill of Rights of 1689. The actions of the British government of the day had injured that sense of justice which flowed from belief in the rights of the free-born Englishman. In particular, it was held that no taxes could be levied without the consent of the people's representatives.

Once the fighting ended, American leaders showed a keen awareness of the dangers of unlimited sovereignty and built into the constitution obstacles to discourage tyrannical government. From this time America's contribution to the evolving critical liberal tradition began to outweigh the mother country's. Above all, it was America that pioneered new developments in constitutionalism. American governments were set firmly under a written constitution, the interpretation of which lay in the hands of a supreme judicial body and not at the mercy of passing majorities. Americans believed, according to Acton, that no nation could ever 'abandon its fate to an authority it cannot control' (1907, p. 56). These measures were partly undermined by the early growth of party spirit in elections, reinforced by the spoils system, but none the less American institutions have remained far more resistant to the growth of arbitrary government than Britain's. As Britain became progressively more collectivist in the latter part of the nineteenth century, America, shielded by its constitution, remained more faithful to the liberalism of Hume and Smith.

Adam Smith and the 'Invisible Hand'
The liberal tradition, and particularly that of the classical economists, is frequently accused by its critics of being a self-serving doctrine supportive of one special interest alone—powerful industrialists. How valid is this claim?

Adam Smith railed against the evils of his day as the

revolutionaries of the seventeenth century had done. He particularly opposed the mercantile system. Ostensibly aimed at maximising the national wealth at the expense of foreigners by promoting exports and discriminating against imports, mercantilism was in reality a system which sacrificed the interests of consumers to those of producers. Consumption, Smith wrote, 'is the sole end and purpose of all production; and the interest of the producer ought to be attended to only so far as it may be necessary for promoting that of the consumer.' But in the mercantile system, he concluded, 'the interest of the consumer is almost certainly sacrificed to that of the producer; and it seems to consider production, and not consumption, as the ultimate end and object of all industry and commerce' (1776, vol. II, p. 155).

Smith's views were not based on high theory, but rather resulted from his observation of the impact of mercantilism on the ordinary citizen. For instance, the manufacture of everyday clothing was deeply affected. On the one hand, the import of cheap raw materials, like linen yarn, was encouraged in order to keep down the wages of English spinners, whilst on the other, the import of finished linen products was discouraged in order to raise prices for the benefit of home manufacturers. The wool manufacturers were even more successful, having secured an absolute ban on the import of wool products.

Manufacturers and traders dressed up their demands for special concessions from government in the language of the national interest, but according to Adam Smith, it was only industries 'carried on for the benefit of the rich and powerful' that were encouraged by mercantilism. Industries which benefited the poor or indigent were frequently neglected or oppressed (vol. 2, p. 139).

Also as a result of mercantilism, commerce, which Smith believed ought to be a bond of union and friendship, had become a source of discord and animosity. He saw little remedy for the 'violence and injustice' of the rulers of mankind, but he thought the 'mean rapacity' and 'monopolising spirit' of merchants and manufacturers could be checked. Although he thought it could not be wholly corrected, it could by the promotion of competition 'very easily be prevented from disturbing the tranquility of anybody but themselves' (vol. I, p. 436). Speaking of protectionism, he writes that, 'it was the spirit of monopoly which originally both invented and propagated this doctrine', and they who first taught it, he says, 'were by no means such fools as they who believed it':

In every country it always is and must be the interest of the great body of the people to buy whatever they want of those who sell it cheapest. The proposition is so manifest that it seems ridiculous to take any pains to prove it; nor could it ever have been called in question had not the interested sophistry of merchants and manufacturers confounded the common sense of mankind. Their interest is, in this respect, directly opposite to that of the great body of the people. (vol. I, pp. 436–7)

His was a plea for the 'system of natural liberty' and against deliberate contrivances imposed by government. The role of government, he thought, should be confined to:

first, the duty of protecting the society from the violence and invasion of other independent societies; secondly, the duty of protecting, as far as possible, every member of the society from the injustice or oppression of every other member of it, or the duty of establishing an exact administration of justice; and, thirdly, the duty of erecting and maintaining certain public works and certain public institutions which it can never be for the interest of any individual, or small number of individuals, to erect and maintain; because the profit could never repay the expense to any individual or small number of individuals, though it may frequently do much more than repay it to a great society. (vol. 2, pp. 180–1)

Today, liberalism is often criticised for encouraging selfishness. This too is based on a misunderstanding. For a civilised society which has progressed beyond mere tribalism to be successful, Adam Smith believed it must harness the powerful and ubiquitous force, self-love or self-interest:

man has almost constant occasion for the help of his brethren, and it is in vain for him to expect it from their benevolence only. He will be more likely to prevail if he can interest their self-love in his favour, and show them that it is for their own advantage to do for him what he requires of them. . . . It is not from the benevolence of the butcher, the brewer, or the baker, that we expect our dinner, but from their regard to their own interest. We address ourselves, not to their humanity but to their self-love. (vol. 1, p. 13)

This is the source of the view that Smith encouraged selfishness. But his argument was a plea for realism about the motives of traders. He was, as we have seen, a very severe critic of the selfishness of merchants and manufacturers, when undisciplined by competition.

Possibly the feature of the British liberal tradition on which most ridicule has been heaped is the claim that individuals intent only on serving their own private interests also serve the interests of others. This insight had been formulated earlier by Bernard Mandeville, in the *Fable of the Bees*, subtitled, *Private Vices, Public Benefits* (1705). But it is best known in the form it was expressed by Adam Smith:

by directing that industry in such a manner as its produce may be of greatest value, he intends only his own gain, and he is in this, as in many other cases, led by an invisible hand to promote an end which was no part of his intention. . . . By pursuing his own interest he frequently promotes that of the society more effectually than when he really intends to promote it. (vol. 1, p. 400)

The belief that the selfishness of producers can be channelled by competition and wise laws so that, despite their selfish aims, they end by serving others has been a vital part of the liberal viewpoint. Hayek's extended analysis of the market's 'invisible hand', is explained in Chapter 5.

NINETEENTH-CENTURY DILUTION

The heart of the liberal tradition is made up of two ideas. The first is that political power should be limited because history has taught that a government free to use its powers as it wants too easily becomes the oppressive tool of special interests. In economics, manufacturers and traders have found it easy to secure royal monopolies or privileges at the general expense. And in religion, Catholic and

Protestant, Independent and Presbyterian alike, have experienced persecution at the hands of a partisan state. The liberal remedy is government limited by law: a rule of law, rather than an arbitrary rule of men.

This is closely allied with a second liberal doctrine, that within a framework of settled law the pursuit of self interest does not lead to disorder. On the contrary, the mutual adjustment of one interest to another often promotes relative harmony. And certainly, whatever harm might flow from the selfishness of men in a free society, still greater suffering would ensue if the power of government was placed at the disposal of any faction or interest.

During the course of the nineteenth century, however, both these ideas lost credence. The continental tradition of egoistic individualism penetrated British ideas, at first through the agency of the first generation of Radicals, Price, Godwin and Paine, and later—and to much greater effect—through Bentham and the Utilitarians, who desired to remodel English laws according to abstract principles without regard to historic rights. The doctrine of the rule of law ceased to be understood and came to be seen as a mere requirement of 'legality'. But the doctrine that a nation should be ruled by *laws* and not by *men* was never a mere assertion that all the actions of a government should be legal. It was partly a procedural requirement, but it was above all the view that the power to make laws was not unlimited. Laws too, were to be appraised in the light of higher more fundamental, principles (pp. 129–31 below).

It was not only the impact of alien ideas that diluted the tradition of critical liberalism, but also the selfish spirit of many Whig aristocrats, the chief carriers of British liberalism. A major preoccupation of advocates of liberty has always been how to stop the state from becoming the tool of sectional interests. From the Glorious Revolution until the Great Reform Act of 1832 England was ruled by aristocrats. There was a good deal of corruption and many landowners enriched themselves at the public expense. But government was limited and its powers were not seriously abused in the manner of the seventeenth century. As even the Marxist historian, E.P. Thomson, acknowledges, although corruption was rife, the impartial rule of law remained a reality, protecting weak and strong alike from arbitrary power (1977, pp. 265–6).

It was not until the end of the Napoleonic Wars in 1815 that the temptation to abuse more fundamentally the power at their disposal became too much for the aristocrats who dominated both the House of Lords and the House of Commons. The war had raised the price of corn, but when the fighting ended the landowners used their monopoly of political power to impose high protective tariffs to prevent prices falling. The manufacturers had lost markets due to the wartime blockade and when they returned to Europe to sell their wares found that they were hampered by the high cost of production at home. The chief cause was the high cost of living, particularly of bread, which forced wages above continental levels. The manufacturers therefore sought an end to the Corn Laws to bring about a reduction in the price of bread. And to prevent further abuse of aristocratic power they sought to end the political monopoly of landed interests.

One of the consequences of the aristocratic abuse of state power was that the manufacturers became the chief carriers of liberal ideas. The liberalism they championed reflected in part their own special interests and in particular their hostility to the landowners. The views of the Manchester School of Liberalism took particularly strong root among the manufacturing class. Adherents of the Manchester School were practical men who favoured free trade and non-intervention in commerce and industry. A campaign for free trade in place of protectionism had begun in the 1820s, but it was not until the 1840s that progress was made. The Anti-Corn Law League, established in Manchester in 1839 under the leadership of Richard Cobden, opposed the prevailing view that Britain should arm itself to fight for trade. International trade, said Cobden, was incompatible with the use of force. It implied mutual reliance, international friendship, and consequently the rejection of any policy built on national pride. The movement enjoyed great success. The Corn

Laws were repealed in 1846 and Britain followed a path of increasingly free trade for the remainder of the century. In domestic affairs, however, the trend was towards collectivism. As the nineteenth century progressed, class rivalry came to dominate domestic politics. Steadily, the old Whig idea that government should remain above the factional fray and to that end should be limited in scope lost its force amidst the struggle between the manufacturers and the landed interests, and amidst the conflict between wage labourers and the manufacturers over government regulation of industry. The strong hostility of the Manchester School to the regulation of hours and conditions of work in factories further reinforced the impression that liberalism was largely a factional ideology, serving only the interests of manufacturers.

Politics became a struggle between classes, with the state machine the prize to be captured and used to advantage. This tendency was reinforced as the franchise was extended during the nineteenth century. Combined with the doctrine of unlimited parliamentary sovereignty politics turned increasingly into a materialistic struggle for sectional advantage at the general expense.

Looking back in 1905, Dicey classified the years from 1865 to 1900 as the 'period of collectivism', and by the end of the century believed collectivism to be firmly entrenched (Dicey, 1905, pp. 62–9, 258–301). In 1890 Sidney Webb confidently asserted that, 'In England the old *a priori* Individualism is universally abandoned' (p. 79). Largely through the English idealist philosophers, led by T.H. Green, the continental tradition of freedom as power became respectable among British liberals. The liberalism of Smith and Hume came to be looked upon as 'negative' in that it left positive outcomes to individual initiative. The tradition of 'positive freedom' believed it was the duty of the state to enhance the power of the weak citizen. To call this 'positive freedom' implies that it is a type of freedom, when in the new liberal view it is no such thing. It represents a view about how the power of the state should be used. The movement for 'positive freedom' originated in the identification of intellectuals with the underdog. The political programme of T.H. Green remained limited but in its concern to bring about the 'best' in men it set no limits on the use of state power. In the hands of T.H. Green's socialist followers, it ended in the glorification of the state as an instrument of social reform. The potential of the state for harm disappeared from the agenda of those who called themselves liberal.

To many it will seem odd to find the nineteenth century being described as a period of liberal decline, for it is generally taught that the last century was the high-point of *laissez-faire*. But the nineteenth century did see the slow dilution of liberal values, and in particular it saw the steady transformation of politics into a struggle for material advantage between classes and with it the disappearance of the idea of the state as the independent protector of the equal rights of every person.

TWENTIETH-CENTURY ABANDONMENT AND RENEWAL

By the First World War liberalism had lost its former sway, even to the extent that liberal ideas had been wholly abandoned by the Liberal Party. By the 1930s liberty was barely understood by British intellectuals, and even America had fallen under the influence of a socialistic 'liberalism'.

However, by the late 1950s the steady pursuit of collectivism yielded such poor results that it prepared the way for a revival of interest in liberty. The liberal tradition, as we have seen, arose out of a particular set of historical circumstances. For this reason it might well have appeared of little relevance in the second half of the twentieth century. Yet what is striking about the liberal tradition is that many leading modern intellectuals have found its principles of central relevance to today's problems. The remainder of this book describes how, in their efforts to understand the failure of collectivism, they have returned to the seventeenth- and eighteenth-century originators of liberalism.

GUIDE TO READING

For a quick overview of the roots of classical liberalism Lord Acton's essay 'The history of freedom in Christianity' (1907, pp. 30–60) is invaluable. In the same volume the essays on 'The history of freedom in antiquity' and 'Nationality' are also useful. Also indispensable are the chapters on 'The Puritan Revolution', 'The Rise of the Whigs', 'The English Revolution', and 'The American Revolution' in Acton's *Lectures on Modern History* (1930). Guido de Ruggiero's *The History of European Liberalism* (1927) is still well worth reading, as is Macaulay's *History of England*, though the hard-pressed student may find some of the detail tedious. *Liberalism* (1964), Hobhouse's classic first published in 1911, is available in cheap modern editions. John Stuart Mill has usually been seen as belonging primarily to the Utilitarian tradition, yet his famous essay *On Liberty*, contains a worthwhile discussion of the non-utilitarian grounds for a policy of non-interference by governments. To understand Mill's contribution it is advisable to read his work in conjunction with John Gray's *Mill on Liberty: a Defence* (1983).

Adam Smith and David Hume should be read in the original. Smith's *The Wealth of Nations* (1776) and *The Theory of Moral Sentiments* (1976 edn.) are both available in cheap modern editions with useful explanatory introductions. Several inexpensive editions of Hume's *Essays* are available. These should be read first in preference to his earlier *A Treatise of Human Nature*.

Among modern discussions of liberalism, Steven Lukes' *Individualism* (1973) is pretty reliable. For a thoroughly hostile account, consult Anthony Arblaster's *The Rise and Decline of Western Liberalism* (1984).

2 Anarcho-Capitalism or the Minimal State?

This chapter considers three closely related traditions of thought. First, it discusses anarcho-libertarianism or anarcho-capitalism, a philosophy based on the absolute or 'natural' rights of the individual. Second, it considers the minimal statism of Robert Nozick, who, also reasoning from a natural rights standpoint, contends that a minimal state can be justified in preference to anarchism. Third, it describes Ayn Rand's 'objectivism'.

LIBERTARIANISM

War is Mass Murder, Taxation is Robbery

The anarcho-libertarian creed, writes Dr Murray Rothbard, rests upon one central axiom; 'that no man or group of men may aggress against the person or property of anyone else' (1978, p. 23). Each person has an 'absolute right' to private property. The term 'property' is used, as John Locke used it, to include both a person's own body, and the 'previously unused natural resources which he first transforms by his labor' (ibid., p. 39).

Today, misleading though it is, we are accustomed to thinking about politics as if there were a left, a right and a centre. Where does anarcho-libertarianism fit? Many of the stands taken by anarcho-libertarians are classified as leftist. The 'non-aggression axiom' means that anarcho-libertarians strongly support 'civil liberties': freedom of speech, publication and assembly. They also oppose the classification of 'victimless crimes' such as pornography, sexual deviation, drug abuse and prostitution, as 'crimes', because they are not violent invasions of other people's property. Conscription, in Rothbard's view, is 'slavery on a massive scale', and because war entails the mass slaughter of civilians, it is seen as 'mass murder' (ibid., p. 23).

The anarcho-libertarian also holds views conventionally classified as right-wing. According to Rothbard, the right of self-ownership and the right to 'homestead' (or set up house on unowned land), comprise the 'complete set of principles of the libertarian system'. Anarcho-libertarianism results from spinning out all the implications of these principles (ibid., p. 39). For instance, if a man owns something in the first place, then he may give it away or exchange it. This principle, writes Rothbard, forms the basis for free contract and the free market economy. The invasion of rights of private property is strongly opposed, whether at the hands of the government or anyone else. Government interference with property rights or with the free market economy through 'controls, regulations, subsidies, or prohibitions' is therefore wholly wrong. Each person has a right to give away his property (bequest) and to exchange it (free contract) without interference. The anarcho-libertarian therefore favours 'unrestricted private property and free exchange', or *laissez-faire* capitalism' (ibid., p. 24).

To many this mixture of 'left' and 'right' will seem odd. But Rothbard defends anarcho-libertarianism as the only consistent political position. It supports the liberty of every individual:

how can the leftist be opposed to the violence of war and conscription while at the same time supporting the violence of taxation and government control? And how can the rightist trumpet his devotion to private property and free enterprise while at the same time favoring war, conscription, and the outlawing of noninvasive activities and practices that he deems immoral? And how can the rightist favor a free market while seeing nothing amiss in the vast subsidies, distortions, and unproductive inefficiencies involved in the military-industrial complex? (ibid., p. 24).

All aggression is consistently opposed, and in Rothbard's view, the state is the 'one central, dominant, and overriding

aggressor'. It should be given no moral sanction to commit
actions that would be regarded as immoral or criminal if
committed by anyone else. In short, 'War is Mass Murder,
Conscription is Slavery, and Taxation is Robbery' (ibid.,
pp. 24-5).

Anarcho-libertarians are particularly critical of the tendency of leftists to distinguish between 'property rights'
and 'human' or 'civil' rights. Socialists uphold civil rights
such as the freedoms of speech and assembly, but deny
the individual property rights. In other words, they uphold
the individual's right to his body, but not to property, yet
in Rothbard's view, the two 'are inextricably intertwined:
they stand or fall together'.

Consider freedom of speech. What use is such freedom
if the government owns all the meeting-halls? In Russia,
for instance, the government allocates meeting-halls to
groups if, and only if, they toe the government line. The
same applies to the freedom of the press. If the government owns all the printing presses, and controls access to
all the paper, no freedom exists:

> there are no human rights that are separable from property rights. The
> human right of free speech is simply the property right to hire an
> assembly hall from the owners, or to own one oneself; the human right
> of a free press is the property right to buy materials and then to print
> leaflets or books and to sell them to those who are willing to buy.
> There is no extra 'right of free speech' or free press beyond the
> property rights we can enumerate in a given case. (ibid., pp. 42-3)

For Dr David Friedman (Milton Friedman's son) private
property is necessary for two reasons. The first is that
people pursue different ends; the second is that some
things are 'sufficiently scarce that they cannot be used by
everyone as much as each would like' (1978, p. 4). It
follows that there must be some way of deciding who can
use what, and when. One way of deciding is violence: 'If I
can beat you up, I get to use the car.' This method, says,
says Dr Friedman, is 'very expensive, unless you like fighting and have plenty of medical insurance' (ibid., p. 5).
A better way is for the use of things to be organised

under a set of rules. The set of rules he prefers is one which regards property as held by individuals. If someone wishes to use another person's property he must persuade him, either by offering something in exchange or convincing him that some cause is worthwhile. If, however, property is held by the government, then it will be used to advance ends sought by the government. Individuals will not be able to pursue their separate ends. Only the particular ends of the dictator, majority, party or person or group in control will be legitimate.

Dr Friedman offers counter-arguments to socialists who dislike voluntary exchange because they see it as rooted in selfishness. There are, says David Friedman, three basic ways of getting other people to help you achieve your ends: love, trade and force. Love includes benevolence and when two or more people voluntarily accept a common goal. Trade is based on reciprocity: 'I agree to help you achieve your end if you help me achieve mine.' Force is straightforward: 'You do what I want or I shoot you.'

Love works well, argues Friedman, but only for a limited range of problems, largely because we can only know a few people really well. This is why most people co-operate by trade. Voluntary exchange or trade is criticised because it is said to be based on selfishness, as if the alternative were love. But this is not so. The real alternative is force. Trade and love are not mutually exclusive. Indeed, trade is neutral between selfishness and unselfishness. If people choose to be self-sacrificing they can be; and if they choose to be selfish, this is also possible if other people will put up with them. A society based on trade respects individual ends and voluntary agreements (1978, p. 19). Force and love are, on the other hand, mutually exclusive, as indeed are force and trade. People who dream about a socialist society, says Friedman, rarely consider that the prevailing values will be chosen by other people. They always imagine that their own will dominate (1978, p. 22). But people are intrinsically different, and for this reason socialism always ends in coercion, and in its more extreme forms, in the use of terror. Trade is antipathetic to force.

It not only tolerates but thrives on the diversity of individual preferences.

The Libertarian Programme

Anarcho-libertarians would entirely dismantle the modern state. Even policing, the administration of justice, and national defence would be provided by private enterprise.

Taxation: Murray Rothbard looks forward to the total abolition of taxes. Government, he says, 'lives and has its being in the practice of forcible theft, which it calls "taxation"'. The task of the anarcho-libertarian is:

> to show that the very existence of taxation and the State necessarily sets up a class division between the exploiting rulers and the exploited ruled. He seeks to show that the task of court intellectuals who have always supported the State has ever been to weave mystification in order to induce the public to accept State rule, and that these intellectuals obtain, in return, a share in the power and pelf extracted by the rulers from their deluded subjects. (1979, pp. 24-5)

Social Security: Rothbard points out that ostensibly progressive taxation tends in reality to be regressive. If the government really wanted to help the poor, it should, in his view, 'Get out of the way' of 'the productive energies of all groups in the population, rich, middle class, and poor alike'. The result would be 'an enormous increase in the welfare and standard of living of everyone, and most particularly of the poor' (ibid., p. 162).

He suggests four ways in which governments might remove themselves. First, taxation should be abolished or drastically reduced. This would create jobs and increase wages which would benefit the poor most of all. Second, there should be equivalent reductions in government spending: 'No longer would scarce economic resources be siphoned off into wasteful and unproductive expenditure.' Instead these resources would be available to supply goods and services desired by consumers. Third, governments should stop subsidising the wealthy, such as industrialists, farmers, beneficiaries of higher education, and so on. Fourth, government should remove its own direct roadblocks standing in the path of the productive energies of the poor: minimum wage laws which price the poor out of the labour market, special privileges to trade unions which help them bar productive and high-paid jobs to poorer groups, licensing laws and other regulations which restrict, for instance, peddling and street trading in the interests of big-city traders and at the expense of eliminating one of the traditional methods by which the poor could get themselves started (ibid., pp. 163-8).

Rothbard strongly objects to the negative income tax scheme recommended as a way of tackling poverty by neoclassical economists like Milton Friedman (Chapter 3). Such a scheme would destroy incentives for those who had to pay for it, and it would encourage more people to accept public dole rather than work, leading to a 'vicious spiral into disaster, heading toward the logical and impossible goal of virtually no one working, and everyone on the dole' (ibid., p. 169). The only 'workable solution', argues Rothbard, is the 'abolition of the welfare dole in favor of freedom and voluntary action for all persons, rich and poor alike' (ibid., p. 170).

Education: The 1970s 'new left' tactic of breaking into schools and shouting 'Jailbreak' may, writes Rothbard, have been 'absurd and ineffective', but it 'certainly expressed a great truth about the schools system' (1978, p. 120.) In common with thinkers who enjoyed wide support from the new left, such as Ivan Illich (*Deschooling Society*, 1973) and Everett Reimer (*School is Dead*, 1971), anarcho-libertarians detest the formalism of schools and see schooling as a kind of prison sentence.

The reason that children are dragooned into the school system is a result of misplaced altruism on the part of the educated middle classes, who believe that the benighted workers should be made to benefit from education for their own good. But the fallacy of 'middle-class school worshippers' is that they confuse formal schooling with *education*. Education is a lifelong process which takes place in many forms, only one of which is formal schooling.

Again, anarcho-libertarians disagree with neoclassical

liberals for not going far enough. Rothbard concedes that Professor Milton Friedman's voucher plan (Chapter 3), by permitting wider parental choice and abolishing the government school system, would be a great improvement on the status quo. But many problems would remain. The immorality of coerced subsidy for schooling would continue, and, more important, no government would subsidise education through vouchers without exercising some control. Schools would require government approval, and conceivably control over the curriculum, teaching methods, and organisation would be greater than it is now (1978, p. 135). Schooling ought not to be compulsory, nor ought there to be a government system.

Policing and Justice: Unlike believers in a minimal state, anarcho-libertarians would also abolish the police and the court system. Private protective agencies, funded by customers' voluntary payments, would emerge to replace the police, now funded by objectionable taxation. Private detective agencies already exist as do commercial security agencies and reveal how the market can supply such services (Rothbard, 1978, pp. 215-22).

The courts of law would be replaced by private arbitration, which is already growing fast. One of the largest arbitration companies is the American Arbitration Association (AAA). Firms sign contracts which provide that all disputes must be settled through AAA. One of the chief reasons for the rapid growth of private arbitration is the speed with which settlements are reached. The official courts, by comparison, function at a snail's pace. (Friedman, D., 1978, p. 110).

In anarcho-libertarian society no single body of law would be imposed. Nor has this always been the case historically (1977, p. 5). Freely competing judiciaries, says Rothbard, were more common than is often supposed. However, both he and David Friedman envisage that a corpus of accepted law would emerge, just as the common law evolved in earlier times. Judges did not *make* law, their task was to *find* it by searching the precedents for the principles of justice which underlay them (Rothbard,

1978, p. 228; Friedman, 1978, pp. 158-61). Rothbard envisages that the natural rights of the individual to his person and property would underlie any future body of 'law' that emerged (1978, p. 228).

A great many objections have been advanced against the anarcho-libertarian view of policing and justice, some of which have been discussed by Robert Nozick (below). The chief objection is that it would deteriorate into private feuding. This has led to the most vigorous of libertarians, such as Ayn Rand, rejecting full-blooded anarchism. David Friedman answers this criticism as follows.

A person who, for instance, has had his TV set stolen would call on his protective agency to recover it. The agency identifies the thief and asks him to return the TV set and make restitution, threatening to return with six burly assistants the next day if he fails to comply. He denies everything and calls his own protective agency who agree to be there in the morning with *eight* men. Is this, asks Friedman what would happen?

Friedman argues that bloodshed would not result because it is expensive. The two agencies would get on the telephone and agree to arbitration. If they did not do so they would be undercut by rival companies who used (cheaper) arbitration in place of (expensive) violence. In practice, he says, such arbitration would have been arranged beforehand and built into protection agreements.

The weakness of Friedman's argument is that it rests on violence always being more expensive than arbitration, but there are surely many situations in which direct action will be more cost-effective than arbitration. Friedman concedes another weakness, namely that plaintiffs and defendants may not agree on a common court. 'Obviously', he says, 'a murderer would prefer a lenient judge.' His answer is that courts should be chosen in advance by protective agencies: 'There would hardly be enough murderers at any one time to support their own protective agency, one with a policy of patronizing courts that did not regard murder as a crime' (p. 164). But this is surely mistaken. For instance, it is not so long ago in American history that a great many otherwise decent Americans regarded the murder of a black man as of no consequence.

Friedman agrees that the acceptance in advance of common rules and common courts is the answer, but he is left promising that such an arrangement *would* emerge. But if no such agreement is arrived at, does not respect for the individual require that common rules be enforced? Ought there not to be a government which supplied, as Locke put it, 'known and indifferent' judges who would settle disputes according to *'established*, settled, known *Law*, received and allowed by common consent to be the standard of right and wrong'? (1963, II, 124-5). This is where Robert Nozick comes in.

NOZICK AND THE MINIMAL STATE

Starting from the same assumptions as the anarcho-libertarians, the American philosopher Robert Nozick has reached very different conclusions. Nozick begins by taking seriously the anarchist case of writers such as Rothbard. Individuals, asserts Nozick, have absolute rights. It follows that there are things no person or group may do to another without violating his rights. And the interesting question for Nozick, as well as the anarchists, is whether this view of individual rights permits a role for the state. Why not, he asks, have anarchy? However, unlike the anarchists, he concludes that 'a minimal state limited to the narrow functions of protection against force, theft, fraud, enforcement of contracts, and so on, is justified', but accepts that 'any more extensive state will violate persons' rights not to be forced to do certain things, and is unjustified' (1974, p. ix).

By what reasoning does Nozick come to a different conclusion from Rothbard?

The 'Immaculate Conception' of the State

He proceeds, like John Locke before him, by postulating a state of nature in which there is no civil government. He rejects both unduly optimistic and unduly pessimistic assumptions about what a state of nature would be like and suggests what would be the best anarchic situation that could realistically be achieved. If it could be shown that the state would be superior to this favourable condition of anarchy, or that the state 'would arise by a process involving no morally impermissible steps' this would provide a justification for the existence of government (1974, p. 5).

His particular starting-point is the state of nature assumed by Locke in his *Second Treatise of Government*. Individuals are in a 'state of perfect freedom to order their actions and dispose of their possessions and persons as they think fit, within the bounds of the law of nature, without asking leave, or depending upon the will of any other man'. The law of nature requires that 'no one ought to harm another in his life, health, liberty, or possessions'. However, Locke writes, some persons do transgress these bounds and in response people may defend either themselves or other victims. The injured party may recover from the offender 'so much as may make satisfaction for the harm he has suffered', and 'everyone has a right to punish the transgressors of that law to such a degree as may hinder its violation'. Retribution should be determined by 'calm reason and conscience' and should be proportionate to the transgression, namely 'so much as may serve for reparation and restraint' (Locke in Nozick, op. cit., p. 10).

These were the 'inconveniences of the state of nature' for which, Locke wrote, 'I easily grant that civil government is the proper remedy'. This, however, is the assumption challenged by the anarchists. Nozick, therefore, reopens the question. If Locke has accurately described the 'inconveniences' of a state of nature, is civil government the best remedy? Or is the remedy worse than the disease? And how does it compare with other remedies that might emerge within the state of nature?

Nozick considers whether a system of mutual protection associations would work. Each person would choose an agency to which they would pay a premium in return for protection, including policing and a judicial system.

Initially a great many mutual protection associations would emerge, all protecting their own members against outsiders. But the particular weakness of private enforcement is that it leads to feuds, an endless series of acts of retaliation and demands for compensation. Men who act as judges in their own cause are inclined to overestimate the harm they have suffered. Nor is there any clear way of bringing a dispute to an end. Moreover, some persons would lack the power to enforce their rights, because some mutual protection associations would be weaker than others.

Because of these drawbacks, Nozick reasons, a situation in which there were several competing mutual protection agencies would tend to encourage the emergence of a single dominant agency. But most significant of all, the dominant protection agency is likely to find itself unable to satisfy its customers unless it has a monopoly. The right of self-defence includes the right to defend oneself against the unfair enforcement procedures of other protection associations, and individuals are likely to look to their own agency for this protection. This leads the dominant protection agency to insist on a monopoly of enforcement rights, for only in this manner can it eliminate unfair procedures. The only sound basis for avoiding feuds is to agree to equal treatment of like cases, and the only way to ensure equal treatment is to establish a single body of law and a single enforcement process.

Thus, according to Nozick, a *de facto* monopoly would arise out of competition among mutual protection agencies. However, it is also probable that a small number of persons would choose to remain outside the monopoly protection association. And they would be unable to enforce punishments or awards of compensation against dominant protection agency members. This would create unequal treatment, as members of the dominant agency would enjoy greater protection than non-members (ibid., pp. 120-1).

However, in Nozick's judgement, this source of resentment and conflict could be overcome if the dominant protection agency compensated outsiders for depriving them of their right of enforcement against dominant agency members (ibid., p. 115). Moreover, this moral requirement to compensate provides a basis for overcoming the second anarchist objection to a state monopoly—that, as well as denying people the right of self-enforcement, it forces them to pay for state protection. This is how it works. It is morally wrong for the dominant protection agency to insist on monopoly enforcement powers whilst simultaneously leaving some persons—those who opted not to pay its insurance premiums—unprotected. It is also wrong to force people to pay for a service they do not want. We can overcome both moral objections in one move if the few persons who refuse to contribute voluntarily to the dominant protection agency are deemed to have paid for their protection by means of the compensation payments to which they are entitled because of their loss of self-enforcement rights. In this manner, reasons Nozick, the minimal state could arise in a morally acceptable way.

In other words an agency maintaining a monopoly over the use of force but providing services only to those who volunteer to pay—an ultra-minimal state as Nozick calls such a situation—would emerge by an 'invisible hand' process which violates no one's rights (ibid., pp. 26, 115). But, reasons Nozick, it would be morally impermissible to maintain such a monopoly without providing services for all. It follows that the transition to a minimal state, in which all are compelled to pay for protection, even though this requires a degree of 'accidental' redistribution, 'morally must occur' (p. 52).

The Distributive State
Having thus justified a minimal state, why, asks Nozick, should the state be no more extensive? To defend his view that the minimal state is all that can be justified he tackles what he takes to be the most influential body of argument for a more pervasive state: the view that governments ought to aim to achieve 'distributive justice'.

First, he challenges the view that the term 'distribution' is neutral. Against the prevailing view that the distribution or dispersal of 'holdings' is unjust if it is unequal (or more unequal than some observer desires) Nozick recommends an alternative 'entitlement' theory of justice. He challenges the assumption which underlies distributionist theories, that 'holdings' are, in any event, always distributed or allocated by some central mechanism or controller:

> In a free society, diverse persons control different resources, and new holdings arise out of the voluntary exchanges and actions of persons. There is no more a distributing or distribution of shares than there is a distributing of mates in a society in which persons choose whom they shall marry. The total result is the product of many individual decisions which the different individuals involved are entitled to make (ibid., pp. 149-50)

Nozick contrasts two theories of justice. Current 'time-slice' (or end-result or end-state) theories assume that the justice of a distribution depends on some structural principle. Often such theories hold that the distribution of holdings at any moment should be equal. By comparison, historical theories ask how a distribution came about and hold that if a person has conducted his affairs in a just manner, this legitimises a differential distribution (ibid., pp. 153-5). It follows that if each person's holdings have been achieved by just means, then the *total* distribution is also just.

Nozick rejects the view that holdings ought to be distributed according to any structural or patterned view, whether the guiding principle is moral desert, usefulness to society, IQ, effort expended, complete material equality or anything else. Moreover, he argues that efforts to bring about all but the weakest end-states will be undermined by voluntary actions (ibid., p. 164). If it were possible for absolute equality to reign at breakfast time, it would be undermined by lunchtime. Consequently, no end-state principle can be realised without continuous detailed interference with individual lives, preventing transfers here and there or confiscating what some people have chosen to transfer to others. The socialist society, he remarks, would have to forbid 'capitalist acts between consenting adults' (ibid., p. 163).

Moreover, an effort to maintain any given distribution will tend to discriminate against giving. For if a stipulated distribution is to be preserved then individuals must be made to spend on themselves, for if they spend on others this will upset the pattern. This, says Nozick, is 'individualism with a vengeance!' (ibid., p. 167). Families are particularly disruptive of centrally ordained patterns, and this, he believes, is a general weakness of end-state theories. They are recipient-oriented and ignore the right to give (ibid., p. 168). Nozick does not attempt to give a precise content to his preferred entitlement theory of justice. Instead he sketches in the ground that would need to be covered. The first requirement is a principle of justice in acquisition, to govern how people may take control of 'unheld' things. The second is a principle of justice in transfer, to regulate how individuals who justly hold certain items may transfer them to others, by voluntary exchange or gift. Any distribution is just if it arises from a previous just distribution by just means. The third principle is necessary because some people are likely not to act according to the first two principles. To cover violations, a principle governing the rectification of injustices is necessary.

Generally Nozick supports a free market economy and regards market transactions as just, but this does not necessarily mean that he is in favour of freezing the distribution of property currently prevailing in every country. Moreover, he concedes that his principle of rectification might justify considerable state intervention in some cases: 'Although to introduce socialism as the punishment for our sins would be to go too far, past injustices might be so great as to make necessary in the short run a more extensive state in order to rectify them' (ibid., p. 231).

Nozick devotes particular attention to John Rawls' theory of justice. Rawls tries to arrive at a principle of justice in distribution which might be accepted by everyone if no one knew what position in society they occupied. He suggests that we put ourselves, as it were, outside society in an 'original position' and that in this condition we attempt to establish principles of justice. In this 'original position', which corresponds to the state of nature in social contract theory, no one knows their status, social class, occupation, wealth, etc. (Rawls, 1973, p. 12).

No one knows who is advantaged or disadvantaged and, therefore, the argument runs, the principles cannot be devised to favour this or that group of persons.

Rawls' particular aim is to lay down a distributive pattern or end-state favouring the poor which permits a degree of inequality (which he believes to be necesssary to encourage productive effort) whilst permitting few sacrifices of 'basic liberties'. There are two principles: First, 'Each person is to have an equal right to the most extensive total system of equal basic liberties compatible with a similar system of liberty for all.' Second, social and economic inequalities are to be arranged so that they are both (a) to the greatest benefit of the least advantaged, consistent with the just savings principle; and (b) attached to offices and positions open to all under conditions of fair equality of opportunity. The first principle has priority over the second, so that liberty can be restricted only for the sake of liberty (1973, p. 302). According to Rawls, the 'just savings principle' cannot be clearly set out, but it has to do with how much one generation saves in order to benefit subsequent generations. In practice, however, it appears that the amount to be saved would be settled from time to time by political decision (ibid., pp. 284-93). The 'general conception' underlying Rawls' scheme is this: 'All social primary goods—liberty and opportunity, income and wealth, and the bases of self-respect—are to be distributed equally unless an unequal distribution of any or all of these goods is to the advantage of the least favoured' (ibid., p. 303).

Nozick mounts a fundamental challenge to Rawls' theory. He questions the assumptions taken for granted by Rawls. First, he asks why individuals in Rawls' original position are presumed to choose rules based on groups rather than individuals (Nozick, 1974, p. 190). Second, he asks why it is assumed that an end-state theory would be preferred, thus ruling out selection of an entitlement or historical theory of justice (ibid., pp. 201-2). And, he asks, why it is obvious that equality of outcome would be preferred. Moreover, Rawls writes as if he believes that total output is primarily a consequence of social cooperation, and because the total product is the result of social co-operation he presumes it is a 'social' responsibility to distribute it. According to Nozick, cooperation consists of a sequence of exchanges, and the ensuing total output is wholly accidental. This total product is not, therefore, common property available for distribution. Why, he asks, 'isn't the appropriate ... set of holdings just the one which *actually occurs* via this process of mutually-agreed-to exchanges whereby people choose to give others what they are entitled to give or hold?' (ibid., pp. 186-7). Ultimately, Nozick believes, all patterned theories, of which Rawls' is the most sophisticated, fail to respect the individual.

Does a Minimal State Lack Lustre?

Nozick draws attention to two 'noteworthy implications' of his standpoint: 'the state may not use its coercive apparatus for the purpose of getting some citizens to aid others, or in order to prohibit activities to people for their *own* good or protection' (ibid., p. ix).

The minimal state adumbrated by Robert Nozick permits taxation for the maintenance of a protective system of law and order but forbids taxation for welfare or social security purposes (1974, p. 115). He writes, for instance, that 'Taxation of earnings from labor is on a par with forced labor' (ibid., p. 169). His objection stands whether the purpose of the taxation is to assist a strictly limited number of needy persons (as Milton Friedman would justify) or whether it is to achieve some predefined material end-state. And he objects whether the redistribution is carried out by means of 'taxation on wages or on wages over a certain amount, or through seizure of profits, or through there being a big *social pot* so that its not clear what's coming from where and what's going where' (ibid., p. 172).

It is common to denounce those who advocate this view as callous. Nozick comments in the preface to *Anarchy, State, and Utopia* that when he first reached the conclusion that the state should neither compel some of its citizens to aid other people, nor undertake programmes for their own good, he felt uneasy. His conclusion seemed 'callous towards the needs and sufferings of others'. And he acknowledges that many share this view. But he emphasises that he only rules out *coercive* methods of helping the poor, the vast array of voluntary methods remain available (p. ix).

Compared with his own view, Nozick is keenly aware of the allure of socialism. It appears to be rooted in a commitment to decency, caring for others, compassion. Even though the reality of socialism wherever it has been tried has been very different, the use of humanitarian rhetoric and the promise of a better life—a socialist utopia—give it a strong attraction.

Nozick questions whether the ideal of a minimal state lacks lustre: 'Can it thrill the heart or inspire people to struggle or sacrifice? Would anyone man barricades under its banner?' (ibid., p. 297). Utopian plans aim at creating the best possible world. But is there any *one* best possible world for all of us? Surely, argues Nozick, the great differences between people—in talent, aptitude, values— mean that at any given moment no single social order could be the best for everyone. And given each person's uncertainty about his own potential and our limited awareness of what the future holds, surely many alternative utopias ought to be on trial at any moment? This is what a minimal state offers. A framework within which we can each pursue our *own* utopia. Each can seek to achieve his own vision of the good life, subject to one limitation—he must secure only volunteers to share it with him. Far from lacking lustre compared with socialism, Nozick finds the minimal state singularly inspiring, It *is* utopia:

The minimal state treats us as inviolate individuals, who may not be used in certain ways by others as means or tools or instruments or resources; it treats us as persons having individual rights with the dignity this constitutes. Treating us with respect by respecting our rights, it allows us, individually or with whom we choose, to choose our life and to realize our ends and our conception of ourselves, insofar as we can, aided by the voluntary cooperation of other individuals possessing the same dignity. How *dare* any state or group of individuals do more. Or less. (ibid., pp. 333-4)

AYN RAND'S OBJECTIVISM

Nozick's political conclusions were shared by Ayn Rand, though on very different grounds (Nozick, 1982). She also rejected anarchism in favour of a minimal state confined to external protection and the maintenance of internal justice: the 'protection of individual rights', she says, 'is the only proper purpose of a government' (Rand, 1964, p. 110). She goes further than Nozick, however, in urging that payment for government services should be voluntary. Nevertheless, she accepts that voluntary funding would only work when 'the basic principles and institutions of a free society' have been established. It would not work today, and is therefore, 'the last, *not* the first, reform to advocate' (pp. 116-8).

Ayn Rand is most noted for her efforts to expound an ethical basis for *'laissez-faire* capitalism'. She called her theory 'objectivism' because it was an attempt to provide an objective answer to the question 'Why do men need a code of values?' Her starting-point is her dislike of the morality which prevailed at the time she was writing. She saw the prevailing orthodoxy as a narrowly conceived altruism which lumped together two moral questions in a single 'package deal': (a) what values should be held; and (b) who benefits from these values? Altruism, she says, substitutes the second question for the first. It declares that actions taken for the benefit of others are good; and that actions for one's own benefit are bad. In so doing 'it evades the task of defining a code of moral values, thus leaving man ... without moral guidance' (1964, p. viii). Observe, she says, the warped moral judgements this produces:

An industrialist who produces a fortune, and a gangster who robs a bank are regarded as equally immoral, since they both sought wealth for their own 'selfish' benefit. A young man who gives up his career in order to support his parents and never rises beyond the rank of grocery clerk is regarded as morally superior to the young man who endures an excruciating struggle and achieves his personal ambition. A dictator is regarded as moral, since the unspeakable atrocities he committed were intended to benefit 'the people', not himself. (ibid., p. viii)

On the contrary, insists Rand, *'concern with his own interests*, is the essence of a moral existence'. But the right to act in pursuit of his own self-interest is not a licence for a person to 'do as he pleases' (ibid., pp. ix-x). The 'standard of value of the Objectivist ethics—the standard by which one judges what is good or evil—is *man's life*, or: that which is required for man's survival *qua* man':

Since reason is man's basic means of survival, that which is proper to the life of a rational being is the good; that which negates, opposes or destroys it is the evil.

Since everything man needs has to be discovered by his own mind and produced by his own effort, the two essentials of the method of survival proper to a rational being are: thinking and productive work. (ibid., p. 23)

Force destroys reason and is therefore immoral. No man, it follows, may *initiate* the use of force, though self-defence is permitted. From this flows the conclusion that the only proper purpose of government is protection of the individual (ibid., pp. 32-3). It also follows, according to Rand, that the principle of trade is the 'only ethical principle for all human relationships'. This is because a trader is a man who earns what he gets and does not take what he does not deserve. He expects to be paid only for his achievements. He treats his fellows, not as masters or slaves, but as independent equals. He deals with them only by unforced exchange, which benefits both parties (ibid., p. 31).

To sum up: according to Rand, human life is an ultimate value, an end in itself. Essential to life is the making of rational judgements or choices. Thus, anything which impedes this rationality impedes life itself. All coercion is therefore wrong and consequently government may do no more than protect its citizens' rights.

Ayn Rand has received little serious attention from philosophers. Her ideas made their effect felt largely through her best-selling novels. Nevertheless a number of contemporary American scholars are influenced by her, notably Tibor Machan, Douglas Rasmussen and Douglas Den Uyl.

Ayn Rand has been important, not so much as a philosopher, but more as a morale booster. In the post-war years, and especially during the early 1960s, the liberal tradition was on the defensive. The men and women who defended individual freedom knew they were not immoral, but they found themselves denounced as cruel, callous, black-hearted ideologues. Then along came Ayn Rand. Not for her a slightly shame-faced insistence that 'capitalism' and the pursuit of profit were unfortunately necessary, however distasteful this may be, to keep the wheels of industry turning. No. Capitalism was the only moral cause worthy of the name. Intellectuals should fight for capitalism, not on practical grounds, but on moral grounds. 'Fight', she said, 'for the value of your person', and for the 'essence of that which is man: for his sovereign rational mind':

Fight with the radiant certainty and absolute rectitude of knowing that yours is the Morality of Life and that yours is the battle for any achievement, any value, any grandeur, any goodness, any joy that has ever existed on this earth' (1961, pp. 54, 192).

GUIDE TO READING

For a first crack at anarcho-libertarianism David Friedman's amusing and succinct *The Machinery of Freedom* (1978) is strongly recommended. Murray Rothbard's most accessible book is *For a New Liberty* (1978). Also of interest is *Power and Market* (1977) and his lengthy, *Man, Economy and State* (1962). Geoffrey Sampson's *An End to Allegiance* (1984) is an informative introduction with a British flavour; and more useful still is Hospers (1971). Tuccille (1971), Machan (ed.) (1974) and (1982) are also well worth consulting. A good bibliography has been produced by Tame, in Seldon (ed.) (1985), pp. 252-61. Nozick's main ideas are contained in *Anarchy, State, and Utopia* (1974). Lucas (1980) especially Chapter 12 provides some effective criticism of Nozick. A valuable set of essays, some critical and some defensive, has been collected by Jeffrey Paul in *Reading Nozick* (1982). This volume also contains Nozick's critique of Ayn Rand's 'objectivism' and a defence of Rand by Douglas Den Uyl and Douglas Rasmussen. Hospers (1967) is one of the few philosophy textbooks to deal with Rand. *For the New Intellectual* gives a good insight into Ayn Rand's contribution. Her best-known novel is *Atlas Shrugged*.

3 Friedman and the Chicago School

The Chicago School was founded in the 1920s by Henry C. Simons and Frank H. Knight. Today Milton Friedman is its most notable representative, though valuable contributions have also been made by many others, including George Stigler, Gary Becker and Ronald Coase.

Of all the members of the liberal counter-revolution, Professor Milton Friedman is the best known. He has attracted not only far wider critical attention from fellow economists, his name is also far better known outside the academic world. His advocacy of both a money-supply growth rule and the retrenchment of government activity has earned him the unremitting hostility of statist socialists and the vested interests which stand to lose as a result of his policies.

To many of these critics Friedman is the archetypal black-hearted right-wing ideologue, utterly lacking in concern for the poor. In fact Friedman's own origins were humble. He was born in Brooklyn, New York, the son of poor Jewish immigrants. Before his birth his mother had worked as a seamstress in a New York sweatshop, and as a student Friedman's poverty forced him to abandon his studies at the University of Chicago, begun in 1932. He was, however, fortunate enough to win a scholarship to Columbia University, where he studied for his doctorate. Like many Americans, therefore, Friedman's commitment to a free society has grown out of his personal experience. Compared with any known alternative, it seems to him that freedom gives greater hope to the poor. With hard work, even the most humble person can succeed.

The chapter is divided into four sections. The first considers the Chicago School's view of the scientific status of economics; the second, Friedman's contribution to the understanding of inflation; the third, his thinking about the role of the state; finally, the contributions of other Chicago School members are briefly described.

THE CHICAGO SCHOOL AND 'ECONOMIC SCIENCE'

Before he attracted attention as an advocate of revised monetary policies, Friedman had already achieved a well-established position as a leader in his field. How does he see his role as an economist?

Friedman's theory of the role and scientific status of economics arises from his wider commitment to liberty. If we are to live together in peace then we need ways of settling our difference without fighting each other. In his view, economic science, or positive economics, can help to make this possible. Friedman distinguishes between 'positive' economics and 'normative' economics. Positive economics is 'in principle independent of any particular ethical position'. It deals with 'what is' not 'what ought to be'. The task of positive economics is to 'provide a system of generalizations that can be used to make correct predictions about the consequences of any change in circumstances' (1953, p. 4).

Friedman's view lies firmly in the Popperian tradition, which rejects the contention that the natural and social sciences are fundamentally different and holds that they share a common method. Friedman concedes that the economist, like all social scientists, is part of the situation he is investigating and that this presents special difficulties. But it does not represent a 'fundamental distinction' between the social and physical sciences' (ibid., p. 5.) The fact that controlled experiments cannot be carried out with the same ease presents still further difficulties. But it does not reduce economics to the status of mere opinion. The researcher has to resort to the evidence thrown up by experience and such evidence may be patchy or less than wholly apposite. It may be complex and more difficult to interpret, and this makes the weeding-out of unsuccessful hypotheses slow and difficult: 'They are seldom downed for good and are always cropping up again' (ibid., pp. 1-11). But often, Friedman argues, such evidence can be as conclusive as experimental findings.

Although Friedman is careful to point out that positive and normative economics are separate enterprises, he does not believe that normative economics can be *wholly* independent of positive economics. Any political conclusion rests on prediction and a prediction, he says, must be based on positive economics. This is why positive economics is important. Differences of view based largely or exclusively on fundamental value judgements can ultimately only be settled by violence, but it has remained Friedman's conviction that 'the basic differences' between economists are 'empirical, not theoretical' (1974a, p. 61). It follows that recourse to the scientific method is vital if we are to solve our problems without violence.

Differences over minimum wage laws provide an example. Underlying the differing standpoints is agreement that it is desirable that there should be a 'living wage' for all. The divergence of opinion is largely the result of different beliefs about the efficacy of this or that measure. Advocates of legal minimum wages believe, that is they predict, that minimum wages will diminish poverty. Opponents believe (predict) that legal minimum wages will generate poverty by increasing unemployment and that this offsets any gain to those who remain in work at the legal minimum (1953, p. 6). Neither side wishes to see people fall below a certain 'decent' minimum, and for Friedman the alternative to minimum wage laws is to subsidise people in work through a negative income tax. This kills two birds with one stone: employment opportunities are maximised whilst poverty is also eliminated.

Similar differences in the predicted consequences of following this or that course of action lie behind disputes over trade union law, the regulation of monopolies, monetary policy, and the effectiveness of state intervention in a wide range of matters. 'I venture the judgement', says Friedman, 'that currently in the Western world ... differences about economic policy among disinterested citizens derive predominantly from different predictions about the economic consequences of taking action ... rather than from fundamental differences in basic values, differences about which men can ultimately only fight' (ibid., p. 5). Value-judgements are not unimportant, but positive economics can help to narrow the gap between opponents.

INFLATION AND UNEMPLOYMENT

Friedman's commitment to a scientific method which emphasises the ability of propositions to yield accurate predictions is no better exemplified than in his investigations of the causes of inflation. His conclusions are based on mammoth studies of the history of monetary policy.

Post-war economic policies pursued by Western governments have been based largely on the thinking of J. M. Keynes and his followers. The idea has been to maintain full employment by attempting to iron out booms and slumps through the manipulation of fiscal policy: on the one hand, during recession, cutting taxes and/or increasing official spending on public works such as roads and railways to reduce unemployment; or, on the other hand, raising taxes or cutting government capital programmes to 'slow down' the economy. It later came to be believed that there was a trade-off between unemployment and inflation. Governments had to balance the one against the other by adept use of fiscal policy. They might find themselves being criticised for making the wrong choice between inflation and unemployment, but either way, it was thought that high unemployment and high inflation could not occur simultaneously.

Two factors brought about a change in this orthodoxy. First, Friedman's investigations of monetary history, originally published in 1963, argued that the cause of the Great Depression—a vital event in the determination of post-war attitudes—had been misunderstood. Second, the results produced by Keynesian policies in the post-war years did not match expectations. In particular, during the 1960s and 1970s, high unemployment and high inflation (stagflation) occurred at the same time. By the mid-1970s inflation was accelerating at an alarming rate. It was at this stage that Friedman's ideas rapidly became influential.

The Keynesian Revolution
The Great Depression was a formative experience for many who lived through the 1920s and 1930s. The long years of high unemployment severely undermined faith in political and economic freedom. For many years before the First World War unemployment had varied in roughly 7–10–year cycles from about 2 to 8 per cent. But from 1921 until 1939 unemployment in Britain never fell below 10 per cent and in 1931 and 1932 it was over 20 per cent.

The reaction of many was bewilderment. Previously it had been assumed that if unemployment rose then wages would fall. It would then become more attractive for some employers to hire workers at these lower rates. Varying wage rates would, therefore, tend to keep the demand and supply of labour in balance. Nineteenth-century evidence clearly supported this view. But the Great Depression did not seem to fit the pattern.

The publication in 1936 of Keynes' *The General Theory of Employment, Interest and Money* appeared to provide an explanation. Employment, said Keynes, depends on aggregate spending, which takes two forms: consumption and investment. People may consume or they may save. If they consume then they create employment. But if they save this will only create employment if their savings are invested. If savings are held in cash or used to purchase interest-bearing securities this does not necessarily create employment.

Hitherto the rate of interest had been understood as the price which kept the availability of funds (savings) for investment in balance with the demand. Keynes took a different view. The willingness to save, he said, depends on factors independent of the rate of interest. There is, therefore, no mechanism by which the demand for investment equilibrates with the propensity to save (1936, p. 167).

Also contrary to prevailing assumptions, he argued that the unequal distribution of wealth militated against full employment. The imposition of death duties at the end of the nineteenth century had led to the gradual removal of extreme disparities in wealth, but further moves in that direction were inhibited by the belief that capital investment depended on savings and that a continued high level of saving depended on the willingness of the rich to save 'out of their superfluity' (ibid., p. 372).

But according to Keynes, the growth of capital was held back by a low propensity to consume (or put the other way round, a high propensity to save). It followed that the accumulations of the wealthy, if they were not invested in physical capital, helped to cause unemployment. He concluded that an increase in death duties, therefore, would *promote* capital growth, and not diminish it as was frequently contended. Not only would huge, and in his view unproductive, estates be diminished, but an increase in revenue from death duties would also enable the government to cut other taxes. This would increase consumption, and—because an increase in the propensity to consume also increased the inducement to invest—it would promote capital growth (ibid., p. 373).

Hitherto, high rates of interest had been regarded as necessary to attract funds for investment (savings). But low rates, Keynes pointed out, would encourage still greater investment. Therefore, he reasoned, the rate of interest should be lowered by government action to promote more investment. He doubted whether 'the influence of banking policy' alone would be sufficient to determine the optimum rate of interest, and argued therefore (if somewhat cryptically) that 'a somewhat comprehensive socialisation of investment will prove the only means of securing an approximation to full employment'. He added, however, that 'beyond this no obvious case is made out for a system of State Socialism which would embrace most of the economic life of the community' (ibid., p. 378).

Keynes' analysis also appeared to discredit another of the price mechanisms previously regarded as vital to understanding the workings of a free market, namely wage rates. Conventionally, variations in individual wage rates were thought to help balance the demand and supply of labour. If individuals accepted 'going rates', experience during the nineteenth century suggested that all except those inevitably between jobs at any given moment would find work. Keynes challenged this assumption. Unless aggregate demand was manipulated by government, he said, a great many individuals could remain unemployed for very long periods. Keynes' views were widely accepted. As Lord Beveridge commented in *Full Employment in a Free Society,* one part of Keynes' analysis was 'accepted by all persons qualified to judge': that the 'demand for and supply of labour in total do not get adjusted automatically either by the rate of interest or by bargains about money wages' (1944, p. 97).

Hand in hand with Keynes' view went the further judgement that the quantity of money in circulation was relatively unimportant, though Keynes himself did not disregard the influence of money. Nevertheless, until the Great Depression, the quantity theory of money (that an increase in the money supply would lead to inflation) was almost universally accepted as valid by economists; but after the publication of Keynes *General Theory* in 1936, it was widely believed that quantity theory had been falsified.

It was also widely believed that the Great Depression in America had demonstrated that controlling the quantity of money was ineffective in maintaining the stability of the economy. This was because prices fell and business declined in spite of what was believed to have been an easy monetary policy. In Keynes' view the Great Depression was the result of a collapse of demand for investment, which reflected the low demand for goods. Monetary policy, he believed, had proved incapable of stimulating the demand required to reduce unemployment. The chief role of

monetary policy was to keep interest rates down in order
to encourage investment.

Mistaken Interpretation of the Great Depression

However, the causes of the Great Depression began to be
re-assessed in the post-war years. In the United States the
Great Depression began in 1929 and ended in 1933.
Output fell by one-third and unemployment rose to 25 per
cent of the workforce. In Britain the impact was less sharp
but more prolonged. It began in 1925 with the return to
the gold standard at the pre-war rate, and continued until
the gold standard was abandoned in 1931, although re-
covery was very slow.

In 1963 Friedman's history of US monetary policy was
first published. (Since 1982 a comparative study of US and
UK monetary policy has been available.) The findings
were stunning. He and Anna Schwartz found that monetary
policy had caused, or at least severely exacerbated, the
Depression in America. Contrary to the impression given
at the time, they found that under the guidance of the
Federal Reserve Board the quantity of money in circulation between 1919 and 1933 had been *reduced* by one-
third, the largest and longest decline in the stock of
money in the period from 1867 to 1960 studied by Friedman
and Schwartz. In the public mind the Great Depression
was interpreted as a great 'market failure', a failure of
capitalism. The conclusion was drawn that the market
economy was fundamentally unstable unless its weaknesses
were rectified by greater government intervention. Friedman
believes his analysis shows this claim to be incorrect. The
Depression in America was the result, not of the failure of
'capitalism', but of 'government failure'. It was caused by
the failure of the Federal Reserve System to perform its
role as intended.

The Depression is widely believed to have begun with
the stock market crash on Black Thursday, 29 October
1929. But according to Friedman this was not the beginning. Business activity had reached a peak in August and
had already fallen by late October. The crash reflected the
puncturing of a unsustainable speculative bubble. This

created considerable caution among potential investors and had a multiplier effect.

These effects of the crash were worsened by the actions of the Federal Reserve System. Instead of expanding the money supply to offset the contraction caused by the collapse, the quantity of money was allowed to decline throughout 1930. Up to October 1930 it declined by 2.6 per cent. Then in the autumn of 1930 came a run on the banks following some bank failures in the Mid-West and South. In December 1930 the Bank of the United States closed. Although it was only a private bank, its name implied official status and this worsened the impact of its failure. Panic spread and 352 banks failed in December 1930 alone.

The Federal Reserve System stood by and let the bank failures occur. If it had purchased government bonds on the open market, the tried and tested device usually employed, this would have given the banks the extra cash to meet depositors' demands. But it failed to do so. In September 1931 Britain abandoned the gold standard and the Federal Reserve System reacted by raising the interest rate it charged banks for loans (bank rate in the UK, the discount rate in the US). This compounded the problem. There was a further banking panic in 1933. In 1929 there had been 25,000 banks. By early 1933 the number had shrunk to 18,000.

Why did the Federal Reserve System make these mistakes? The Federal Reserve System had functioned well in the 1920s. It had maintained stability using the money supply to counterbalance changes in trade. According to Friedman, it failed to continue this policy during the vital Depression years due to the rivalry between the Federal Reserve Bank of New York and the Federal Reserve Board in Washington. The Board in Washington was determined to establish its leadership, after many years in which New York had set the pace. As part of this power struggle the Board rejected the course urged by the New York Federal Reserve Bank, the open market purchase of government securities. It was not until 1933 that the tried and tested solution was attempted, and a new system of monetary controls initiated.

Thus, the Great Depression, widely interpreted at the time and subsequently as a failure of 'capitalism', was in reality a consequence of the failure of a government agency. In the view of Friedman and Schwartz, the Federal Reserve System failed to perform its allotted task. Their evidence also refutes the later Keynesian claim that 'money does not matter'. On re-examination, writes Friedman, the Great Depression was 'a tragic testament to the effectiveness of monetary policy, not a demonstration of its impotence' (1970, p. 12).

Keynesianism Refuted by Post-War Experience

Keynesianism dominated economic thought in Britain from the Second World War until the 1970s. Gradually, however, the evidence against Keynes' view mounted. In Friedman's judgement three experiences were decisive in bringing about the counter-revolution. The first was that the post-Second World War depression predicted by many Keynesians did not happen. This 'stagnation thesis' anticipated that once the massive wartime levels of military spending ceased there would be a corresponding collapse of demand resulting in depression and deflation. But there was no such collapse. The second experience was the failure of post-war 'cheap money' policies. Both the United States and Britain tried to keep interest rates low to encourage investment, but the policy had to be abandoned in both countries as inflation took hold.

The most decisive experience, however, was the occurrence of 'stagflation'. Until the mid-1960s it was assumed by virtually all economists that there was a stable relationship between the level of unemployment and the rate of change of wages. It was expected that high levels of unemployment would be accompanied by falling wages and low levels of unemployment by rising wages. Wage changes in turn affected prices. This theory was usually expressed in the form of a Phillips curve, first suggested by A.W. Phillips in 1958. His famous graph plotted the rate of change of wages against unemployment. The rate of change of wages corresponds roughly to price changes and for this reason the graph is commonly shown as plotting the rate of price change against unemployment, missing out the intermediate step of wage changes. The Phillips curve appeared to offer policy-makers a clear choice. They could have low unemployment with higher inflation; or higher unemployment with lower inflation.

However, experience failed to bear out the hypothesis. High unemployment, it turned out, could be accompanied by high inflation, a phenomenon which came to be called 'stagflation'. In response to this new evidence, Friedman was one of those who developed an alternative hypothesis. First, he reasserted the importance of the distinction between real and nominal wages. And second he emphasised the importance of the *perceived*, as opposed to the *real* or *nominal* changes in wage rates. If there is, for instance, an unanticipated change in aggregate demand each producer is likely to interpret this as special to his product. He may decide to produce more at the higher price and he may be willing to pay higher nominal wages, because what matters to him is, not wage costs generally, but the particular cost of the wages of his employees as against the new higher product price. It may well be that he perceives a higher nominal wage as a lower real wage (i.e. as a proportion of the price he can obtain for his product). What counts for the employee is the real purchasing power of his wage. He may perceive a rise in nominal wages as a real increase and this may attract more workers to a particular sector or company.

But, as Friedman writes, 'only surprises matter' (1977b, p. 12). Workers who interpret a nominal increase as a real increase are deceived in the short run only. Employers too will realise their mistake and each will adjust to the new rate of inflation, or rather the new rate of *perceived* inflation. This means that at any moment workers and employers will assume (predict) a certain rate of inflation, and build this into their calculations. The result is that it takes still higher inflation to 'trick' them again into interpreting a general increase in prices as peculiar to them.

Thus, what matters is not inflation as such but unanticipated inflation. This means that there is no stable relationship between inflation and unemployment and that public policy can not be based on trading off one against the other. We do not, says Friedman, have a choice between inflation and unemployment: 'We have been misled by a false dichotomy: inflation or unemployment. That option is an illusion. The real option is only whether we have higher unemployment as a result of higher inflation or as a temporary side effect of curing inflation' (1980, p. 282).

How then, can we explain the *apparent* link between inflation and unemployment? There is, in Friedman's terminology, a 'natural rate of unemployment', which depends on real factors—how smoothly the labour market adjusts, the extent of competition or monopoly, restrictive practices, and generally, how well producers are meeting the requirements of consumers. A government can have a temporary effect on the rate of unemployment by changing the money supply, but in the long-run there is no escape from the 'natural rate' by monetary manipulation alone (1977b, pp. 13-15). (The natural rate can, however, be affected by removing barriers to the efficient working of the market.)

Thus, if unemployment is below the natural rate as a result of the expansion of the money supply, a reduction in the quantity of money in circulation will cause unemployment to increase until the natural rate is reached. 'Full employment' cannot be achieved without regard to the 'real' factors which determine why one company thrives while others struggle, why employers hire and fire workers, and why employees prefer this to that job. And because workers and employers adjust their expectations to the perceived rate of inflation, the numbers in employment can only be kept above the natural rate for any length of time by *accelerating* inflation.

Friedman acknowledges that his 'natural rate' hypothesis cannot account for the more recent development of what he calls 'slumpflation'. Higher inflation has been accompanied, not merely by higher unemployment, but by still higher unemployment than the 'natural rate' hypothesis would suggest. He believes this is because the economic climate appears to many actors to be volatile. The government intervenes here and there to control prices or wages, and market forces are unable to function. The economic system cannot operate at its best amidst constant uncertainty. It becomes generally less efficient and unemployment ensues at a still greater level than the natural rate theory predicts (1977b, p. 31). This is borne out by experience in the USA since 1979, during which time monetary growth has been volatile. Milton and Rose Friedman describe changes in the quantity of money during this period as more unstable than in any five-year period since the last war (1985, p. 92).

To sum up: inflation is a consequence of increasing the money supply in excess of the rate of growth of real aggregate output; and unemployment, except in the short run, depends on 'real' factors—restrictive practices, entry barriers, ease of movement, and above all, the extent to which resources are productively used and consumer wants well served.

The Quantity Theory of Money

Thus, for Friedman, the lesson of the Great Depression and of post-war economic policies is that control of the quantity of money in circulation is vital to the maintenance of economic stability. If a government relies upon fiscal policy alone—regardless of whether a budget deficit is funded by borrowing or printing money—it may not produce the intended result. Only an increase in the money supply will be expansionary (1970, p. 17). This is because, if the government borrows to cover a deficit at the market rate, any money it raises cannot be spent again by the lenders. A deficit alone cannot, therefore, create expansion. But if the government prints money to cover a deficit then expansion will (temporarily) follow. The determining factor is the money supply, not the deficit alone.

Friedman's view is not new. Indeed, before the publication of Keynes' *General Theory*, the quantity theory was widely taken for granted. In Friedman's opinion, all the historical evidence supports the conclusion that the quantity of money in circulation determines inflation. The quantity theory is amply demonstrated, not only by the history of the use of paper money, but also by experience of the use of commodities, like gold, silver, tobacco and seashells as money. For instance, from the early years of the seventeenth century until the second half of the nineteenth century, tobacco was the basic medium of exchange in Virginia and neighbouring colonies. It so happened that the price tobacco could fetch in England was higher than the cost of production and naturally planters set out to produce more. Inflation was the result, and within 50 years of colonisation the prices of goods in tobacco had risen 40-fold. As tobacco continued to buy less of other valued items tobacco farmers set out to cut down production. Laws were passed requiring part of the crop to be destroyed, and some turned to crime, roving the countryside in gangs destroying tobacco plants. This reached such a scale that in 1684 the Assembly passed a law stating that for eight or more persons to travel around destroying tobacco plants constituted treason, for which they were liable to be hanged (Friedman and Friedman, 1980, pp. 250–1).

Blame for inflation is often placed outside government, but this is a mistake. According to Friedman, it cannot be blamed on avaricious trade unions, greedy businessmen, or Arab sheikhs. Each of these may cause a rise in particular prices, but not a rise in the *general* level of prices. Nor, if exchange rates are flexible is inflation imported, though Friedman accepts that this claim was often correct when all leading nations were simultaneously on the gold standard. But today the quantity of money is fixed by governments printing paper money or making book-entries.

The relationship between an increase in the quantity of money and inflation is not simple. Friedman concedes that there is not a 'precise one-to-one correspondence between the rate of monetary growth and the rate of inflation' (1980, p. 255). The consequences may take years to show. This is because a great many factors affect *individual* prices and therefore at any moment will affect the *average* price level. But, he says, it is essential to distinguish clearly between *relative* prices and the *general* level of prices. If, for instance, oil goes up in price and the quantity of money remains constant then people have less to spend on other items. The effect of the oil price increase will therefore be balanced out over a period as the shortage of money to spend on other items leads to downward pressure on these other prices. There will be no long-run impact on average prices. If however, the quantity of money increases at the same time as, say, a sharp increase in the price of oil, then the oil price rise will not be counterbalanced by falls in other prices, and the *general* level of prices will increase.

The Cure for Inflation

According to Friedman, there is only one cure for inflation: a slower rate of increase in the quantity of money. Just as it takes time for inflation to develop so it takes time for inflation to be cured. Unpleasant side effects of the cure are unavoidable.

He compares inflation with alcoholism: the good effects come first, only next morning does a hangover ensue. With inflation the initial effects seem good: the greater quantity of money enables whoever has access to it to spend more, jobs are more plentiful, business picks up. But then prices start to rise: workers find that their higher money wages buy less goods, businesses find their costs have risen, and put up prices still further. Prices continue to go up, but demand stagnates. As with alcohol or drug abuse, the temptation is to increase the dose. But it takes ever-larger quantities of money to give the economy the same 'kick' (1980, p. 271). Only surprises matter and as people catch on, only larger doses of inflation will reduce unemployment. However, governments have been unwilling to administer the required higher dose because, as inflation gets into double figures, so it tends to become a political issue. Consequently the general trend in inflation has been up for the last 20 years, and successively higher inflation has been accompanied by higher unemployment (1985, p. 89).

The analogy with alcohol can be extended, for if the supply of money is curtailed then withdrawal symptoms follow: a lower rate of growth and temporarily high unemployment. This makes it very difficult to cure inflation once it has started. But there is another problem, namely that not everyone loses by inflation. The government, in particular, benefits, because it can spend more on buying the votes of favoured groups in the population, whilst appearing not to take the money from anyone else. This is one reason why some governments have failed to control inflation, despite setting out to do so.

Moreover, inflation takes time to remedy. We have already seen how unanticipated inflation sends false signals to producers. Individual product or service prices are normally going up or down reflecting changes in demand and supply. Used to interpreting price changes as signals that demand and supply conditions have changed, the general increase in prices initially confuses suppliers into thinking that demand has gone up. As a result the initial side-effect of increasing the money supply is to give the impression of greater prosperity. But soon producers realise that price increases do not necessarily signal changes in demand for their product. When workers, manufacturers and retailers discover they have been 'fooled' they adjust accordingly by putting up prices still further. A price–wage spiral is the outcome. Everyone adjusts their expectations accordingly (1980, pp. 274-6). Thus, inflation takes time to remedy because these expectations cannot be changed overnight. It takes time—possibly years—to satisfy employers, employees and customers that the general price level is stable and that price changes are *particular* to individual products.

Fine-Tuning or Steady Growth
Some economists favour the use of monetary policy for 'fine-tuning' the economy, varying the quantity of money to counterbalance other forces making for booms or slumps. Friedman counsels against such arbitrary intervention be-

cause he believes our understanding is still too limited: 'our present understanding of the relation between money, prices and output is so meagre ... there is so much leeway in these relations, that such discretionary changes do more harm than good.' He prefers instead of fine-tuning, a policy under which the quantity of money would grow at a steady rate—'month-in, month-out, year-in, year-out'—to provide a stable monetary framework (1970, p. 26). Monetary policy can only accomplish so much: 'Just as I believe that Keynes' disciples went further than he himself would have gone, so I think there is a danger that people who find a few good predictions have been made by using monetary aggregates will try to carry that relationship further than it can go.' A steady rate of monetary growth cannot produce perfect stability, but it can 'provide a framework under which a country can have little inflation and much growth' (ibid., pp. 27-8).

Side-Effects

Can anything be done about the side-effects of controlling the money supply? The side-effects of curing inflation cannot be avoided, argues Friedman, but they can be mitigated. The most important device for mitigating the side-effects has already been mentioned, to slow inflation '*gradually but steadily* by a policy announced in advance and adhered to so it becomes credible' (1980, p. 277). This enables people to adjust gradually.

For instance, in place of the volatile monetary policy pursued by the Reagan administration, Milton and Rose Friedman would have preferred President Reagan to have kept his pledge to introduce a 'stable, sound and predictable monetary policy'. They believe the Federal Reserve System should have reduced monetary growth from around 8.5 per cent in early 1980 to 5 or 6 per cent in 1982, and that it should have continued to reduce it slowly thereafter. The result would have been a longer recession than the six-month one from January to July 1980. But the revival would have been longer, more like three years, instead of the one year from July 1980 to July 1981. Unemployment would initially have risen faster but would not have reached the levels actually attained. There would have been no decline in real per capita income and wages. Interest rates would have been lower, possible by 3–5 per cent. The cost of this policy of steady reductions in monetary growth would have been a slower reduction in inflation, possibly around 2 per cent a year less. But it is far outweighed by the advantages: more people in work, less pressure to increase government spending and a more stable economy (1985, pp. 91-2).

Index-linking of contracts, including contracts of employment, mortgages and other loans, and tenancy agreements is strongly recommended to cushion the impact of change. Friedman believes it is especially important to index tax brackets so that governments cannot change the burden of taxation without a vote. It also gives government a disincentive to inflate, since their gain from doing so would be smaller. Similarly, government borrowing should be in the form of purchasing-power securities so that governments cannot cheat people by allowing the real value of the sums borrowed from its citizens to erode. For Friedman such measures are a moral requirement. Their main purpose is to improve our political institutions. Inflation is, he says, 'a form of taxation without representation' (1974c, p. 73).

Many Keynesians now accept that if the money supply is expanded more rapidly than the rate of growth of output, then inflation will result. But, they are not prepared to accept Friedman's cure. A common reaction has been to argue for the continued manipulation of aggregate demand (through fiscal, monetary and exchange rate policies) in order to reduce unemployment, whilst accepting that additional measures are necessary to prevent real wage increases from preventing a fall in unemployment. Professor J. E. Meade, for example, urges the establishment of 'impartial wage tribunals' in place of 'uncontrolled monopoly bargaining' (1985, p. 28). Such a scheme would ensure that any increase in total money expenditures would lead, not to an increase in money earnings and the general level of prices, but to 'an increase in employment, output and sales at uninflated money wage-rates and prices' (ibid., p. 17). (Further discussion of the political impact of 'monetarism' can be found in Chapter 8.)

FRIEDMAN AND THE ROLE OF THE STATE

His belief that economics can help opponents to settle their differences peacefully has guided Friedman in his work, not only on monetary policy, but also on the wider role of the state, though here he has not carried out the empirical work which is the hallmark of his work on monetary policy. Friedman has published three works in which he considers the relationship between freedom in economic matters and individual freedom in general. In 1962 he published *Capitalism and Freedom* which was based on some lectures delivered in the mid-1950s. In 1979 he first published jointly with his wife, Rose, *Free to Choose,* based on their successful TV series in which they explore a series of political reforms aimed to enhance individual freedom of choice. In 1983 this was followed by the first edition of *The Tyranny of the Status Quo,* in which he and his wife discuss why Western democracies have found it so difficult to contain the power of the state.

Economic and Political Freedom

Capitalism and Freedom criticises the notion that political freedom can be maintained whilst destroying economic freedom. The chief manifestation of this deluded view, Friedman says, is democratic socialism, advocates of which condemn the denial of individual liberty typical of Soviet communism whilst simultaneously recommending Soviet economic policies. But no society which is socialist, Friedman argues, can maintain individual freedom. The historical evidence indicates that 'capitalism' is a necessary, though not a sufficient, condition for political freedom (1962, pp. 9-10). Civil liberty has survived nowhere for long unless ordinary citizens also enjoyed economic freedom.

In Friedman's view this is no historical accident. The preservation of individual freedom requires the elimination of sources of coercion, with government ranking as the most menacing potential source. It follows that new liberals should seek to eliminate concentrations of power, and especially political power, to the fullest possible extent. If this is not possible they should at least seek the dispersal of power. It is especially vital that economic activity should be removed from the control of governments. If the government's economic power is limited, this enables economic strength to become a check on political power rather than a reinforcement of it (ibid., p. 15).

Consider freedom of speech. In a free society it is, says Friedman, 'enough to have the funds' to buy space in newspapers or to print your own propaganda. In a society with a state controlled press and state controlled paper mills, this would not be enough (ibid., p. 18). In a free society, with resources dispersed among the people, it is easier for the individual to defy the government of the day—or any powerful private person or agency—than in a centralised society. Similarly, if the state or some element of it starts to persecute any section of its population, as happened in the McCarthyite era, the dispersal of economic power can mitigate the impact of official repression. Some film-makers, for instance, continued to employ the victims of McCarthyism, thus diluting the impact on them (ibid., pp. 20-1). If the Soviet government chooses to persecute someone there is no escape.

How Much Equality?
The chief reason that western countries have lost sight of the dangers of concentrated political power is that the pursuit of equality has come to be highly valued. The story of the United States, suggest Milton and Rose Friedman in *Free to Choose,* 'is the story of an economic miracle and a political miracle that was made possible by the translation into practice of two sets of ideas' (1980, p. 1). They are referring to the ideas of Adam Smith and Thomas Jefferson.

The Friedmans admire Jefferson's commitment to limited government described in his first inaugural address: 'a wise and frugal government, which shall restrain men from injuring one another, which shall leave them otherwise free to regulate their own pursuits of industry and improvement' (ibid., p. 4). It is this sentiment which, they believe, has made America a prosperous nation in which citizens are free to find happiness by making the most of their talents.

Adam Smith showed why the pursuit by each individual of his own aims did not degenerate into anarchy. Many economists assume that there is a 'fixed pie' and that one party to an exchange can only gain at the expense of the other. Smith's key insight, according to the Friedmans, was that if an exchange is strictly voluntary it will not take place unless both parties believe they will benefit from it (ibid., pp. 1-2, 13). It follows that no external force is necessary to produce cooperation among individuals who can all benefit from free exchanges.

Following Hayek, Friedman emphasises the centrality of prices. The mechanism that achieves the coordination without coercion of voluntary endeavour is the price system. It enables people, who do not need to know each other or like each other, to combine their efforts to achieve their separate goals. Prices perform three functions. They transmit information about what consumers want, the prices they will pay, and about the availability of raw materials. Second, they provide an incentive to adopt the least costly methods of production. And third, they determine who gets how much of the product—the distribution of income (ibid., p. 14).

However, the values of Smith and Jefferson have, in the view of the Friedmans, been progressively abandoned to the detriment of Western civilisation. Instead of fearing government, as did the American founding fathers, Western intellectuals have increasingly been 'attracted by the good that a stronger government could achieve—if only government power were in the 'right' hands' (ibid., p. 5). They fear that this tendency, if continued, will lead to a relapse into tyranny and misery, still the state of most of humankind. The chief culprit has been the modern thirst for equality.

The American Declaration of Independence gives some

warrant for the pursuit of equality but, the Friedmans argue, the equality the founding fathers had in mind was a very different kind from the equality of *outcome* sought today. For the founding fathers, all were equal in the sight of God and before the law. In later years, equality came to mean 'equality of opportunity', by which was meant that there should be no arbitrary barriers—birth, nationality, colour, religion, sex—standing in the path of talent. Both equality before the law and equality of opportunity proved compatible with the enjoyment of the freedom to shape one's own life. But in later years intellectuals began to demand equality of an entirely different order, 'equality of outcome'. Equality of this provenance is not compatible with liberty (ibid., p. 128).

The Friedmans' first criticism is that advocates of equality of outcome do not in practice advocate strict equality. No one maintains that everyone, regardless of age or sex, should have identical rations of food, clothing, and so on. The goal is rather 'fairness'. The difficulty with the pursuit of 'fairness' is that it lies in the eye of the beholder: 'If all are to have "fair shares", someone or some group of people must decide what shares are fair—and they must be able to impose their decisions on others, taking from those who have more than their "fair" share and giving to those who have less' (ibid., p. 135). In practice this means that political power determines the share-out.

The Friedmans also point out that many advocates of equality of outcome have a vested interest. The intellectuals for whom equality of outcome has become 'almost an article of religious faith' are the same individuals who have the most to gain from their advocacy of it. They earn high incomes promoting equality of outcome through the media or administering the programmes established in pursuit of it. The Friedmans recommend that, as a test of their sincerity, such intellectuals should renounce their high incomes and join one of the egalitarian communes dotted around America. Only then will the Friedmans believe that self-interest does not lie behind the preaching of the merits of enforced equality (ibid., p. 142).

Finally they point to the record of 'capitalism' in raising the living standards of the poor. In capitalist societies the professed ideals of egalitarians have been more
nearly reached than in socialist ones. Few people, say the
Friedmans, 'can fail to be moved by the contrast between
the luxury enjoyed by some and the grinding poverty
suffered by others' (ibid., p. 146). But they reject the view
that 'capitalism' is to blame. 'Nothing', they say, 'could be
further from the truth.' Wherever free markets have been
permitted to operate, the ordinary man 'has been able to
attain levels of living never dreamed of before' (ibid., p.
146). In free societies the poor have risen in both absolute
and relative terms.

The Friedmans conclude that a society that puts equality
of outcome before freedom will end up with neither equality nor freedom. But a society that puts freedom first 'will,
as a happy by-product, end up with both greater freedom
and greater equality'. This is because, whilst a free society
does not prevent some people from achieving positions of
advantage, it does prevent such positions from becoming
institutionalised. Incumbents are 'subject to continued
attack by other able, ambitious people'. Freedom 'pre-
serves the opportunity for today's disadvantaged to become
tomorrow's privileged and, in the process, enables almost
everyone, from top to bottom, to enjoy a fuller and richer
life' (ibid., pp. 148-9).

The Unintended Results of Statism
The Friedmans find it particularly striking that the results
achieved by collectivism have been very different from
those intended. A new class of bureaucrats has emerged,
they say, secure in their jobs and protected from inflation;
the trade unions have come to represent the best-paid
aristocrats of labour and not, as trade union propaganda
suggests, the poor and downtrodden. High taxation has
encouraged fiddling and lowered respect for the law generally (ibid., p. 144). State interference has produced perverse results across the board, in social security, education,
health and consumer protection.

Consumer Protection: Consumer protection legislation can all too easily be 'captured' by producers. This was notoriously so in the case of the Interstate Commerce Commission. Its regulation of rail traffic produced price increases which satisfied no one except the producers, and its later regulation of long-distance trucking ruined competition in that industry. It illustrates what the Friedmans call the 'natural history' of government intervention:

a real or fancied evil leads to demands to do something about it. A political coalition forms consisting of sincere, high-minded reformers and equally sincere interested parties. The incompatible objectives of the members of the coalition (e.g., low prices to consumers and high prices to producers) are glossed over by fine rhetoric about the 'public interest', 'fair competition' and the like. The coalition succeeds in getting Congress ... to pass a law.The preamble to the law pays lip service to the rhetoric and the body of the law grants power to government officials to 'do something'. The high-minded reformers experience a glow of triumph and turn their attention to new causes. The interested parties go to work to make sure that the power is used for their benefit. They generally succeed. (ibid., p. 201).

The Food and Drug Administration's (FDA's) regulation of pharmaceutical products is identified as having produced particularly harmful results. The Friedmans cite the evidence of Dr William Wardell of the Center for the Study of Drug Development at the University of Rochester that the delayed arrival of Beta-blockers in the United States, due to administrative problems at the FDA, cost around 10,000 lives a year. Also cited is the conclusion drawn in the light of a major study of the empirical evidence by Sam Peltzman, an erstwhile colleague at Chicago, that the harm done by the FDA greatly outweighed the good (ibid., pp. 206-7). The reason that the FDA causes harm is that officials err on the side of caution. As the Friedmans say, if an official approves another thalidomide his name 'will be spread over the front page of every newspaper'. But if he refuses aproval of a drug that is capable of saving many lives, no one will know about his mistake: the 'people whose lives might have been saved will not be around to protest' (ibid., p. 208).

The extent to which Friedman would retain a state regulatory apparatus in these areas is not entirely clear. He concentrates his efforts on drawing attention to the disadvantages of state regulation, but it does not follow that full-blooded deregulation would always be a good thing. Although some of Professor Friedman's pronouncements imply that he would deregulate on a massive scale, in reality he concedes that the decision whether to use the government machine or rely on voluntary cooperation is partly pragmatic: 'In any particular case of proposed intervention, we must make up a balance sheet, listing separately the advantages and disadvantages' (1980, p. ix). Consequently, when Professor Friedman has turned his mind to the practical details of reform his proposals have sometimes contained strong collectivist elements. His proposals, for negative income tax and education vouchers (see Chapter 6), for instance, concede a good deal to the collectivist case. But his discussion of consumer protection legislation strongly implies that he would sweep away the whole regulatory edifice and rely on competition to throw up suitable safeguards. He is very reluctant to concede that an alternative to the heavy-handed regulation of the FDA may be a reformed regulatory aparatus. Yet there is much evidence to suggest that the regulatory systems of other nations offer considerable advantages compared with the FDA.

The US Government General Accounting Office found that several important new drugs were introduced abroad earlier than in the USA. The mean time between application and approval in America was 23 months, compared with five months in the UK. A report by the Industry Analysis Division of the US Department of Commerce concluded that 'improvements in the regulatory testing and approval process offer the potential to significantly increase the incentives for R & D investments in the pharmaceutical industry' (US Government, 1984, pp. 48, 63). They also found that due to the stringent regulatory climate, many American companies had been transferring their research and development work to other countries.

Thus, the particular regulatory process employed by the

FDA appears to be the root of many of the problems to which Friedman draws attention, and the possibility that a process more akin to the British system may overcome these problems ought not automatically to be written off. In marked contrast to his policy recommendations for the control of inflation, which are based on well-documented research, Friedman's conclusions for consumer protection are nowhere near as well supported.

Social Security: According to Milton and Rose Friedman, many government transfers of income have been going in the wrong direction. Social Security policy in America is an excellent example, they say, of Director's Law: 'Public expenditures are made for the primary benefit of the middle class, and financed with taxes which are borne in considerable part by the poor and rich' (1980, p. 107).

In the Friedmans' view, most welfare programmes should never have been enacted. Without them, many beneficiaries would have been self-reliant individuals instead of wards of the state. They propose a scheme to bring about an orderly transfer of people from 'welfare rolls to payrolls' (ibid., p. 119). There are two elements. First, they recommend the replacement of the existing 'ragbag of specific programmes' by a single comprehensive programme of income support in cash. Second, they advocate the winding-down of Social Security and gradually requiring people to make their own arrangements for their retirement. Such an arrangement would, they say, provide a minimum for all regardless of the reasons for their need, while doing 'as little harm as possible to their character, their independence, or their incentive to better their own condition' (ibid., p. 120).

The comprehensive cash support scheme they propose would be integrated with income tax. At present each person is entitled to personal tax allowances, but if they earn less than these amounts the allowances are useless. Under the Friedmans' negative income tax scheme, if a person's income fell below the level of their personal allowances they would receive a payment from the tax authorities equivalent to the difference between their allowances and their actual income (or some percentage of the difference).

Why Do Governments Fail?

The fundamental error, the Friedmans believe, has been to fail to see danger in the concentration of power: 'We have been forgetting the basic truth that the greatest threat to human freedom is the concentration of power, whether in the hands of government or anyone else. We have persuaded ourselves that it is safe to grant power, provided it is for good purposes' (1980, p. 309). To emphasise the point they quote Justice Louis Brandeis:

Experience should teach us to be most on our guard to protect liberty when the government's purposes are beneficial. Men born to freedom are naturally alert to repel invasion of their liberty by evil-minded rulers. The greater dangers to liberty lurk in insidious encroachment by men of zeal, well-meaning but without understanding.

The Friedmans' contention is, not only that collectivism has in practice tended to serve the interests of powerful producers rather than the intended beneficiaries of intervention, but also that collectivist intervention is bound to produce this result. The reason that special interests tend to prevail lies in the nature of modern democracy. A system which operates by enacting detailed and specific legislation tends to give undue political power to small groups with highly concentrated interests. There is 'an invisible hand in politics that operates in precisely the opposite direction to Adam Smith's invisible hand. Individuals who intend only to promote the *general interest* are led by the invisible political hand to promote a *special interest* that they had no intention to promote' (ibid., p. 292).

Milton and Rose Friedman have extended their analysis in their most recent book, *The Tyranny of the Status Quo* (1985). Drawing on the experience of President Reagan, Mrs Thatcher and President Mitterrand, they argue that a new leader has a honeymoon period of six to nine months in which to make radical changes. Failure to act decisively during this time will mean that it is too late to act at all, because the 'tyranny of the status quo' quickly re-asserts itself. The reason is that any measure which affects significantly a *concentrated* group tends to have effects on members of that group which are 'substantial, occur promptly, and are highly visible'. Effects on individual members of the general population tend to be 'trival, longer delayed, and less visible':

Quick, concentrated reaction is the major source of the strength of special interest groups in a democracy—or for that matter any other kind of government. It motivates politicians to make grandiose promises to such special interests before an election—and to postpone any measures adversely affecting special interest groups until after an election (1985, p. 14).

Each such group, they say, is 'a corner of an iron triangle of beneficiaries, politicians, and bureaucrats'. This situation cannot be corrected by electing the 'right' politicians, although the role of the US presidency holds out some hope, for only the president has an incentive to serve the general interest. But ultimately little can be achieved without constitutional reform to limit the powers of government (1985, pp. 157-8).

ECONOMIC 'IMPERIALISM'

One of the characteristics of the Chicago School has been the extension of economic analysis outside the discipline's normal boundaries. Professor Gary Becker's (1976) investigations of the family have strayed so far from normal territory that Becker has been accused of economic 'imperialism'.

George Stigler—like Friedman, a Nobel prize winner—is a leader of Chicago's positivism, with its emphasis on the meticulous empirical testing of established theories. The 'sole test', he says, 'of the usefulness of an economic theory is the concordance between its predictions and the observable course of events' (1949, p. 23).

Stigler has undertaken empirical work in a number of fields. In recent years he has looked at the attitude of private industry to government regulation. Writing in 1982, he found there were 88,000 employees of 57 federal agencies regulating the US economy—a threefold increase on ten years earlier (1982, p. 8). This figure excludes the Internal Revenue Service and state and local regulators. He postulates that 'efficiency-destroying' regulation of the economy is not in the interest of consumers, and especially poor consumers. Consumers, he says, do not gain from the regulation of public utilities, financial institutions, labour markets, or imports and exports (ibid., p. 9). Producers, he says, have generally sought regulation themselves, often while maintaining the illusion of opposition. Close study often reveals that producers benefit greatly from government intervention. Some state licensing laws, for instance, require barbers to have more hours training (as many as 1200) than an airline pilot. It would appear, comments Stigler (who is noted for his sense of humour) that it is less difficult to navigate around the earth than it is around the human skull. He cites a second humorous example. A scheme was introduced by the US Department of Agriculture to compensate beekeepers whose bees died as a result of pollution. The result has been the 'complete disappearance of bees who die a natural death' (ibid., p. 9).

Racial Discrimination

Thomas Sowell is not on the staff of the University of Chicago but is a product of that university, having studied there for his doctorate. His most important contribution has been to the study of racial discrimination.

He scrutinises the common assumption that ethnic minorities owe their incomes to racial discrimination. First, he shows that some ethnic groups in America have incomes above the national average, notable the Jewish, Polish and Chinese peoples. Others, such as blacks, Mexicans, Puerto Ricans and Filipinos have incomes below the average. It cannot therefore be assumed that every ethnic group owes its average income wholly to discrimination. There must be other factors at work in place of, or as well as, discrimination. Sowell points out

that the average income of each ethnic group is itself a
statistical artefact because a wide range of disparate individuals are lumped together (1981, p. 9). Age, for instance, makes a great difference to income, and the median
incomes of the various ethnic groups differ radically. Many
higher-paid jobs require years of training and experience.
This is chiefly why families with heads in the age group
45–54 had incomes on average 93 per cent higher than
families headed by persons under 25 years of age in 1974.
It follows that if an ethnic group has a high proportion of
young members it is likely to be under-represented in
occupations requiring lengthy training, such as law and
medicine. The median age of Jews, for instance, is 46 and
of Puerto Ricans 18. This partly explains why Jewish
people earned 172 per cent of the national average income, whilst Puerto Ricans earned 63 per cent (ibid., pp.
9-11).

The average income of an ethnic group also conceals
inter-generational differences. Older blacks and Puerto
Ricans, for instance, enjoyed much less schooling than
young blacks and Puerto Ricans now do. Consequently,
older blacks are represented less frequently than other
groups who enjoyed longer schooling in occupations for
which educational qualifications are a prerequisite. But the
position is changing for younger blacks.

Sowell has also examined the history of discrimination.
He shows how in the years after the abolition of slavery
the profit motive undermined efforts by many southern
whites to hold down the pay of blacks, to cheat black
employees in company stores, and to impose unfair contracts on them by taking advantage of their illiteracy.
Gradually, the employers who did not cheat their staff and
who paid better wages attracted higher calibre employees.
Bad employers could not attract the staff they wanted or
in some cases could attract no staff at all. Their reaction
was to raise wages, because in the end profit spoke louder
than prejudice. Gradually the condition of blacks improved
(ibid., p. 37).

According to Sowell, economic theory predicts that
profit-maximising organisations would discriminate less

than non-profit organisations. If a candidate for a job was likely to be good for profits then a profit-seeking company would hire him regardless. Evidence from the railroads supports this view. When the railroads were profit-making companies blacks were *over*-represented, but when government took over blacks tended to be excluded (ibid., p. 48). In the past the federal government has adopted especially discriminatory policies. From around 1910 to 1930, reflecting white opinion, there was increasing discrimination by the federal government. Blacks were excluded, for instance, from the army and navy. But there was no comparable retrogression in private competitive industries during the same period (ibid., p. 49).

The general conclusion that Sowell draws is that a free market works to the advantage of potential victims of discrimination. The worst discrimination in the past has been perpetrated by governments under pressure from majority white opinion. In a free market, racial prejudice may be no less vehement, but the countervailing pressure of the profit motive cuts across it, to the lasting advantage of the victims of prejudice.

The Economics of Property Rights
Ronald Coase is reputed to be the originator of two new branches of economics: the economics of law, and the economics of property rights. Both branches were inspired by his seminal paper, 'The Problem of Social Cost', published in the *Journal of Law and Economics* in October 1960. And both owe much to his editorship of the *Journal of Law and Economics* since 1964. The most important of these new branches is the economics of property rights, to which I now turn. Richard Posner (1972; 1981) of the University of Chicago Law School has led the economics of law, which analyses law from an economic standpoint. He examines the law, and especially common law, as a device which works in favour of economic efficiency, rather like the price mechanism.

The economics of property rights has been developed by a number of writers. It is a critique of the neoclassical approach to externalities, formulated initially by A.C. Pigou.

Put at its simplest, the neoclassical argument is that individuals, as they go about buying and selling, take into account their private benefits and costs. But in addition to these private benefits and costs there are also side-effects, some beneficial and some harmful. Economists variously call these side-effects externalities, diseconomies, third party effects or neighbourhood effects. Because externalities are not taken into account in private dealings it is argued that the government must step in by means of regulations or taxes and/or subsidies, to ensure that external costs and benefits are not ignored. In the view of this tradition, externalities represent a failure of the market.

The economics of property rights challenges the neoclassical view by pointing out that many externalities are not the result of the failure of the market. According to Professor Coase, some negative externalities go uncompensated because of government intervention. He uses the example also selected by Pigou in the *Economics of Welfare* (1929, p. 136), namely a railway engine emitting sparks which burn nearby woodland and for which the owner of the land is not compensated. Pigou regards this as a 'natural' situation which he contrasts with one modified by state intervention to force the railway company to pay compensation. However, Coase points out that if a farmer received no compensation for the loss of woodland burnt down as a consequence of flying sparks from a steam engine in 1920 (when Pigou's first edition was published) this would have been a result, not of a 'natural' situation but of earlier government intervention. From 1860 railway undertakings with statutory authority to use steam-engines were not liable at common law for damage caused by sparks, whereas previously they had been. In 1905 an exception was made. An owner of agricultural land or crops was permitted to sue for damages if (a) the damage did not exceed £100 (£200 from 1923); (b) he notified the rail company of the occurrence of the damage within seven days; and (c) he made a claim within 21 days (Coase, 1960, p. 30). This means that Pigou falsely stated the problem. He uses this example to show how it is possible 'for State action to improve upon 'natural' tendencies' (Pigou, 1929, p. xii). He is referring to ways in which the state directs the free play of self-interest with the intention of producing more beneficial outcomes (ibid., pp 129-32). But it is clear that the situation he describes in 1920 was the product, not of the unsatisfactory market, but of unsatisfactory state intervention.

The contribution of the new property rights theorists has been to point out that this applied to many other externalities. A very considerable number of public nuisances which at some stage have been actionable at law have been authorised by statute, as long as there has been no negligence. The list of nuisances exempt in Britain in 1960 included the escape of sewage, some types of river pollution, and the catch-all, 'annoyance caused by things reasonably necessary for the excavation of authorised works' (Coase, 1960, p. 24). More recently airport and new road schemes have aroused considerable public antipathy. Such schemes are undertaken or authorised by governments, and the reason that they stir up such public anger is because governments look upon the nuisances created by official action with greater leniency than they do those created by private endeavour.

Thus, the new property rights theorists challenge the widespread assumption that externalities are the result of the free play of self-interest and that state action to check or channel self-interest is automatically the answer. Many externalities are the result of earlier state intervention, and reform of outstanding government initiatives may well be the solution rather than still greater extensions of government power.

In particular, property rights theorists object to the common socialist assumption that externalities are an inherent product of private property and that 'communal ownership' is therefore preferrable. Socialist analyses of property tend to stress the importance of ownership, and for this reason socialists believe it essential to bring property compulsorily into government hands. For the new property rights theorists such thinking fails to see the true character of property. To focus on the ownership of physical property—land, buildings, machinery—is to neglect the

importance of *rights* to *use* it. Rights to use land can exist
without ownership, as for instance when a person has a
right to walk across land belonging to someone else. We
should focus, therefore, on the bundle of rights connected
with particular property. It is conceivable that property
could formally be privately owned but that every significant use to which it might be put required government
permission. Similarly, property could be state-owned, with
a very large measure of real discretion lying in the hands
of private individuals. For this reason, any examination of
externalities should take careful account, not so much of
who owns the property, but who possesses which particular rights to use it. Failure to do so has produced some
misleading interpretations of many of our environmental
problems.

The new property rights theorists strongly object to the
identification of private rights with anti-social behaviour.
This claim is, they say, 'as mischievous as it is popular'
(Alchian and Demsetz, 1973, p. 24). On the contrary,
they argue, *communal* rights can encourage immoral behaviour. For instance, the cruel clubbing to death of seals
in Canada is a result of the policy of the Canadian government. No one has private rights in the seals. Killing takes
place on a first come, first served basis, until the stipulated
quota is reached. The result is that hunters work rapidly
to kill as many as they can before time runs out.

Private rights can be socially useful, argue Alchian and
Demsetz, because they may encourage people to take into
account social costs. This is because the 'social' cost becomes a private cost. A great many externalities, in this
view, are the result of a failure properly to specify property rights, with the result that private transactions cannot
resolve or internalise external costs and benefits. This applies especially to the depletion of 'common' resources,
such as the killing of whales to the point where they face
extinction, or over-fishing, or the destruction of forests.
These are problems which have emerged because of the
absence of private property rights. No one has private
rights to the fish, the whales and many forests. Pollution
or destruction occur, it is said, not because of 'market

failure', but because there is no market, only a no-man's land. The solution is to allocate the property rights to private persons. The cost of resource depletion would then be a private cost, and it would therefore pay owners to conserve. The same reasoning applies to water pollution, which is often the result of permitting common access to waterways.

John Burton, the research director of the Institute of Economic Affairs (IEA), has suggested how a private property solution could help to solve one of the environmental tragedies of all time, the steady spread of the Sahara Desert into neighbouring semi-arid areas which are currently able to support agriculture and cattle rearing. In much of the affected areas there is no private property, and most inhabitants lead a largely nomadic existence. Consequently it pays no one to ensure that land is not over-grazed. And it pays no one to plant grass or trees to prevent soil erosion. If private property were introduced, argues Burton, this would change. People would have a stake in the future, and the spread of the Sahara could be checked (1978, pp. 83-9).

Why are private property rights not an answer to every externality? According to the new property rights theorists, this is chiefly because the 'transaction costs' are too high. Where such costs—namely, the cost of negotiating, agreeing terms, drawing up and enforcing the contract, etc.— are less than the potential benefit, private bargaining will take care of many externalities. For instance, Steven Cheung has shown how the complex 'externalities' of bee-keeping are internalised. Professor J. E. Meade used apple farming and beekeeping to demonstrate the wide gap between private and 'social' costs. The bees take the pollen from the apple blossom, and so the apple farmer unwittingly feeds the bees. At the same time the bees fertilise the apples. According to Meade this is a situation theoretically requiring taxes and subsidies to bring private and 'social' costs into balance. However, Cheung found in the state of Washington that apple farmers and bee-keepers come to a variety of arrangements. In practice apple blossoms provide little honey, but the pollination services of bees are highly valued. In such cases longstanding agreements existed under which apple growers paid beekeepers for placing their hives on their farms during the spring. The value of the honey extracted was taken into account in arriving at rental payments (1978, p. 62).

In other cases transaction costs are too high for externalities to be handled by private agreement. Smoke pollution is a classic case. So many people are affected that it is difficult for the polluter to identify them all, let alone agree a price with them for continuing to pollute (Posner, 1973, pp. 24-5). In such cases it may be permissible for the government to step in.

GUIDE TO READING

The best starting-point is *Free to Choose* by Milton and Rose Friedman, in which their views about the role of the state and the causes of inflation are set out in a highly readable form. *Capitalism and Freedom* is equally suitable for the general reader. The Institute of Economic Affairs has published a number of pamphlets in which Friedman's ideas on monetary policy are presented in language accessible to the general reader and the student just starting out. The most useful are *The Counter-Revolution in Monetary Theory* (1970), *Monetary Correction* (1974b) and *Inflation and Unemployment* (Friedman's Alfred Nobel Memorial Lecture) (1977b). More technical discussions can be found in 'The Quantity Theory of Money—a Restatement', one of the essays in *Studies in the Quantity Theory of Money* (1956), and also in 'A Theoretical Framework for Monetary Analysis', in Gordon (ed.) (1974). This volume also contains essays critical of Friedman's views, and his reply. His standpoint on the scientific status of economics can be found in 'The Methodology of Positive Economics', in Friedman (1953). For a short survey of Friedman's economic thought, consult Burton (1981).

A good introduction to Becker's works can be found in Shackleton (1981). Nick Bosanquet's *After the New Right* (1983) (Chapter 3) is a critique of Friedman from a left-wing perspective. Chapter 48 of Lipsey (1983) provides an accessible, critical account of Friedman's 'monetarism'. For a totally unrepentant Keynesian critique of monetarism, consult the speeches of Nicholas Kaldor in the House of Lords (Kaldor, 1983) and the same author's *The Scourge of Monetarism* (1982), an attack on the monetary policies of the Thatcher government. For a neo-Keynesian alternative view which claims to have re-established the 'quintessentially Keynesian principle of effective demand as the determinant of real output and employment', consult Godley and Cripps (1983), or anything by members of the Cambridge Economic Policy Group.

Further criticism of Friedman's monetary policy can be found in two IEA papers, *Inflation: Causes, Consequences, Cures,* Lord Robbins *et al.* (1974); and *Is Monetarism Enough?*, Minford *et al* (1980). For Hayek's criticism of Friedman, consult 1978a, pp. 76-81. Samuel Brittan's *How to End the 'Monetarist' Controversy* (1982) is instructive, and Eamonn Butler's recent textbook, *Milton Friedman* (1985), is also useful. Chapter 8 of the present book contains further discussion of monetary policy. A criticism of *Capitalism and Freedom* by a political scientist can be found in C. B. Macpherson's *Democratic Theory: Essays in Retrieval* (1973), Essay VII, 'Elegant Tombstones'. Friedman's view of freedom is also criticised by David Heald (1983, Chapter 4). Chapter 3 of Heald's book also contains a worthwhile discussion of monetarism from what Heald calls a 'left-Keynesian' standpoint.

4 The Public Choice School

Public choice theory, sometimes called the economics of politics, applies some of the methods of economics to the study of political behaviour. About half the adherents of the school are political scientists and half economists. The school's headquarters is the Centre For the Study of Public Choice, formerly based at the Virginia Polytechnic Institute and State University and now located at George Mason University in Virginia. Its leaders are Professor Gordon Tullock, editor of the journal *Public Choice*, and Professor James Buchanan.

The essence of public choice theory has been summed up by Professor Buchanan:

> In one sense, all of public choice or the economic theory of politics may be summarised as the 'discovery' or 're-discovery' that people should be treated as rational utility-maximisers in all of their behavioural capacities. This central insight, in all of its elaborations, does not lead to the conclusion that all collective action, all government action, is necessarily undesirable. It leads, instead, to the conclusion that, because people will tend to maximise their own utilities, institutions must be designed so that individual behaviour will further the interests of the group, small or large, local or national. The challenge to us is one of constructing, or re-constructing, a political order that will channel the self-serving behaviour of participants towards the common good in a manner that comes as close as possible to that described for us by Adam Smith with respect to the economic order. (1978, p. 17)

Thus, as with the other schools comprising the 'new right', the public choice school represents a revival of interest in classical liberalism. As a modern movement it dates from the late 1950s. Early work in the public choice tradition was, in Buchanan's phrase, *demand*-driven; that is, its focus was on the ways in which individual preferences could be made to count in collective decisions. There was a particular emphasis on the ways in which voter pressures led to political outcomes. Later work was concerned with the *supply* of government goods and services. The behaviour of administrators was analysed, not as if they were dispassionate servants following orders from their political masters, but as though they were self-interested persons like anyone else with private preferences which affected their conduct in making and administering policy.

Amongst early demand-side contributions, Anthony Downs' book, *The Economic Theory of Democracy* (1957), proved seminal. Political parties, he argued, were very like entrepreneurs. They formulated policies which they believed would maximise their votes, in much the same way that private companies manufacture the products they believe will maximise profits (1957, p. 295). His early work was criticised by William Riker, who argued that parties do not *maximise* votes, but only seek to put together a 'minimum winning coalition' (1962, pp. 33, 100). Duncan Black's attempt to study scientifically the voting behaviour of members of committees (1958) was also an important starting-point, though it was subsequently much neglected. Buchanan describes Black as 'a prophet without honour in his own country' (1978, p. 3). The public choice school, however, did not emerge as a distinctive tradition until the mid-1960s, through the work of Buchanan and Tullock.

THE REALITIES OF COLLECTIVE CHOICE

According to Buchanan and Tullock, what is distinctive about the public choice school is that it examines more carefully 'the political, or government and bureaucratic structures, rules, and procedures (the *institutions*) through which policy decisions are made, and less the *content* of the decisions themselves' (1981, p. 82). Public choice theorists are not so much interested in the outputs of government, but rather in identifying the constraints under which governments operate and understanding what this means for public policy-making.

The Voters

Early work focused on voting and party behaviour, and a good deal of theoretical work discussed the mechanism of majority voting. Much of this work is highly mathematical but this can safely be ignored by all but specialists.

An important element is the 'median voter theorem'. This predicts that a political party seeking to win a majority of votes on a particular issue will select as its party platform the preferred course of the median voter (i.e. the one in the middle of any range, for instance, voter number four in a range of seven). If the number of voters was seven then adopting the position of the number four voter would give a political party a majority of four to three. If the median voter theorem is true, it follows that in a two-party system, party programmes will tend to converge—a prediction borne out by experience (Tullock, 1976, pp. 14–25).

Tullock also examines the consequences of political ignorance. It has long been recognised by political scientists that voters are frequently poorly informed about the issues debated during election campaigns. Tullock has suggested that this is a rational response to voters' real circumstances. This can be seen by comparing the power of the citizen making a choice of product in the market with the power of the citizen making an electoral choice. In the market the consumer benefits if he becomes well informed about the range of products available. Not all do become well-informed, some remain ill-informed, and many others rely on third party endorsements; but the point is that time spent gathering information benefits the consumer. This is not so with an electoral choice. The power of the individal is so small that however well-informed he is, his influence on the outcome will remain very small, and probably insignificant (Tullock, 1970, pp. 116–18).

The 'Choice in Welfare' Surveys

The most valuable studies of the strengths and weaknesses of electoral choice have been carried out by Ralph Harris and Arthur Seldon of the Institute of Economic Affairs. Much public choice analysis of electoral behaviour is marred by its excessively theoretical character and especially its concern with mathematical model building. Invariably such models erect a huge edifice on questionable assumptions. In sharp contrast, the Harris–Seldon studies are built on extensive surveys conducted over a fifteen-year period from 1963 to 1978.

The reasoning behind the surveys was this. When people spend in the market they have direct, detailed control and can exploit the choice offered by competing suppliers. But when services are provided by government, expenditure is determined by politicians and officials, and the individual has no detailed control:

In place of the daily choice between myriad suppliers, the voter has a single option between two or three political parties at elections every four or five years. Instead of the consumer's freedom to shop around and buy items of varying brands from differing outlets on a pick-and-choose, *á la carte* basis, the citizen must cast his one vote for a single political supplier and swallow the entire manifesto package on a *table d'hôte*, take-it-or-leave-it basis for years on end. Where the commercial firm must accurately label his products and publish their prices, all political parties regularly promise 'free' services without revealing the cost that will be exacted through all kinds of taxes. While commercial advertisers are prohibited from falsely describing their goods or those of their competitors, most political salesman think nothing of bidding for votes with half-truths, quarter-truths, and outright untruths. (1979, p. 68)

Because no post-war government has attempted to discover citizens' preferences, Harris and Seldon set out to provide the next best thing, a test of opinion using market research techniques. Their surveys were unlike the usual attitude surveys of opinion pollsters. They did not merely

ask general questions about health and education; respondents were also questioned about a series of priced
alternatives.

The macro questions reveal declining support for the
present method of funding health care and education. In
1963, 1965, 1970 and 1978 respondents were asked to
choose between the following three alternatives:

1. The state should take more in taxes, rates and contributions and so on to pay for better or increased
   (health/education) services which everyone would
   have.
2. The state should take less in taxes, rates and contributions and so on to provide services only for people
   in need and leave others to pay or insure privately.
3. The state should continue the present service but allow
   people to contract out, pay less contributions and so on
   and use the money to pay for their own services.

Table 1: Policy for Health: 1963–78

Base: total sample	2005	2018	2005	1992
	1963	1965	1970	1978
Policy option	%	%	%	%
A. Keep present system	41	32	29	20
B. Concentrate on poor	24	25	24	18
C. Allow contracting out	33	34	46	54
'Don't know'	2	9	1	7

Source: Harris and Seldon, 1979, p. 45.

Table 2: Policy for Education: 1963–78

Base: total sample	2005	2018	2005	1992
	1963	1965	1970	1978
Policy option	%	%	%	%
A. Keep present system	51	41	44	15
B. Concentrate on poor	20	16	20	17
C. Allow contracting-out	27	32	35	60
'Don't know'	2	11	2	8

Source: Harris and Seldon, 1979, p. 50.

The health findings are set out in Table 1. They reveal a steady decline in support for the present method of funding health services, from 41 per cent in 1963 to only 20 per cent in 1978 (1979, pp. 44–5). Similar findings were obtained for education, as Table 2 reveals. Support for the present system fell from 51 per cent in 1963 to 15 per cent in 1978 (ibid., p. 50).

The micro survey of education used the device of the voucher to test opinion. The value of the voucher was related to the annual cost of statutory state secondary schooling. In 1965 it cost £150, in 1970 the figure was £225, and in 1978 it was £450. Parents were asked if they would take a voucher valued at either one-third or two-thirds of the average state school cost and add to it to pay fees for private education (ibid., p. 85). In 1978 the exact questions were:

If the state gave you £150 a year for each child aged 11 or more which could only be spent on secondary education—and you would probably have to pay another £300 yourself to make up the fees—do you think you would accept that offer or not?

And what if the offer were £300 so that you might had to add only another £150; do you think you would accept that offer or not?

The 1963 results are unfortunately not comparable with subsequent years, because in that year respondents were asked about vouchers worth either 'half' or 'most' of the cost of school fees. In subsequent years they were asked about vouchers worth one-third or two-thirds of the cost. In 1965 15 per cent of male heads of households said they would pay one-third of the school fees if the state gave them two-thirds. In 1978 this had increased to 51 per cent. As expected, the numbers saying they would accept the offer varied by price (ibid., p. 91). The full findings are set out in Table 3. Very similar results were obtained for medical services. These findings are in Table 4 (1979, p. 107). The policy conclusions drawn by Harris and Seldon are considered in Part II of this book.

Table 3: Suppressed Demand for Choice in Education, 1963–78
Proportion of male heads of households[a] who would add to
school vouchers to pay annual day fees (with women in 1978)

	1963[b] men		1965[b] men	1970[b] men	1978 men	1978 women
Base	1187		1218	1309	602	372
	%	%	%	%	%	%
Would add ⅔ to ⅓ value voucher	10[c] 26[d] } 36		15	27	29	30
Would add ⅓ to ⅔ value voucher	25[c] 21[d] } 46		30	43	51	52

Notes: a. With children of school age under 19 years.
   b. Excludes the small proportion who intended to pay
      for private education.
   c. 'Very interested'.
   d. 'Interested'.
Source: Harris and Seldon, 1979, p. 91.

*Table 4: Suppressed Demand for Choice in Medicine, 1963–78
measured by acceptance of part-value vouchers*

	1963[a]		1965[a]	1970	1978
Base	1559		1663	2005	1992
	%	%	%	%	%
Would add ½ to ½ value voucher	7[b] 20[c] } 27		23	26	51
Would add ⅓ to ⅔ value voucher ('most' in 1963)	17[b] 21[c] } 38		30	31	57

Notes: a. Excluding those who said they were members of
      private health insurance schemes.
   b. 'Very interested'.
   c. 'Interested'.
Source: Harris and Seldon, 1979, p. 107.

THE DECISION-MAKERS

In more recent years the public choice school has focused,
not so much on the behaviour of voters, but on the be-

haviour of the wielders of power: the politicians and the bureaucrats. Professor Tullock is critical of traditional economics for employing a 'benevolent despot' model of the political order. Instead of seeking to identify the optimal policy and proceeding to recommend this to government, Tullock prefers to analyse government as an apparatus, like the market, in which actors try to achieve their private ends. Public choice theory assumes that all individuals in government 'serve their own interests within certain institutional limits' (1976, p. 2).

Once said these assertions seem almost obvious. But they strongly contradict the post-war orthodoxy, especially in Britain. The dominant attitude was typified by these remarks made by the eminent socialist historian, G.D.H. Cole, in a pamphlet first published in 1947 and still being reissued by the Labour Party in the 1970s. Writing about the imminent nationalisation of some major industries, Cole comments that managers and technicians as well as wage earners will be 'inspired by a different feeling when they are working for a public which regards them as holding a public trust, and they will work the better as a result' (1947, p. 23). Moreover, he expected that the coming of state socialism would *reduce* the extent of bureaucracy:

If we keep Capitalism we shall have to keep hosts of people preventing the capitalists from exploiting the public. Under Socialism we shall be able to do with many fewer bureaucrats, because the main industries will be organised directly as public services for the common benefit. (1947, p. 28)

Politicians: According to public choice theorists, just as businessmen are looked upon as acting according to the 'profit motive', so politicians should be regarded as having a 'vote motive'. Politicians may, for instance, switch their allegiance from one idea or policy to another according to the possibility of winning political power. Tullock points out that this need not be a bad thing, for in this way the political process tends to give the people what they demand (Tullock, 1976, p. 25).

However, the general conclusion suggested by the public

choice school is that politicians do not reflect the views of voters. Some do, and it may be that all must to a degree, but there are a number of countervailing pressures. In the first place, politicians are people who entered politics to have an influence on outcomes, not merely to mirror the opinions of others. For this reason, Buchanan argues, all-important budgetary outcomes will not fully reflect voter preferences (1975, pp. 156–7).

More significantly, the pressure exercised by politicians is uni-directional, tending always to favour budgetary expansion. Why is this? According to Buchanan there are three broad types of politician: the ideologue, who seeks to 'do good' as he sees it; the 'seeker after acclaim', whose motive is intrinsic enjoyment of office; and the profiteer, who pursues personal gain from office. The ideologue tends to favour the use of the state machine to further his aims. There are anarchist ideologues, who conceivably might counterbalance statist utopians, but anarchists tend not to seek public office. The 'seeker after acclaim' will find he can secure more votes by pleasing special interest groups and less by cutting taxes. The efforts of the profiteer will similarly tend to promote higher expenditure (ibid., p. 158).

In Buchanan's view, the use of the power of the state to serve private interests has external costs. By diminishing each person's capacity to direct his or her own life, efficiency is curtailed to the extent that it depends on free initiative. Moreover the process of serving private interests has a tendency to accelerate. For if one private interest stands by and allows others to accumulate special benefits at the general expense, then any group slow to move will end up much worse-off. Once this process starts then everyone must join in or lose out. Political parties, therefore, become vote-seeking coalitions which respond to pressure groups by a process of vote-buying at the common expense.

A further important element in the distortion of political preferences, according to the public choice school, is 'logrolling'—that is, the process by which one legislator agrees to support a colleague's favoured measure without necessarily being in favour of it on merit, in return for like support on some other issue. This largely secret process tends to reduce the thoroughness of policy appraisal, and to discourage a proper weighing of costs and benefits (Tullock, 1976, pp. 41–55).

Bureaucracy: Professor William Niskanen notes that competition is widely regarded as a useful spur to effort in the private sector, and asks why the same view is not held about government bureaucracies: 'Is it plausible that businessmen and bureaucrats are such different people that profits are a necessary incentive in private firms but that the "public good" is a sufficient incentive in government bureaus, that competition is a necessary discipline in private firms but that monopoly is a desirable characteristic of bureaus?' (1978, p. 164).

In Professor Niskanen's view, 'Neither businessmen nor bureaucrats have any inherent motivation to be efficient' (1973, p. 51). Whether or not they turn out to be efficient depends on the constraints and incentives under which they operate. It is therefore important to understand what these are. There are two main factors: the relationship between a bureau and its 'sponsor'; and the aims of the individual bureaucrat and the incentives and constraints under which he functions.

A government bureaucracy is funded by a single or dominant collective organisation and funded by tax revenues, or at least more or less compulsory contributions (1973, p. 13). The sponsor (the government) has no alternative supplier, and the bureau has no other source of funding. In economics this is called a 'bilateral monopoly'. It makes for a special kind of relationship: it is 'awkward and personal—characterised by both threats and deference, by both gaming and appeals to a common objective' (ibid., p. 14).

In understanding businessmen it has proved possible without too much distortion to assume that they seek to maximise their utility (their private benefits) by pursuing profit. This leaves much that they may do out of account, but the attribution of a simple profit motive has proved a useful predictive mechanism. There is no entirely satis-factory simplifying device for bureaucrats, but some assumptions are possible. Niskanen assumes that public officials value income, pleasant working conditions, power, prestige, the public good and an easy life in about the same proportions as everyone else. Bureaucrats, he says, are like other people, they 'appear to shirk when they can get away with it and are efficient when they have to be' (1978, p. 167).

Often an increase in the size of the bureau will satisfy many of the personal aims of officials. Consequently budget-maximisation often has the predictive value to the private sector profit motive. 'Size-maximisation' or 'empire building' may also lead to improved service of the con-sumer, for one way of justifying expansion is to satisfy the consumer, or at least to give the impression of providing good service (Tullock, 1976, pp. 29–30).

However, because of their grasp of technical know-ledge, bureaucrats can increase the supply of their service beyond the political demand for it, get away with in-efficiency, and enhance their own salaries. Writing in 1979, Tullock believed the evidence to be sparse but reckoned that as a 'rough rule of thumb' a service would cost the government about twice as much as it would a private competitive producer (1979, p. 34). Professor Niskanen's view is similar. The constraint under which bureaucrats operate is that they must supply the output expected by their sponsor (1971, pp. 41–2; 1973, pp. 26–7). but notwithstanding this, he finds that bureaus are invari-ably too big: 'All bureaus are too large. For given demand and cost conditions, both the budget and the output of a monopoly bureau may be up to twice that of a competitive industry facing the same conditions' (1973, p. 33).

Two main factors explain why this is so. First, a govern-ment sponsor has available to it no *priced* alternatives: it must 'take it or leave it' (1973, p. 31). Second, the budget scrutiny process is usually dominated by a specialised com-mittee, which in turn is dominated by individuals with a high interest in service expansion (ibid., p. 32).

To sum up: public choice is contrasted with the normative analysis of public policy. It does not examine which public policies should be carried out, but rather investigates more directly 'the means through which policy programmes are chosen and implemented' (Buchanan and Tullock, 1981, p. 82). Broadly, the 'positive' (factual) conclusion drawn by the public choice school is that 'commonly *the government alternative is inherently inferior to the market*' (ibid., p. 81). The motivations of both politicians and administrators tend to promote budget aggrandisement. This has opportunity costs—measured by foregone alternatives in which people might have invested if they had not been so heavily taxed. And because many government services are monopolistic, consumers tend to be less well served than if competitors are able to threaten the continued existence of poor performers.

TRY THE MARKET OR IMPROVE THE SYSTEM?

Two possible normative conclusions could be drawn from the empirical findings of the public choice school. The first is that government activity should be shifted into the market; and the second, that the structure of government should be reformed to improve its efficiency. Mr Nicholas Bosanquet, in his critique of the new liberalism, *After the New Right* (1983), accuses the public choice school of neglecting the reform of government services because of its preference for privatisation, but a number of public choice theorists have devoted attention to internal bureaucratic reform. Niskanen, for instance, considers the alternatives to bureaucracy under three headings, broadly approved by other public choice theorists: internal reform; the evolution of (market) alternatives; and political or constitutional reform.

Internal Reform: The internal working of bureaus could be improved by introducing personal reward systems for senior managers, or encouraging competition between bureaus. Competition between bureaus, Niskanen found, helped to increase the information available to politicians, due to inter-bureau rivalry for budget allocations. A monopoly bureau can more readily suppress information about costs, its failures, and the risks, incurred by its favoured strategies. Competition also increases the range of technologies used to supply services. A monopoly bureau is more likely to rely on a smaller range of techniques, with a possible loss of efficiency. Tullock also favours inter-bureau competition, and has advocated experimentation with competition between regional bureaus in the administration of social security programmes to throw up comparisons by which performance could be judged (1979, p. 37).

However, the trend in the US has been almost entirely opposed to inter-bureau competition and in favour of consolidation. Consolidation of bureaus to achieve 'better coordination', a pattern followed in the US during the 1960s and 1970s, increases 'the probability of doing everything right only at the cost of increasing the probability of doing everything wrong', says Niskanen (1978, p. 165). He cites the formation of the Department of Defense (DOD), Health, Education and Welfare (HEW), Housing and Urban Development (HUD) and Transportation. As consolidations they did nothing to improve prospects for tackling the problems each agency faced. (Subsequently HEW has been split into two, the Department of Education, and the Department of Health and Human Services.)

However, a degree of competition remained. Competition between the Departments of Labor, Health, Education and Welfare (HEW) and Housing and Urban Development (HUD) in the 1970s made it possible to make 'an intelligent choice among a jobs strategy, an incomes strategy and a cities strategy'. In general, he finds that competition among bureaus 'may reduce the probability that the expected task is accomplished, but it increases the probability, that the *right* task will be accomplished, often in unexpected ways' (1978, p. 169).

The personal rewards of officials may also be manipulated to encourage the pursuit of efficiency. A bureau could, for instance, be given a budget and an expected output. Senior managers could be allowed to retain a

proportion of the difference between the approved budget
and the incurred cost. Services which might be amenable
to this treatment are welfare payments, tax returns and air
traffic control. A slightly more acceptable alternative
might be a system of 'deferred prizes', awarded according
to performance over a specified period and payable, say,
five years after leaving (1973, pp. 44–6).

Niskanen's studies of local government services, including schooling, conclude that unit costs vary with the
absolute size of local government and some studies of
policing support this view. Niskanen concludes that inefficiency is not a necessary characteristic of the supply of
government services. For a specified output, costs can be
reduced by increasing competition among bureaus, by contracting with private firms, and by reducing the absolute
size of official organisations (1975, pp. 637–8; 1978, p.
167). According to Tullock, waste due to the overpayment
of officials could be tackled by cutting salaries until voluntary resignations roughly matched applications from suitably
qualified persons (1979, p. 37). And in some circumstances,
information disclosure, along the lines of 'freedom of information' legislation, may help considerably (1976, pp.
36–40). Tullock also advocates the promotion of a 'competitive market in government'. There are many units of
local government and to a degree competition for population already exists. Many parents, for example, take into
consideration the quality of local schooling when weighing
up where to live (1970, p. 121).

Market Alternatives: The second approach suggested by
Niskanen is the development of alternative, primarily
market, sources of supply. He does not, however, advocate the contracting out of whole services, for this would
reduce the comparisons thrown up by competition.

One of the targets of the public choice school has been
the tendency of economists to assume that if the market
proves unsatisfactory in some respects it should be wholly
replaced by government. It became commonplace to look
upon any market failure as a sufficient justification for
government intervention. There was no corresponding

awareness of the weakness of government. The public choice school insists that the choice of a market or government solution should rest on a proper weighing of the costs and benefits of both alternatives, government and market. The choice is seen as largely pragmatic, measured by a calculation of the good and harm that government intervention, on the one hand, and the market, on the other, may cause. Government, however, is believed to suffer from a fundamental flaw.

The chief difference between government and market environments is that the limitations within which individuals operate differ. In Professor Tullock's view, the constraints put upon individual conduct in the market are at present more 'efficient' than those under which politicians and civil servants operate. By 'efficient' he means that 'individuals in the market are more likely to serve someone else's well-being when they seek to serve their own than they are in government' (1976, pp. 7, 27). One of the objectives of the public choice school is, therefore, to discover the reforms that would bring the efficiency of government closer to that of the market. Part II considers 'privatisation' proposals in more detail.

Political and Constitutional Reform: Its emphasis on institutions means that public choice aims at 'more comprehensive, and long range, reform as opposed to piecemeal, pragmatic change' (Niskanen, 1973, p. 84). Public choice theorists have focused particularly on constitutional reform to set limits to detailed government interference. The leading contributions to the discussion of constitutional reform in the United States are Buchanan's *The Limits of Liberty* (1975) and *Democracy in Deficit* (co-authored with Richard Wagner in 1977). They especially favour amendment of the American Constitution to impose a balanced budget rule. No government, federal or state, would be permitted to function by means of a budget deficit. The domination of budget review committees by representatives of vested interests could partly be overcome by the random assignment of members. In addition independent review agencies could be established to function as countervailing 'vested interests' (Niskanen, 1973, pp. 59, 61). To overcome the inherent bias of majority voting in favour of 'high-demand groups', Niskanen suggests that all appropriations should be subject to a two-thirds voting rule and the President should make greater use of his veto (1971, pp. 227–8; 1973, 62).

In *The Consequences of Mr Keynes* (1978) Buchanan, Wagner and John Burton consider similar ideas in the British context (below, p. 195). Some British public choice theorists, however, do not share this enthusiasm for constitutional reform, believing it to be ill-suited to British conditions (Rowley, 1983, pp. 144–55).

SUMMARY

The chief insight of the public choice school is that there is no escape from private motivations. Under any arrangements, and whatever the scope of government, private motives will guide conduct. If the state controls the distribution of material holdings then private groups do not somehow cease to be powerful—they organise to control the state, in order to protect and advance their own interests.

To expand the power of the state does not, therefore, eliminate selfishness, as some academics suggest. For instance, Le Grand and Robinson in their best-selling textbook, *The Economics of Social Problems* claim that: 'There can be little doubt that the market fosters personal attributes, such as greed and a lack of concern for one's neighbour, that are incompatible with altruistic behaviour' (1984a, p. 267). This implies that government interference always promotes altruism. It is certainly true that some institutions do encourage altruism, but a state which presents itself as a mechanism which can be captured for the self-interested reallocation of other people's holdings is not one of them. This is because, however the state presents itself, and however pervasive it becomes, the struggle for private advancement continues in other guises. More importantly, the distributive state lacks any mechanism for checking the excesses of self-interested groups. Selfishness is undesirable, but as Adam Smith argued, competition can at least prevent self-interested groups from 'disturbing the tranquility of anybody but themselves' (1776, vol. I, p. 436).

GUIDE TO READING

D.C. Mueller's *Public Choice* (1979) is a valuable textbook guide, although the student approaching public choice for the first time will probably find the IEA publication *The Economics of Politics* (Buchanan *et al.*, 1978) easier. The *Vote Motive* by Gordon Tullock (1976) is also useful. A brief survey of Buchanan's contribution can be found in Locksley, 1981. For a collection of recent essays on public choice consult Buchanan (1986). For a critical, but sometimes unreliable, account consult Bosanquet (1983), Chapter 4. Brian Barry's *Sociologists, Economists and Democracy* (1978) contrasts the 'economic' and 'sociological' approaches to the study of political behaviour, though he focuses chiefly on the work of Downs. J.F.J. Toye (1976) offers a similar criticism. A very worthwhile discussion of the public choice approach can be found in Heald (1983), Chapter 5.

The case for constitutional reform in Britain has most recently been argued by John Burton (1985). A critique of the Harris–Seldon surveys can be found in Taylor–Gooby (1985), pp. 38–48.

5 Hayek and the Austrian School

As well as being a notable philosopher of liberalism, Hayek is also part of a tradition of specifically economic thought called the Austrian school. His role within this school is considered at the end of the chapter.

HAYEK AND LIBERTY

Until the beginning of the Second World War, Hayek had been concerned primarily with technical economic questions, but the rise of Nazism in the 1930s produced a change in his priorities. He became convinced that the true character of the German National Socialist movement was wholly misunderstood in English 'progressive' intellectual circles. Born in Vienna in 1899, he had by the outset of the Second World War spent around half his adult life in Austria and half in England. His close contact with British intellectual circles, following hard on the heels of his days in Austria where he had been well placed to understand the Nazi phenomenon, convinced him that the ideas which had fed the rise of Nazism were growing in influence in Britain. Written at the height of the fight against the Nazis between 1940 and 1943, the *Road to Serfdom* warned that the unquestioning faith of intellectuals in central planning and central direction was preparing the way for totalitarian rule.

The freedom that had made the West a successful civilisation and which remained the wartime slogan of the allies against Hitler's Germany had been, Hayek contended, long since abandoned by British intellectuals and even as men fought and died in its name was little respected by them. According to a new preface written in 1976, he had not intended to give the impression of believing that *any* movement in the direction of socialism was bound to lead to totalitarianism. But he had intended to warn that 'unless we mend the principles of our policy, some very unpleasant consequences will follow which most of those who advocate these policies do not want' (1976a, p. ix). In particular he believed that Britain had reached a stage where it was more important to clear away the obstacles which governments had placed in the path of a once free people, and thereby to release the creative energy of individuals, than it was 'to devise further machinery for "guiding" and "directing" them'. It was necessary to create conditions *favourable to* progress rather than to *plan* progress (ibid., p. 177). This concern that freedom was being unwittingly thrown away determined the direction of his intellectual efforts for the remainder of his long life.

Hayek had not always been sceptical of socialism. His view had been altered by Ludwig von Mises' book, *Socialism*, which he had read in 1922. Before that Hayek describes himself as one of many young idealists who had returned to their university studies after the First World War believing that the civilisation in which they had grown up had collapsed and determined to build a better world. The socialist movement, he wrote, 'promised to fulfil our hopes for a more rational, more just world': 'And then came von Mises' book. Our hopes were dashed. *Socialism* told us that we had been looking for improvement in the wrong direction' (Foreward to von Mises, 1981, p. xix).

In 1960 the University of Chicago, where he taught from 1950 until 1962, published his *The Constitution of Liberty* in which he developed the themes he had outlined in *The Road to Serfdom*. In *The Constitution of Liberty* Hayek wrote that for nearly 100 years the basic commitment to freedom on which western civilisation had been

built had been falling into disregard and oblivion. Few had
any clear conception of what freedom was (1960, pp. 1–2).
Not only was the mood of the Western intelligentsia one
of disillusionment with freedom, disparagement of its
achievements, and exclusive concern with the creation of
'better worlds', Western ideas had also been transmitted
throughout the rest of the world at precisely that stage in
history when Western intellectuals had lost faith in the
very traditions that made the West worth copying. His
wartime fear that this loss of faith in freedom was leading to totalitarianism without anyone realising it had not
lessened with the passage of time.

Hayek therefore set out to restate clearly the case for
and character of freedom; to consider how liberal philosophy could be applied to the concrete problems of the
day; to analyse how prevailing values were (often uninten-
tionally) undermining it; and to examine how it could best
be maintained.

Hayek's Restatement of the Ideal of Liberty

In Hayek's judgement, it has been respect for freedom of
a particular kind that has enabled the West to become the
most prosperous and humane civilisation ever. Above all,
Western civilisation has been built on respect for the self-
directing individual. For Hayek, freedom is the absence of
coercion, a situation in which the individual is not dependent on the 'arbitrary will of another' (1960, p. 12). This
has often been called 'negative' freedom and contrasted
with 'positive' freedom, and for some, the use of the
epithet 'negative' suggests that it is an inferior kind of
freedom compared with 'positive' freedom. But merely
because freedom describes the absence of an undesirable
state of affairs does not diminish its worth. As Hayek was
later to write, freedom is one of the 'three great nega-
tives': peace, freedom and justice (1979a, p. 130). No one
would argue that peace was an unattractive commodity
merely because it describes the absence of war. To avoid
any connotation of approval or disapproval I shall call
Hayek's concept of freedom, 'plain freedom'.

Hayek strongly criticises those who speak of positive

freedom as if it were a species of the genus freedom. This produces confusion, and dangerous confusion at that, for those who speak of positive freedom have in mind the range of options open to a person. To contemplate the avenues open to someone is, however, to consider the extent of their *power* and not the degree of 'plain freedom' they enjoy. The confounding of power with freedom is one of the errors which has led to the undermining of liberty in the West, as government has used the might at its disposal, not to protect the plain freedom of individuals, but to alter their power *vis-à-vis* other citizens. Few liberals objected when all that was involved was the protection of people from extreme poverty, but steadily interventions have grown in magnitude. Recently, under the guise of appealing to 'social justice' the depredations of the state have multiplied many times over—a problem to which I shall return later in this chapter.

Vital to Hayek's conception of liberty is the maintenance of plain freedom through law. As Chapter 1 argued, the classical liberal view has been that a free society can only be maintained if the government's power is used in support of it. But once this has been conceded, the question becomes how to prevent the state from abusing its power. To some writers this question has seemed to be the same as asking 'Who should rule?', as if this or that group or person might be more likely to refrain from abusing the power of the state. British liberals, however, tended not to see this as the real issue. In the light of the revolutions of the seventeenth century, when royal tyranny was followed in quick succession by the abuses of the Roundheads, only to be succeeded by yet further royal abuse, British liberals concluded that no *person* should rule. Instead, there should be a government of *laws*. The necessity for safeguards against the abuse of power by the government of the day forms a still stronger part of the American tradition, where a written constitution safeguarded by a powerful Supreme Court has been placed in the path of potentially marauding majorities.

The Factors Undermining Liberty

It was only after he had completed *The Constitution of Liberty* that Hayek came to see more clearly why individual freedom had failed to retain the support of the idealists to whom, he says, 'all the great political movements are due'. He identifies three reasons.

The first is a failure to be aware of the limits of human knowledge. The character and fallibility of our knowledge means that detailed central direction of economic and social life is unworkable and must always produce unexpected results. Knowledge is dispersed, and so our institutions must be decentralised.

The second problem is the modern demand for social or distributive justice, which has produced a willingness to use the coercive apparatus of the state, not to see fair play between citizens according to settled rules, but to adjust directly the material positions of particular persons and groups in accordance with the government's preferences. This puts every person's life-chances at the mercy of arbitrary political judgements.

The third factor is the modern notion that political freedom requires unlimited popular sovereignty, or unlimited government. Particularly damaging is the tendency for the same authority that makes the rules of justice to also direct the day-to-day affairs of government (1973, p. 2).

1. The Limits of Human Knowledge: Hayek's 'plain freedom' has been progressively undermined by collectivist thought. The principal culprit is the assumption that governments aiming to create a better world can deliver planned changes in our institutions and in the distribution of material goods. Hayek does not argue that we are at the mercy of circumstances; or that we must put up with things as they are; nor is he romantic about the past or about tradition. His view, put at its simplest, is that in attempting to improve the world we should display that degree of caution justified by the true complexity of social affairs. A genuine commitment to creating the 'good life' requires that we should first take the trouble to understand how society works. So Hayek's aim has been to understand the mechanism by which progress, in material as well as moral well-being, can best continue.

There are two ways of looking at how civilisations 'hang together' or 'work', or put the other way round, do not disintegrate as a result of selfish squabbling. Both emerged as medieval communalism broke down and men sought release from ancient ties which seemed to impede their efforts to improve their lives. The first (Russell's self-assertive tradition) holds that we have unlimited power to realise our wishes. If necessary the whole social order can be remade from scratch: to 'grasp this sorry scheme of things entire'. The second—the tradition of Locke and Hume—acknowledges that there are limits to what we can deliberately bring about because there are limits to what we know. We do not have to put up with the problems and evils which surround us, but if we wish to bring about change for the better we should be aware of the limits of our understanding. It is vital to understand this because, writes Hayek, 'the effect of allowing ourselves to be deluded by the first view has always been that man has actually limited the scope of what he can achieve. For it has always been the recognition of the limits of the possible which has enabled man to make full use of his powers' (1973, p. 8). Hayek calls the first liberal tradition 'constructivist rationalism' and the second, 'evolutionary rationalism'. He links each to a conception of 'social order': a 'made' order and a 'spontaneous' order.

To understand Hayek's view we must appreciate something of the background to his theories, and in particular we must appreciate the historical links between competing theories of knowledge and individual freedom. Philosophers have long debated the nature of knowledge, disputing with particular force its sources and how to appraise rival claims about truth or falsity.

When we say that this or that is true or false, what are we doing? One view is that the discovery of knowledge takes place wholly in the mind. Each object in the external world has a true nature or essence which we can arrive at by introspection. Knowledge consists of these essences. In the view of Karl Popper, this theory, often

called Platonic realism (Popper prefers to call it 'essential-
ism'), lends itself to 'epistemological pessimism'—the
theory that only a few people can acquire knowledge. This
standpoint is linked to political authoritarianism. Because
most people are doomed to ignorance, they should, it
follows, submit to rule by the wise.

In the seventeenth century, however, authoritarianism
in politics, religion and science was under attack. If
knowledge was not laid down from on high by kings and
bishops, contemporary philosophers asked, what was the
source of our knowledge? Two kinds of answer were given.
One tradition flowed from the work of René Descartes,
whose *Discourse on Method* was first published in 1637.
Descartes and his followers replied that the individual
must apply the method of doubt to all assertions. This
would lead him to discover that he cannot doubt his own
existence, and from this certain foundation the individual
could begin to discover truth. Truth was distinguished
from falsehood because truth was 'clear and distinct', like
a mathematical proof. The individual should, therefore,
reject as false any notion that did not seem clear and
distinct. As to truth, its ultimate source was God, and
this established its reliability, for if what was clear and
distinct was false than God was deceiving us—and this was
utterly impossible. Philosophers have called this view
rationalism.

For Francis Bacon, the first of the empiricists, the
source of our knowledge was not man's reason—the con-
templation of clear and distinct ideas—but experience.
This view was also subversive of established authority, but
insisted that in challenging prevailing orthodoxies—in
daily life as well as in science—we should use our senses.
Scientific theories, it was believed, were built up inductively bit by bit through painstaking observation. The
empiricist view gained rapidly in stature as a result of
the huge advances of experimental science and especially
due to the prestige of Newtonian physics, which by the
eighteenth century seemed wholly beyond challenge. The
empiricist view that all knowledge derives from experience
was put clearly by Hume:

If I ask, why you believe any particular matter of fact which you relate, you must tell me some reason; and this reason will be some other fact, connected with it. But as you cannot proceed after this manner *in infinitum*, you must at last terminate in some fact which is present to your memory or senses; or must allow that your belief is entirely without foundation (*Inquiry Concerning Human Understanding*, section V, part I in *Essays, Literary, Moral and Political*).

And more succinctly in the same work he says, 'all our ideas are nothing but copies of our impressions ... it is impossible for us to *think* of anything, which we have not antecedently *felt*, either by our external or internal senses (section VII, part I).

Hume, who believed in the truth of Newtonian physics, did, however, see that induction was logically invalid. Hume showed that when we say that 'A causes B' all that we are entitled to claim is that in our past experience A and B have frequently appeared together or in rapid succession and that no instance has been observed of A not being accompanied or succeeded by B; but however many instances we have observed of A accompanying B we are not entitled to assume they will be conjoined in the future. This left Hume with a problem. Hume believed that Newtonian physics was indubitably true, as did all his contemporaries and indeed all scientists until Einstein, well over a century later. He also knew that Newton believed he had arrived at his theories inductively. And it appeared to him that in both science and in daily life we did actually arrive at knowledge by induction, or at least by a process that looked like induction.

How could this be explained? Hume's reply was that we placed our confidence in custom or habit. Experience was the basis of our knowledge, as the enormous success of experimental science suggested, but we arrived at our theories not by a process of valid logical inference, but by placing our confidence in custom. In the past each of us has observed many repetitions of the association of this object with that, and from this repetition we infer that we can expect their conjunction in the future. But this is not a rational process:

All belief of matter of fact or real existence is derived merely from some object present to the memory or senses, and a customary conjunction between that and some other object; or in other words, having found, in many instances, that any two kinds of objects, flame and heat, snow and cold, have always been conjoined together: if flame or snow be presented anew to the senses, the mind is carried by custom to expect heat or cold, and to *believe*, that such a quality does exist, and will discover itself upon a nearer approach.

'All inferences from experience', he concluded, 'are effects of custom, not of reasoning' (*Inquiry Concerning Human Understanding*, section V, part I).

This is where Kant comes in. Immanuel Kant's most important book is *The Critique of Pure Reason*, first published in 1781. Like Hume he accepted the indubitable truth of Newtonian physics, but could not accept that habit or custom played the role Hume claimed.

Philosophers distinguish between analytic and synthetic statements. An analytic statement is one that is true by virtue of the meaning of the terms used, or more precisely a proposition in which the predicate (what is said of the subject) is part of the subject. To deny the truth of such a statement is self-contradictory. For instance, the expressions 'the fat man is a man', and 'the tall woman is a woman' are analytic. To maintain that a tall woman is not female is self-contradictory. A synthetic proposition is one that is not analytic. The statement, for instance, that Nelson was the victor at Trafalgar is synthetic. Before Kant, philosophers had regarded synthetic propositions as derived from experience, but Kant did not accept this. For him a statement could be synthetic but known *a priori* (that is, without benefit of experience). The laws of mathematics, for example, are known *a priori*, as are the relations of lines in geometry.

Hume had shown that induction was not analytic as previously supposed. Kant accepted this but continued to assert that a cause-and-effect relationship could be known *a priori*. He argued that when we look at the outer world we look at it through given concepts which enable us to understand it. There are things-in-themselves (noumena) which cause sensation (sight, touch, etc.) and there are phenomena, which are the things that appear to us in perception. Phenomena fall into two parts: one due to the object (noumena) and one due to our mental apparatus which organises perception. Space and time are the most important such categories. We look at the world through these, much as we might look through coloured spectacles. They are rather like pigeon holes, by means of which we order the world as we view it. In addition to space and time there are other *a priori* concepts, of which Kant identifies twelve types, including quantity, quality and relations of cause and effect.

To sum up: David Hume accepted that induction was not logically valid, but nevertheless held that all knowledge rested on experience. Kant argued that there is always an element of experience in our acquiring of knowledge or perception, but that there is also an element that is given by our mental apparatus. Thus, some of the properties detected in the outside world by an observer may be due to the observer:

> our reason can understand only what it creates according to its own design: that we must compel Nature to answer our questions, rather than cling to nature's apron strings and allow her to guide us. For purely accidental observations, made without any plan having been thought out in advance, cannot be connected by a ... law—which is what reason is searching for. (Preface *Critique of Pure Reason*, 2nd edn, quoted in Popper, 1972, p. 189)

But Kant's view is also unsatisfactory, and this is where Hayek and his close friend and associate Popper have made important contributions. According to Karl Popper, these earlier theories of knowledge were influenced by a doctrine he calls 'epistemological optimism': the notion that knowledge is easily arrived at. The early empiricists, for instance, looked upon nature as a kind of open book. Kant recognised that we could not derive laws from observation statements and inferred that we interpret observable facts in the light of theories we supply: 'Our intellect', he says, 'does not draw its laws from nature ... but imposes them upon nature' (Popper, 1972, p. 180). Popper believes this goes too far, and prefers a more tentative formulation: 'Our intellect does not draw its laws from nature, but tries—with varying degrees of success—to impose upon nature laws which it freely invents' (1972, p. 191).

In Kant's view, our reason imposes laws on nature and is invariably successful in doing so. For Popper, we must invent theories and try them out. Such theories can and do come from anywhere. We can regard our theories as knowledge and place reliance on them, not because custom justifies it (as Hume thought), or because certain concepts or theories are given to us *a priori* (as Kant thought), but because we vigorously test them. And we must do this by trying to refute them. Theories cannot be derived logically from observations but they can clash with observations. If experience contradicts a theory then it stands refuted. Theories able to withstand repeated attempts to refute them can be relied upon, but only for the moment. We are left, not with final truth, but with the best corroborated theories. We have to learn to live with the uncertainty surrounding our knowledge.

Hayek initially took a different view, but came to accept Popper's argument. His contribution has been to suggest where our theoretical concepts have come from. Hayek follows Kant in holding that we can never look at the world except through our concepts, or by using theories, or without supposition. This even applies to our basic senses like sight, touch and smell. There is not, as Hume believed, available to us a body of basic sense impressions or elementary sense data untainted by conceptual thought. All our experiences are theory-laden. Hayek is interested in what these concepts are and how they change. They are not purely private, and hence he is no solipsist; they are public. Yet, they are also unknown to us in that they are not part of our conscious thinking. But he cannot accept Kant's view that these categories are known to us *a priori*. They are not unchanging.

Hayek's explanation, emphasised particularly strongly in his most recent unpublished work (*The Fatal Conceit*, forthcoming) is that our conceptual apparatus is the product of evolution. Successful societies have flourished through having hit upon concepts which 'worked' in practice. Social orders whose concepts were ill-adapted to survival failed. Thus, in Hayek's view, we have (a) the external world; (b) the observer armed with theories; and (c) the theories themselves. The theories or concepts are not wholly private products of the mind (as in Cartesian rationalism) and nor are they fixed (as in Kantian apriorism); they are public and can be improved upon, but only at one remove, by means of long-run evolution: 'it is not merely a part but the whole of sensory qualities which is ... an "interpretation" based on the experience of the individual or the race. The conception of an original pure core of sensation which is merely modified by experience is an entirely unnecessary fiction' (Hayek, 1952, p. 42).

In *Law, Legislation and Liberty* Hayek acknowledges the similarity of his view with Popper's 'world 3'. According to Popper there is the world of physical objects (world 1), the world of conscious thought processes and experiences (world 2), and the world of objective knowledge, such as books, films and computer memories (world 3). The knowledge of this latter 'world 3' is independent of each person and can be improved upon by open criticism (Popper, 1975 pp. 153–90; 1976, pp. 180–7). Hayek differs from Popper, however, in that he has less confidence in our ability to improve world 3 by open criticism: 'The mind is embedded in a traditional impersonal structure of learnt rules, and its capacity to order experience is an acquired replica of cultural pattern which every individual mind finds given. *The brain is an organ enabling us to absorb, but not to design culture*' (Hayek, 1979a, p. 157; emphasis in original). Popper rejects comprehensive 'social engineering' because of the fallibility of human knowledge, but is prepared to support 'piecemeal social engineering'. Hayek is more sceptical, believing the scope of human theoretical knowledge to be severely limited. But though Hayek stresses how limited our knowledge is, he is not an epistemological pessimist in the Platonic sense. The limits of human knowledge cannot be overcome by any person. We are all in the same boat. Thus, far from providing a basis for authoritarianism, Hayek's pessimism is a powerful argument against allowing any (inevitably fallible) person from exercising coercive power over others.

The Implications for Political Theory: Conventionally, liberalism has been justified on three closely related grounds: the moral rightness of individual freedom due to the inherent dignity of the individual; the practical virtues of free markets; and the importance of limiting by law the power of government to harm its citizens. Hayek's contribution has been to elucidate a fourth basis for a liberal order, the limitations of human knowledge and understanding.

The view which prevails today is based on thoroughly different assumptions. He calls this view constructivist rationalism. This philosophy emerged in the seventeenth century under the influence of René Descartes. As we have seen, he sought to apply the principles of mathematics to social affairs. In the Cartesian tradition everything that could not be demonstrated to be 'true' according to reason thus defined was dismissed as 'mere opinion'. Men conducted themselves rationally only to the extent that their actions were determined by known and demonstrable truths. To conform with tradition or custom was looked upon with utter contempt. The best law, for instance, was the product of a single mind: 'the greatness of Sparta was due not to the pre-eminence of each of its laws in particular, ... but to the circumstances that, originated by a single individual, they all tended to a single end' (Descartes, quoted in Hayek, 1973, p. 147n).

Today constructivist rationalism continues to dominate political theory and day-to-day politics. Governments speak of controlling or steering the economy and socialists aspire to use the state machine to bring about a 'fundamental and irreversible' shift in the balance of power and wealth in favour of manual workers. Such thinking, says Hayek, is misguided.

Hayek calls the alternative view evolutionary rationalism. It holds that the institutions which prove to be of service have not been deliberately designed but have emerged or evolved. Sometimes institutions or practices were adopted with no apparent justification, and sometimes they were accidentally maintained because they 'worked' in the sense that the people among which they emerged prevailed over others. There are two mechanisms by which success is measured: the migration of individuals to popular cultures; and the emulation of successful cultures by others.

Civilisation, Hayek says, was not planned or created by man. The view than men have built civilisation stems from the erroneous view that human reason stands apart from society: 'But the growth of the human mind is part of the growth of civilisation; it is the state of civilisation at any given moment that determines the scope and the possibilities of human ends and values. The mind can never foresee its own advance. Though we must always strive for the achievement of our present aims, we must also leave room for new experiences and future events to decide which of these aims will be achieved' (1960, p. 24).

For Hayek, not only is man's mind a product of the civilisation in which he has grown up, human knowledge or understanding is limited in two senses. First, the knowledge which can be manipulated by any one mind is only a small part of the knowledge which at any moment contributes to the success of any person's actions. There are a great many particular facts of which we take advantage, but each person is actually aware of very few. No person understands all that has gone into making the world what it is. No single person, inside or outside government, can know all the facts of which advantage is actually being taken as each person co-ordinates their endeavours with the efforts of other persons:

Most of the advantages of social life ... rest on the fact that the individual benefits from more knowledge than he is aware of. It might be said that civilisation begins when the individual in the pursuit of his ends can make use of more knowledge than he has himself acquired and when he can transend the boundaries of his ignorance by profiting from knowledge he does not himself possess. (1960, p. 22)

In Hayek's view, man's actions are adapted not only to the particular facts each person knows but also to a great many others he does not know and cannot know. This adaption is brought about, not only by known connections between means and ends, but also by following simplifying signals like money values, or by obeying customs, habits, rules, morals, laws or institutions, the origins of which are often unknown (1973, pp. 11–12).

This is the second sense in which our knowledge is limited. We know little of the institutions which are central to the spontaneous coordination of human endeavour. Our emotions, skills, morals, traditions, habits and laws are all adaptations to past experience, each of which may be unknown to us, let alone understood. Hayek is suggesting that our knowledge is essentially practical knowledge, 'knowledge how' (1967, pp. 43–4). Much of what proves serviceable to us cannot be articulated by us, in much the same way as the person who does a cartwheel is unable to explain precisely what enabled him to do it: the speed of his run up, the angle of trajectory at take off, at what precise moment to bend or straighten the elbows, and so on.

According to Hayek, discussion of such questions has been severely hampered by wide acceptance of a misleading distinction between 'natural' and 'artificial' (or man-made) phenomena. Until Bernard Mandeville and David Hume were writing in the eighteenth century, all that was man-made was assumed to have been the result of deliberate decision. This tendency to think of the social order as the product of a thinking mind remains powerful today: society 'acts' or 'treats' or 'rewards' or 'remunerates' persons, or it 'values', 'owns' or 'controls' objects or services, or is 'responsible for' or 'guilty of' something, or that it has a 'will' or 'purpose' or is 'just' or 'unjust', or that the economy 'distributes' or 'allocates' resources (1973, p. 28). All suggest that society is like a person, which it manifestly is not.

In reality there are, not two, but three categories: (a) phenomena that are natural; (b) those that are the result of human *design*; and (c) those that are the result of human *action* but not of human design, as Adam Ferguson expressed it (Hayek, 1973, p. 20). Using this more sophisticated understanding of social phenomena, Hayek identifies two kinds of social order: 'made' orders, which are deliberately constructed from outside usually by the issuing of orders; and 'spontaneous' orders, which do not result from any commands.

A 'made' order serves a predetermined purpose. It is relatively simple in that it is confined to that level of complexity its controller can survey, and it is concrete in the sense that it can be perceived by inspection as when one looks at an organisation chart. An army is a 'made' order, and so is a factory. Communism rests on the assumption that a society can be organised as if it were a made order.

A 'spontaneous' order (or 'extended' order, as Hayek now prefers) may attain any level of complexity; it does not manifest itself to our senses, but may be understood as an abstraction; it has no particular predetermined purpose though many people within it will be pursuing a great many particular purposes. In it individuals are not instructed how to act but permitted to use their talents as they believe best within rules believed to facilitate free initiative.

The order or regularity or predictability is maintained because rules—embodied, perhaps, in laws, habits, customs, morals or institutions—are observed in practice. This does not mean they are written down or even known by the people who are guided by them. Here there is a parallel with language. We all, for the most part, obey rules of grammar, but most of us could not say what the rules were, yet the fact that we obey them enables us to understand each other. The particular example he has in mind is the power of religion. The Protestant ethic dictated that hard work in this life would be rewarded after death. Hayek, who is an agnostic, regards this as superstition, but he emphasises that such myths frequently play an important part in determining the success or failure of particular societies.

The units of a spontanous order are individuals and

organisations aimed at particular ends. One such organisation is government. According to Hayek, one of its 'particular ends' is to function rather like the maintenance squad of a factory: 'its object being not to produce any particular services or products to be consumed by citizens, but rather to see that the mechanism which regulates the production of those goods and services is kept in working order' (1973, p. 47).

In Hayek's view, government interference to improve a spontaneous order may be counter-productive: 'What the general argument against "interference" thus amounts to is that, although we can endeavour to improve a spontaneous order by revising the general rules on which it rests, and can supplement its results by the efforts of various organizations, we cannot improve the results by specific commands that deprive its members of the possibility of using their knowledge for their purposes.' This is because the government does not have the particular knowledge of the several actors (1973, p. 51). If force is used to restrict the freedom of ingenuity of individuals it undermines the mechanism which makes progress and adaptation to change possible—the free use of initiative. Reformers, in this view, should resort, not to interfering with the rules of the spontaneous order, but to achieving their aims through private organisations.

Hayek's spontaneous order is the same notion as Adam Smith's invisible hand. Smith's theory has frequently been ridiculed but there was never any suggestion that the spontaneous order was the best possible state of affairs: 'neither Smith nor any other reputable author I know', says Hayek, 'has ever maintained that there existed some original harmony of interests irrespective of those grown institutions' (1967, p. 100). Moreover, although the idea has been derided by socialists, they none the less sometimes use similar explanations. For instance, socialists hold that urban land values are created by 'society' and are not the result of any effort on the part of the owners. For this reason taxation of urban land values is often urged. Robert Nozick has shown how widely 'invisible hand' explanations have been used (1974, pp. 20–1).

To sum up: if we are to avoid making mistakes we must take the limits of our knowledge into account as we seek to improve our lives. For Hayek, the free play of dispersed ingenuity and initiative is vital, not only in narrowly commercial matters. but in every sphere of life: 'It is because every individual knows so little and, in particular, because we rarely know which of us knows best that we trust the independent and competitive efforts of many to induce the emergence of what we shall want when we see it.' Although this may be humiliating to human pride, 'we must recognise that the advance and even the preservation of civilization are dependent upon a maximum of opportunity for accidents to happen' (1960, p. 29). We never know who will turn out to be successful or what will count as success in the future.

2. *The Impossibility of 'Social Justice':* The second factor undermining freedom today is the pursuit of 'social justice'. Earlier liberals understood that for justice to be of value it must be impartial. For David Hume the value of 'plain justice' lay precisely in that it took no account of persons. Because of this, men and women with conflicting interests—some selfish, some altruistic—could work together.

Hayek believes that 'plain justice' is barely understood in the West. When the term is used today it is invariably to complain about some concrete state of affairs such as the pay of some particular set of employees, or the housing conditions of some group. But strictly speaking, Hayek argues, only human conduct can be called just or unjust: 'If we apply the terms to a state of affairs, they have meaning only in so far as we hold someone responsible for bringing it about or allowing it to come about. A bare fact, or state of affairs which nobody can change, may be good or bad, but not just or unjust' (1976b, p. 31). Natural occurrences, for instance, can neither be just nor unjust. 'To speak of justice', Hayek says, 'always implies that some person or persons ought, or ought not, to have performed some action; and this "ought" in turn presupposes the recognition of rules which define a set of cir-

cumstances wherein a certain kind of conduct is prohibited
or required' (1976b, p. 33).

The distribution of material possessions at any given
moment is not something that can be the subject of such
rules, because it is not the result of any person's deliberate actions: 'It has of course to be admitted that the
manner in which the benefits and burdens are apportioned
by the market mechanism would in many instances have
to be regarded as very unjust *if* it were the result of a
deliberate allocation to particular people. But this is not
the case' (1976b, p. 64).

The expression 'social justice', Hayek believes, should
be wholly extinguished from the language:

the phrase 'social justice' is not, as most people probably feel, an
innocent expression of good will towards the less fortunate ... it has
become a dishonest insinuation that one ought to agree to a demand of
some special interest which can give no real reason for it.

Ultimately, the 'systematic pursuit of the *ignis fatuus* of
"social justice" which we call socialism is based throughout on the atrocious idea that political power ought to
determine the material position of the different individuals
or groups—an idea defended by the false assertion that
this must always be so and socialism merely wishes to
transfer this power from the privileged to the most numerous class'. The 'great merit' of the market order, in
Hayek's judgement, was that during the last two centuries
it deprived everyone of such power (1976b, p. 99).

Hayek's views have come under sharp criticism from
advocates of 'distributive justice'. Some critiques are little
more than ritual denunciations which accuse Hayek of
being callous or even cruel, but there have also been some
scholarly critiques from a socialist standpoint. Professor
Raymond Plant's Fabian Society pamphlet (1984) is a
good example. He accepts that overall material outcomes
are not intended by anyone, any more than the weather is
intended. But he argues that this observation is beside the
point. The important question is not how market outcomes
were *caused* but how we *respond* to them. We can be just

or unjust in our reactions to the misfortunes experienced by others.

Plant also argues that, although market outcomes are not intended they may be predictable. Those who already command resources and economic skill, he says, are most likely to benefit (1984, p. 4). This objection is much weaker than his first, for very clearly if at any given moment some people have more resources at their disposal than other people, then those already well endowed will have an advantage. But this does not only apply to markets. It also applies to every type of society so far known. Whether you live in a pluralist democracy or under democratic socialism, or in the Communist bloc, there will be an advantage in possessing power and wealth. This advantage explains why the middle classes benefit disproportionately from the welfare state, as many collectivists frequently observe. There is no escape from human differences, and consequently no escape from differences of material wealth and power, but what we can do is to ensure that those who hold power at any time can be easily dislodged for poor performance. With political power this is the role of free elections, and with economic power it is the role of competition. Bad performers in the market can find themselves driven out of business by alternative suppliers more attuned to the wishes of fellow citizens.

But let me return to his first point, which has more force. Hayek's view, says Plant, that the benefits and burdens of the market are not distributed by some identifiable agency but rather by the impersonal forces of the market 'may be true but is irrelevant' (1981, p. 151). What really matters is how we respond to the misfortunes of others. And it is possible to describe our reactions to misfortune as either just or unjust.

This claim is valid, but care should be taken not to assume that the existence of hardship or misfortune provides a rationale for government intervention. It provides a moral basis for action to help any person suffering misfortune. But it still leaves unresolved what sort of action should be taken. If it could be shown that private action to assist the poor or victims of misfortune was always less adequate than government action, then a case could be made for state intervention, but no such general claim can be made. Indeed, in some cases private action may be superior. Thus, the existence of misfortune morally requires that help be offered, but what form this should take is a pragmatic question, depending on which available types of help are most effective.

3. The Danger of Unlimited Sovereignty: The search for social justice goes hand in hand with the notion of democracy as unimpeded national self-rule, which derives from the self-assertive tradition of liberalism. In Hayek's view we have tried democracy the wrong way. After the overthrow of absolute monarchy the aim of constitutional government was to limit governmental powers by a variety of devices: the separation of powers; the rule of law; government under the law; and the rules of judicial procedure. Above all, coercion was only justified according to uniform rules applicable to all. However, it came to be believed that if government was selected by a popular vote rather than on the hereditary principle, all these safeguards were unnecessary. This new faith in majority rule meant in reality a return to unlimited government. The notion that a democracy, because it had to obey the majority, could only do what was in the general interest turned out to be false. Indeed, says Hayek, it is '*impossible*' for a body with unlimited powers and under a necessity to buy the votes of particular interests to serve the general interest:

Such a body, which does not owe its authority to demonstrating its belief in the justice of its decisions by committing itself to general rules, is constantly under the necessity of rewarding the support by the different groups by conceding special advantages. The 'political necessities' of contemporary democracy are far from all being demanded by the majority. (1979a, p. 101)

Yet the compulsion habitually employed in western democracies is frequently not acknowledged as such. For example the back cover of a recent book by Tony Benn entitled *Parliament, People & Power* and subtitled *Agenda For a Free Society* (1982) calls for a transformation of the British state so that it will become the 'unfettered expression of the popular will'. It is assumed that such an unfettered Parliament is compatible with a free society.

Unfreedom occurs when a person lies at the mercy of the arbitrary will of other persons, and for this reason, as Chapter 1 argued, liberals have preferred a 'government of laws' to a 'government of men'. So far so good. But laws, Hayek has averred, may be arbitrary too, and in the modern world this has become a very considerable problem. Any law will not do. A particular kind of law alone will maintain plain freedom. Hayek distinguishes between two kinds of law: 'rules of just conduct' and 'commands' or 'directions' (1960, p. 148 *et seq.*; 1973, Chapter 5). Plainly if law means nothing other than the commands of the government of the day, whether elected or otherwise, the individual remains as much at the mercy of the arbitrary will of others as in the days of the divine right of kings. Many modern laws are in reality commands aimed at achieving particular ends. Confusion arises because these commands have the form of abstract law.

A *command* or direction is given with a particular concrete end result in mind. A *rule* is made or followed with no such concrete outcome in view. It regulates the conduct of all persons towards others and must conform to certain principles. Rules of just conduct must be promulgated in advance and never applied retrospectively. They should be formulated to apply to everyone equally and apply to an unknown number of future instances. They should not discriminate between named persons or groups. These principles are more than just formal requirements. They demand that a person formulating rules of just conduct should adopt a particular attitude of mind, namely the Kantian 'categorical imperative'. Rules of just conduct should be universalised by putting oneself in the position of those affected by the law. This is the attitude required by ancient maxims, such as 'do as you would be done by' or 'do unto others as you have them do unto you'. These meta-rules for the formulation of law should not, there-

fore, be dismissed as merely formal or procedural requirements. They lay down the kind of mental process a law
maker must go through in any genuine search for a true
rule of just conduct.

As we have seen, rules of just conduct, which may also
be laws, lay down a view of right conduct towards others.
It is vital that they largely take the form of *prohibitions* of
known types of harmful conduct (1976b, p. 35). The pro-
hibition of stated types of harmful action leaves men and
women free to pursue *any other* course of action not
specified, with the result that human initiative is not stifled
more than is absolutely necessary. This is possible, says
Hayek, 'only by the state's protecting known private
spheres of the individuals against interference by others
and delimiting these private spheres, not by specific assig-
nation, but by creating conditions under which the individual can determine his own sphere by relying on rules
which tell him what the government will do in different
types of situations' (1960, p. 21; also 1979a, p. 100).

Coercion is made as innocuous as possible by enabling
the individual to know in advance in what circumstances
he will be coerced by the state: thus most of the time the
'individual need never be coerced unless he has placed
himself in a position where he knows he will be coerced'.
Through general rules the threats of coercion issued by
the state become part of the stock of information which
the individual uses to make his own plans (1960, p. 21).

How to Maintain Individual Freedom
In order that freedom might be maintained Hayek proposes constitutional reform. It is first of all necessary to be
clear about what is being aimed at. If the ideal being
sought is a nation of free and responsible people this
requires that a particular view of the role of government
be taken. There are two main types of relationship between government and society. The first assumes that any
outcome is a matter for government policy. Life, the
'good life', is to be arranged by the government: material
rewards, conditions at work, health, education, social

security. Every important element of life is the subject or potential subject of a government decree.

The second kind of government–society relationship holds that concrete results—who lives where, who works for who, who gets paid what, how ill health is handled, who lives in what types of house, who worships in this or that way, how any particular product should be made and who can make it, etc.—are not for governments to prescribe, but for people to arrive at by voluntary agreement. Hayek has suggested what sort of constitution might enable a government–society relationship of the second type to be accomplished and maintained.

All governments, however discriminatory their actions in reality, claim to be acting fairly or justly or in the public interest. The practical problem is how to submit these claims to the test. As we have seen, Hayek suggests that a government should be required to demonstrate 'its belief in the justice of its decisions by committing itself to general rules' (1979a, p. 101). Because such rules are general they apply to everyone equally, and specifically to the lawmakers and their supporters. In this view the paramount duty of the state is to prevent one section of the population from tyrannising over any other, whether by using private power or the power of the state. The state, in this view, should be non-sectional.

How might such a state be accomplished? The mechanism proposed by Hayek for achieving a non-sectional state follows the practice of the ancient Athenians, a method also recommended by J.S. Mill (1972, p. 238). In Athens at the height of the democratic period the *Ecclesia* or popular assembly could only pass *psephisms*, or decrees on particular matters of policy. A separate assembly, the *Nomothetae* was charged with revising the laws, understood as rules of just conduct or *nomos*. In order to separate the promulgation of decrees dealing with particular matters from the making of rules of just conduct Hayek suggests the establishment of two new popular assemblies: one charged with governing in the sense of carrying out a programme of action; and the other charged with formulating the *nomos*. He believes that people would choose very different representatives for the two assemblies:

In choosing somebody most likely to look effectively after their particular interests and in choosing persons whom they can trust to uphold justice impartially the people would probably elect very different persons: effectiveness in the first kind of task demands qualities very different from the probity, wisdom, and judgement which are of prime importance in the second.

Hayek also suggests a device by which members of the legislative assembly could be shielded from party discipline and from needing to earn a living once their term of office was completed, a vital safeguard if they are to be fearlessly impartial. He suggests that everyone reaching the age of 45 in a given calendar year should have a vote for candidates in the same age group whose term of office would be fifteen years. The result would be an assembly of persons aged between 45 and 60, one-fifteenth of whom would retire every year (1979a, pp. 112–13).

Hayek and Conservatism
Hayek's strong emphasis on the limits of human understanding and his stress on our reliance on evolved institutions has raised in the minds of many academics the question whether Hayek has more in common with the conservative than the liberal tradition. Conservatives have strongly emphasised the weakness of man and stressed the value of tradition as contrasted with attempts at deliberate remodelling of the social order.

Let me deal first with one claim, namely that Hayek's evolutionism is a kind of Social Darwinism. In a spontaneous order, says Hayek, change occurs not as a result of the deliberate plans of government but by evolution. This is why he refers to the rationalism characteristic of a spontaneous order as 'evolutionary'. Today there is a reluctance to use the concept of evolution due to its association with late nineteenth-century Social Darwinism. But the mistake of advocates of the cruder versions of this doctrine was to focus on the selection of the 'fittest' individuals. In Hayek's thinking, evolution applies to institutions not individuals. He is, therefore, not a Social Darwinist.

Consider now how Hayek's thought compares with modern conservatism. Roger Scruton, the most notable of contemporary conservative writers, attacks liberalism and socialism alike. But he speaks of liberalism as if it were the full-blooded libertarianism of Rothbard (see Chapter 2), attacking particularly the notion that social institutions can sensibly be made to conform to a political idea, and arguing that instead tradition must be taken into account. 'In all its variants, and at every level', he writes, 'liberalism embodies the question: "Why should *I* do *that*?"' The liberal answer is either that the individual must rationally consent to do what is in question, or that he must do it because respect for the rights of others demands it (1984, p. 196; emphasis in original). For Scruton, men are 'born into a web of attachments; they are nurtured and protected by forces the operation of which they could neither consent to nor intend':

Their very existence is burdened with a debt of love and gratitude, and it is in responding to that burden that they begin to recognise the power of 'ought'. This is not the abstract, universal 'ought' of liberal theory ... but the concrete, immediate 'ought' of family attachments. It is the 'ought' of piety, which recognises the unquestionable rightness of local, transitory and historically conditioned social bonds. Such an 'ought' is essentially discriminatory; it recognises neither equality nor freedom, but only the absolute claim of the locally given. (ibid., pp. 201–2)

According to Scruton, liberal individualism 'sees the individual as potentially complete in himself, and possessed of reason, which he can use either well or ill' (ibid., p. 72). Its prevailing weakness is:

that it reposes all politics and all morality in an idea of freedom while providing no philosophy of human nature which will tell us what freedom really is. It isolates man from history, from culture, from all those unchosen aspects of himself which are in fact the preconditions of his subsequent autonomy. When the liberal tries to make concrete the ideal of freedom which he proposes, he finds himself always constrained to endorse ... the habits and predilections of a particular way of life—the way of life of the emancipated urban intellectual ... Such a philosophy presents no idea of the self, over and above the desires which constitute it: it therefore has no idea of self-fulfilment other than the free satisfaction of desire. (ibid, p. 120)

Are Scruton's dismissals of 'liberalism' also dismissals of Hayek's 'critical rationalism'? Hayek's view is fully respectful of tradition, nor does he regard individuals as self-contained. Writing in the 1940s, Hayek dealt with what he called 'the silliest of the common misunderstandings' of individualism. He distinguishes between two traditions, true and false individualism. True individualism is 'primarily a *theory* of society, an attempt to understand the forces which determine the social life of man, and only in the second instance a set of political maxims derived from this view of society'. It does not postulate 'the existence of isolated or self-contained individuals, instead of starting from men whose whole nature and character is determined by their existence in society'. If that were true, he says, 'it would indeed have nothing to contribute to our understanding of society'. On the contrary, true individualism is 'directed primarily against the properly collectivist theories of society which pretend to be able directly to comprehend social wholes like society, etc., as entities *sui generis* which exist independently of the individuals which compose them'. By tracing the combined effects of individual actions we discover that many institutions 'have arisen and are functioning without a designing and directing mind' and that 'the spontaneous collaboration of free men often creates things which are greater than their individual minds can ever fully comprehend' (1949, pp. 6–7). This true individualism stands opposed to the 'false' constructivist rationalism of Descartes and his followers.

Scruton is criticising the 'naive', 'self-assertive' constructivist rationalists, but Hayek has attempted to take the argument further. Yes, argues Hayek, tradition and custom are important. It even makes sense to respect tradition when we can give no direct reason for doing so, other than the recognition that it may embody the wisdom of ages past without our being aware of it.

But to what extent is Hayek really a conservative? He has undoubtedly adjusted the liberal ethic in response to conservative attacks. His stress on the role of tradition owes much to conservative thought. And in his most recent work (as yet unpublished) his evolutionary theory has been given pride of place. Nevertheless, I shall argue that there are some very clear differences between the conservative view and Hayek's liberalism. Above all, he is searching for a realistic liberalism in place of naive liberalism, or in John Gray's terminology, 'hubristic rationalism'. He strongly rejects the mystification and intuitionism which lies at the heart of the thinking of conservatives like Roger Scruton, qualities which give the conservative ethic a decided 'now you see it, now you don't' character.

Moreover, in an essay published in 1960, Hayek explicitly refutes the suggestion that he is a conservative. The 'decisive objection' to conservatism is that 'by its very nature it cannot offer an alternative to the direction in which we are moving' (1960, p. 398). Liberals may not, in common with conservatives, approve of current developments, but they differ in that they want 'to go elsewhere, not to stand still' (ibid., p. 399). Conservatives differ from liberals in their attitude to change and this in turn affects their view of authority. In Hayek's view, conservatives exhibit a 'timid distrust of the new as such', whereas the liberal position is based on 'courage and confidence' (ibid., p. 400). This fear of change is at the root of conservative fondness for authority and of its lack of understanding of economic forces. All order appears to the conservative to be the result of authority. The conservative cannot accept that order can arise spontaneously.

Furthermore, because the conservative holds that authority is vital to the maintenance of order he is not as concerned as the liberal to limit the arbitrary potential of government, but only to see that the 'best' people get control of it. This is based on the judgement that some people are superior and that they should control other people's lives. The liberal does not deny that some people are superior in some respects, but disagrees that 'anyone has the authority to decide who these people are' (ibid.,

p. 402). Ultimately, the difference lies in the attitude taken to knowledge:

> what I have described as the liberal position shares with conservatism a distrust of reason to the extent that the liberal is very much aware that we do not know all the answers and that he is not sure that the answers he has are certainly the right ones or even that we can find all the answers. He also does not disdain to seek assistance from whatever non-rational institutions or habits have proved their worth. The liberal differs from the conservative in his willingness to face this ignorance and to admit how little we know, without claiming the authority of supernatural sources of knowledge where his reason fails him. (ibid., p. 406)

Tradition should be respected, but this does not mean that each person, wherever he is, must simply put up with his lot. The Hindu woman does not, for instance, have to submit to *suttee* (widow-burning) on the death of her husband. The status quo is not always good. Traditions, in Hayek's view, are important, but they are on trial. They are in competition with one another, and the test of their success is their ability to hold or attract people who are otherwise free to move, and their ability to find emulators. It must be conceded that movement between nation states is difficult, but emulation is less difficult. And if government is decentralised movement is made more easy. Federal systems offer most scope for free movement. In Australia, for instance, the different tax laws of the state governments have resulted in competition for mobile citizens (Ray, 1984, p. 60).

Hayek has also sought to identify a criterion by which individuals can judge the relative desirability of different societies. The Good Society, he says, 'is one in which the chances of anyone selected at random are likely to be as great as possible'; or, put another way, 'the best society would be that in which we would prefer to place our children if we knew that their position in it would be determined by lot' (1976b, p. 132).

Notwithstanding his increased emphasis on evolutionary forces which he regards as little open to human manipulation, Hayek in his later years remains essentially liberal. Hayek differs sharply from liberals like Rothbard who place reason above all else, but he is very far from adopting a conservative hostility to reason as such:

> None of these conclusions are arguments against the use of reason, but only arguments against such uses as require any exclusive and coercive powers of government; not arguments against experimentation, but arguments against all exclusive, monopolistic power to experiment in a particular field—power which brooks no alternative and which lays a claim to the possession of superior wisdom—and against the consequent preclusion of solutions better than the ones to which those in power have committed themselves. (1960, p. 70)

HAYEK AND ECONOMICS

So far only the general principles of Hayek's thought have been considered. This section considers the practical application of his thinking in that all-important sphere, economics.

Friedrich Hayek is the leading exponent of the Austrian (or Neo-Austrian) tradition of economic thought. The founder of this school was Carl Menger (1840–1921) whose teachings were published in his *Principles of Economics* in 1871. His main followers were Friedrich von Wieser (1851–1926) and Eugen von Bohm-Bawerk (1851–1914). Hayek and Ludwig von Mises (1881–1973) were the most prominent among the next generation of Austrians. Today Hayek continues to be the most eminent of a number of Neo-Austrian thinkers, including Murray Rothbard, Ludwig Lachmann and Israel Kirzner.

Central to the Austrian view of economics is their 'subjectivism'. Classical economists believed that value (the price at which goods and services are exchanged) was dependent upon the costs of production. Ricardo, Mill and Marx favoured the version of this theory that saw the labour input as decisive in determining value. Ludwig von Mises rejected this view, urging that value was subjective. It reflected, he said, the preferences, prejudices, casual likes and dislikes, and the predicaments, of individual actors.

Hayek accepts that prices are subjective and extends

this belief to social phenomena generally. He says, for instance, that, 'so far as human actions are concerned the things *are* what the acting people think they are' (1979b, p. 44). This has implications for his view of the scientific status of the study of social phenomena. At one stage he was convinced that the natural and social sciences were fundamentally different because the subject-matter was fundamentally different. Social phenomena were not amenable to objective study in the same way as physical objects. He did not, however, accept the Austrian alternative of praxeology, which believed that economics could proceed by deduction from certain axioms about 'human action'.

Later Hayek was influenced by Popper's insight that the method of the natural sciences was not inductive, but hypethetico-deductive, and came to the view that the gap between the natural and social sciences had been narrowed (1967, p. viii). He did not, however, change his view that social phenomena were fundamentally different from physical phenomena, or that this put severe limits on what the social sciences could accomplish. The great complexity of social phenomena compared with the physical world, means that we can never observe all the 'data'. Competition, for instance, is valuable precisely because it enables unknown persons to back their own judgement and come up with potentially attractive new ways of providing for their fellows. We can never observe all the actions that make competition useful. Nor can this problem be overcome by treating people as members of 'statistical collectives': 'For this reason economic theory is confined to describing kinds of patterns which will appear if certain general conditions are satisfied, but rarely if ever derive from this knowledge any predictions of specific phenomena' (1967, p. 35).

Such predictions of patterns are testable and useful, but economic theory cannot go beyond this to the production of anything resembling scientific laws, and nor can it be regarded as a kind of policy science enabling us to manipulate the national economy. Hayek is, therefore,

very much out of step with the economic orthodoxy of
recent decades.

Macro or Micro?

Since the late 1930s, and especially since the Second
World War, economists have been overwhelmingly concerned with macro-economic questions: national income,
GDP, aggregate demand, the unemployment level, aggregate prices. In particular they have sought to understand
how governments can maintain full employment by manip-
ulating aggregate demand. Hayek and other members of
the Austrian School have long regarded this concern as
fundamentally misconceived.

Hayek attributes the ascendancy of macro-economics to
Keynes' *General Theory* more than to any other single
work. Keynes' 'final conceptions', Hayek writes, 'rest entirely on the belief that there exist relatively simple and
constant functional relationships between such "measurable" aggregates as total demand, investment, or output,
and that empirically established values of these presumed
"constants" would enable us to make valid predictions'
(1978b, p. 285).

But Hayek believes there is 'no reason whatever' to
assume that such relationships as may appear to exist
are constant. Aggregate demand, investment, output and
unemployment, depend on the micro-economic conduct of
actors within the economic systems. All aggregates depend
on the infinitely complex choices being made daily by
consumers as they select this or that product, workers as
they move from job to job, trade unions as they bargain
for improvements in wages and conditions here and there,
and companies as they seek new opportunities for profit in
markets at home or overseas. Macro-economics neglects
to understand these complexities. In particular it fails to
take into account the largely subjective character of price
determination, and the signalling function of relative
prices.

However, because it is based on apparently measurable
phenomena, macro-economic theory *appears* to be more
scientific than micro-economics. But, writes Hayek:

it has achieved this pseudo-exactness at the price of disregarding the relationships which really govern the economic system. Even though the schemata of micro-economics do not claim to achieve those quantitative predictions at which the ambitions of macro-economics aim, I believe by learning to content ourselves with the more modest aims of the former, we shall gain more insight into at least the principle on which the complex order of economic life operates, than by the artificial simplification necessary for macro-theory which tends to conceal nearly all that really matters. (1978b, p. 289)

Wasteful Competition?

Hayek's view of the character and importance of competition is equally at odds with the opinions of the bulk of economists. Economics textbooks conventionally discuss competition by contrasting the extreme cases of 'perfect competition' and monopoly, with most of the real world seen as in between. Textbook discussions usually hinge around two main concerns. First, they consider whether or not a particular firm has to put up with the price as determined by the market, or whether it has some leeway in price fixing or the control of output. And second, they discuss whether or not the efficient level of output has been achieved. The efficient level of output is said to be that point at which marginal costs coincide with prices. At this point, if a firm produces more, then it must charge a higher price, in which case competitors can undercut it. Hayek's criticism is that analyses which look at markets in this manner too readily overlook the chief advantage competition offers. Competition is useful, he says, in just the same way that a sporting competition is useful. It enables the most proficient performer to emerge. But the focus on the efficient level of output so central to the economic analysis of competition distracts attention from its advantages in the ordinary sense of the term. 'It is difficult', Hayek writes, 'to defend economists against the charge that for some 40 to 50 years they have been discussing competition on assumptions that, *if* they were true of the real world, would make it wholly uninteresting and useless. If anyone really knew all about what economic theory calls the *data*, competition would indeed be a very wasteful method of securing adjustment to these facts'

(1978, p. 179). Hayek's criticism of perfect competition has not only been neglected, he has on occasion had the very opposite view attributed to him. In a Fabian Society pamphlet, David (now Professor) Collard, an economist at the University of Bath, describes the 'new right' view thus: 'The economic vision of the New Right is the economists' model of perfect competition in which rational consumers indicate their preferences to profit-seeking producers by means of prices under conditions of perfect information' (1968, p. 3).

In reality Hayek argues that textbook discussions of 'perfect competition' have done a great deal of harm. He writes, for instance, that 'it is evidently neither desirable nor possible that every commodity or service that is significantly different from others should be produced by large numbers of producers' (as perfect competition dictates) (1979, p. 66). On the contrary, competition is 'like experimentation in science, first and foremost a discovery procedure'. The issue is, 'how we can best assist the optimum utilization of the knowledge, skills and opportunities to acquire knowledge, that are dispersed among hundreds of thousands of people, but given to nobody in their entirety' (1979a, p. 68). The knowledge he has in mind consists of 'a capacity to find out particular circumstances, which becomes effective only if possessors of this knowledge are informed by the market which kinds of things or services are wanted, and how urgently they are wanted' (1978b, p. 182). This is why Israel Kirzner describes the essential quality of the entrepreneur as having crucially to do with 'alertness' to opportunities for production (1980, pp. 5–26).

What are the achievements of competition? First, it encourages the emergence of new *products*: 'everything will be produced which somebody knows how to produce and which he can sell profitably at a price at which buyers will prefer it to available alternatives'. Second, it encourages the emergence of more efficient *producers*: everything that is being produced is more likely to be produced by 'persons who can do so at least as cheaply as anybody else who in fact is not producing it'. Third, it encourages lower *prices*: everything will be sold at prices lower than, or at least as low as, those at which it could be sold by anybody else (1979a, p. 74).

Central to the success of competition is pricing. At any given moment it is very difficult for any person to establish whether or not it will prove attractive for him to make one product rather than another, or to adopt one technique rather than another. Prices are the key: 'It is only through prices he finds in the market that he can learn what to do and how.' It is only prices that inform him 'constantly and unmistakeably ... what goods or services he ought to produce in his own interest as well as the general interest of his community or country as a whole' (1984, p. 28).

The way in which prices simplify complex phenomena to a single criterion is disliked by some critics of the market. Reducing everything to the 'cash nexus' is said to encourage selfishness, whereas there are other considerations which may be more important than financial ones. First of all, it should be clear that Hayek does not only favour commercial dealings. He strongly supports the voluntary sector and urges that we preserve 'between the commercial and the governmental' sectors a third, independent sector, to include charitable, voluntary and mutual aid associations. Above all he is concerned that 'public spirit' should not always be identified with demand for or support of government action (1979a, pp. 50–1).

But he recognises that prices do fail to take into account much that is important. They are simplifying devices. But this is their merit. They send signals to producers which enable them to meet the needs of others. A producer may only wish to make money by obtaining cheap raw materials, but he serves the customer, whose needs might not otherwise be met.

But most important of all is that competition enables us to cope with the unforeseeable. We live in a complex world which no one can comprehend in its entirety. The prosperity of the world depends upon meeting our wants in ways which make the best use of available resources. At any given moment (though not of course in the long-run) there is only so much wealth. If resources are wasted on producing one item there is so much less for other goods, and this effect ripples across the world. Britain, for instance, has reserves of gold ore but it can only be produced at very high cost. It is better that the British should use their resources to produce goods at prices which are attractive to uncoerced consumers at home or abroad. The same applies to coal. If Britain uses its resources mining coal that meets no one's needs, it wastes its resources and diminishes its prosperity, and in turn diminishes the total prosperity of the world.

The market, if it is not impeded by special interests abusing the powers of government, is a mechanism that encourages the discovery of the most economic ways of meeting our needs. But, vital to Hayek's view, is that the most economic ways of meeting needs remain to be discovered and are always changing in ways we cannot foresee.

Freedom, Social Justice and Economic Discipline
For Hayek there is a paradox in the prevailing attitude to freedom. Many people, he writes, 'seem to believe that freedom consists of being able to do whatever they like and still enjoy all the benefits of an advanced society in which they must cooperate with others'. But modern society 'could not prosper—or even survive for long—if it allowed the mass of its members that kind of freedom'. This is because modern prosperity 'requires all of us to observe an impersonal discipline':

More than once in our lifetimes, some of us have to do things we may dislike—changing our jobs, our homes or our neighbourhoods, or accepting a smaller income than we had come to expect.... And all this is hard to bear because it seems the consequence of causes and events a long way off about which we know nothing: a change of habit in another industry or a technical invention in another country.

But it is important to recognise what is happening when we accept this discipline: we are obeying the discipline of other people's wants or other countries' production methods. And these are ultimately the sources of our wealth (1984, p. 27). Moreover, if we try to escape the impersonal discipline of other people's wants we are left only with still worse alternatives: central direction, which may vary in its stringency from western socialism to totalitarianism; or a syndicalist-corporatist response in which big business and the big unions rule the roost in their own narrow self interest. To demand 'social justice' or to imagine that our circumstances could be otherwise is based on a misunderstanding of how markets work.

Today we speak routinely of 'the economy' and of the government directing or regulating or managing 'the economy'. For Hayek such talk is misconceived. There is no unitary 'economy' which can be directed as if it were an organisation with a single hierarchy of ends. He suggests that we use a different term, catallaxy, which derives from the Greek word *katallattein*. This meant, not only 'to exchange' but also 'to admit into the community' and to 'change from enemy into friend'. Thus a catallaxy is a special kind of order produced by people and organisations going about the production, distribution and exchange of goods and services, acting within the laws of property, tort and contract and mutually adjusting their plans and activities to those of others (1976b, pp. 108–9).

What do we do about the misfortune this need for constant adjustment to the needs of others can produce? Through no fault of their own some persons may find their skills no longer required or that they can no longer command the income they once did. It is no answer to protect existing interests, as experience shows. For Hayek such adjustments are the price that has to be paid for our common progress. In the end everyone is better-off. Falling income or loss of job signals a failure to serve others. To protect people from this 'negative feedback' is to undermine the mechanism that encourages people to serve each other. The prospect of reward is an incentive to serve. This incidentally, does not mean that Hayek opposes state assistance of the poor. On the contrary, he favours the maintenance of a national minimum below which no one should be allowed to fall.

Although a free society cannot protect the existing

position of every person in it, it is the best arrangement known to us for improving equally the chances for all. We should regard as the most desirable order of society, he says, 'one which we would choose if we new that our initial position in it would be decided purely by chance (such as the fact of our being born into a particular family)' (1976b, p. 132).

Thus, Hayek makes two very strong moral claims for a free society. First, it is the best method known to us for improving the life-chances of the vast majority of people. And second, it is the best method known to us for channelling the efforts of all into the service of others.

Inflation
Inflation, in Hayek's judgement, is one of the great enemies of freedom, because it reduces the ability of the ordinary citizen to control his or her own life. In his frustration at the long record of failure by governments to control inflation he has suggested that governments should be deprived of their monopoly of the issue of money. This would cure the recurring bouts of acute inflation and deflation which, he says, have 'plagued the world for the past 60 years'. These cycles have been blamed on 'capitalism', but in reality they are the result of repeated failures by governments to maintain reliable money (1978a, p. 126).

Under his plan, people would be able to choose from among a variety of currencies and this would inhibit governments from debasing their own. To set the ball rolling he proposes that the countries of the Common Market bind themselves by formal treaty not to place any obstacles in the way of free dealing in one another's currencies. Such a scheme, he says, is less Utopian than the proposal, already under active consideration, to introduce a single European currency. It would contain inflation because 'any deviations from the straight path of providing an honest money would at once lead to the rapid displacement of the offending currency by others'. Individual countries would be deprived of the 'various dodges' by which they temporarily conceal the effects of their actions by protecting their currency, and would be constrained to keep their currency more stable (1978a, p. 19).

Experience of inflation also bears out his conviction that micro-economic study is the only way to arrive at accurate understanding. An increase in the money supply, for instance, does not have a direct effect on the *general* level of prices. Additional money enters the economy at *particular* points and therefore has an effect on *particular* prices. It therefore distorts the vital signalling role of the market. Relative prices no longer convey to producers how best they can meet the requirements of consumers, and the market ceases to direct the efforts of all into the service of others. An industry thus affected also becomes vulnerable to a later collapse. The evil day is postponed, but not cancelled. This is what happened to many nationalised industries, like shipbuilding and steel. Investment was sucked in which was not justified by demand and which was only available because the government had printed extra money.

Friedman's view differs from Hayek's. According to Hayek, they differ so much on monetary policy that, in spite of their friendship, they avoid the subject (*The Times*, 9 May 1985). Friedman, like Hayek, mistrusts governments because they have used inflation to deceive the electorate. They have expanded the money supply to fund spending deficits. This enables them to spend more without obviously forcing voters to spend less. In particular it enables the government to raise revenue without raising taxes, especially if tax brackets are not adjusted upwards as inflation rises. And governments have used inflation to generate employment, which, as we have seen is only a short-run effect.

However, Friedman believes that, in the American context at least, a constitutional amendment would suffice. He recommends that the annual growth in the monetary base should be kept within the range of 3–5 per cent and favours the calling of a constitutional convention to consider a number of amendments, not only to require fixed monetary growth, but also to require the government to balance the budget, and replace progressive income tax by a flat-rate tax (a balanced budget law has now been passed) (1985, p. 159).

Hayek, as we have seen, does not share Friedman's faith in such measures, and he accuses Friedman of remaining a Keynesian in one sense. Friedman believes there is a relatively straightforward causal relationship between changes in the quantity of money and the general level of prices. Hayek insists that there can be no direct relationship between mere aggregates, because an aggregate is itself artificial. It is already at one remove from reality. There can, therefore, be no direct relationship between two sets of artificial phenomena. To seek causal relationships we must return to the detailed data of everyday life, particular prices and actual wages. To make matters worse, the quantity of money is a particularly difficult aggregate. In the age of the credit card and computer banking, money is very difficult to define, and the quantity in circulation very difficult to measure and control. There is, writes Hayek, 'no such thing as *the* quantity of money' (1978a, p. 77).

Hayek's conclusion is that it is futile to imagine that governments will behave responsibly and maintain sound money, because, he says, they have too much to gain from inflation. He proposes that the maintenance of sound money should no longer be a government responsibility. However, he has also entered the debate about short-run monetary stabilisation, because he accepts that his plan is unlikely to be accepted for many years. And in practice he accepts that governments can reduce inflation by controlling the money supply, but he emphasises that we must always be aware that the relationship is not a causal one. It is very rough and ready, and the sooner we turn our eyes to micro-economic realities the better. Even leaving aside this fundamental difference, Friedman and Hayek also differ about short-run monetary stabilisation. Friedman advocates a gentle step-by-step reduction in the rate of monetary growth to reduce the short-run dislocation that tighter monetary control causes. Hayek believes this merely prolongs the agony and has urged that governments should decelerate monetary growth swiftly. In the

early part of Mrs Thatcher's term of office Hayek predicted that unemployment at levels of 10 per cent or more
over a period of three years or so would have a destabilis-
ing effect, and would lead to pressures to do a U-turn.
Much higher levels of unemployment could be tolerated,
he says, so long as it was only for six months or so.
In the event, the Thatcher government has followed the
Friedmanite path and at the time of writing, in the early
months of 1986, Hayek's predictions have not been borne
out. High levels of unemployment have been tolerated for
several years, without producing political instability or a
U-turn but as the next general election approaches it is
likely that unemployment will become the dominant issue
and that the government will respond by quietly abandoning its strategy in order to buy a short-run reduction in
unemployment. (Further discussion of Hayek's economic
thought can be found in Chapter 8.)

CONCLUSION

To sum up: Hayek in many ways remains an enigma. He
is at .heart a classical liberal—or an Old Whig, as he
prefers. When he sees unfreedom, he wants to remedy it,
and when he sees injustice he wants to help. The world
could be a better place, he believes, and will only become
so through human endeavour. At the same time he is
deeply conscious of the limits of human theoretical knowledge and increasingly he has come to understand both
changes in our institutions and the development of our
intellectual apparatus as evolutionary processes over which
individuals have little or no direct control. In his latest
unpublished work he appears at times to place humankind
wholly at the mercy of evolutionary forces. Yet we know,
from his pronouncements in the last few years, that he is
no fatalist and that he continues to discuss and advocate
schemes for political and economic reform. The conclusion
is bound to be drawn that there is in Hayek an unresolved
tension. On the one hand, there is the conservatism which
says that we are stuck with a good many of our institu-

tions and that to meddle with them too readily is asking
for trouble; and on the other, is the liberalism which says,
I see around me denials of liberty, and I see injustices,
here is my remedy.

GUIDE TO READING

The best introduction to Hayek's thought is his own *The
Constitution of Liberty* (1960). The reader can then turn to
Law, Legislation & Liberty (1973). A more detailed treatment of many of the questions raised in these two books
can be found in *Studies in Philosophy, Politics and Economics* (1967) and in *New Studies* (1978b). The hard-pressed
student can find succinct presentations of Hayek's thought
in a number of IEA papers, particularly *1980s Unemployment and the Unions* (1984) and *Full Employment at Any
Price?* A three-hour video in which Hayek talks to the
journalist John O'Sullivan is also obtainable from the
IEA.

John Gray's *Hayek on Liberty* (1984) (now available in
a 2nd edn) is the best secondary introduction to Hayek's
thought. Also useful are Eamon Butler's *Hayek* (1983)
and Norman Barry's *Hayek's Social and Economic Philosophy* (1979). Professor Barry (1981) has also produced a
short survey of Hayek's thought. A sometimes misleading
critique of Hayek from a left-wing standpoint can be
found in Bosanquet's *After the New Right*, Chapter 2.
Raymond Plant's Fabian pamphlet (1984) is a very useful
critique. For a criticism of Hayek's view on distributive
justice, consult Lucas (1980), Chapters 8, 12 and 13. A
criticism of Hayek from a neo-conservative standpoint can
be found in Kristol (1978) Chapter 7 and Epilogue. On
the Austrian School generally, Alexander Shand's *The
Capitalist Alternative* (1984) is valuable, and so is W.
Duncan Reekie's *Markets, Entrepreneurs and Liberty*
(1984). Taylor (1980) is a useful short guide.

Part II
PRACTICAL POLITICS

6 Political Impact: Education and Social Security

INTRODUCTION

Bit by bit, in recent years new liberals have put forward a wide variety of proposals for the transformation of western countries. A central role in generating this emerging liberal programme has been played by research institutes devoted to investigating the potential of markets to meet human wants.

Britain has the Institute of Economic Affairs, founded in 1955, the Adam Smith Institute, established in 1977, and the David Hume Institute, which opened in Edinburgh in 1985. The IEA has firmly established itself as a non-partisan research institute with a reputation for scholarly independence. Its emphasis on the production of academic research papers and remaining aloof from day-to-day politics is not shared by the younger Adam Smith Institute. It eschews what it calls the 'linear' approach of the IEA and follows a more vigorous 'micro-political' strategy, dilligently searching out the next incremental step which can be taken towards a more free society and, informed by public choice theory, targeting the interests that might benefit from it. Both Institutes play a role reminiscent of the Fabian Society within the socialist movement.

In Australia, Sydney has the Centre For Independent Studies and Centre 2000. In Perth there is the Australian Institute of Public Policy, and Melbourne's Monash University has the Centre of Policy Studies. Canada has the Fraser Institute. In the USA there is the Heritage Found-

153

ation in Washington, the Pacific Institute For Public Policy
Research in California, the Center for the Study of Market
Alternatives in Idaho, and the more outspokenly libertarian
Institute For Humane Studies in Virginia. Dallas is home
for both the Fisher Institute and the National Center for
Policy Analysis.

In Europe institutes inspired by the IEA have been
founded in Brussels (the Institutum Europaeum), Paris
(the Institute Economique de Paris), Stockholm (Timbro),
Italy (the Centro de Ricerche Economique Applicate),
Greece (the Centre for Political Research and Information) and Spain (the Instituto de Economica de Mercado).
Peru has the Instituto Libertad y Democracia and Argentina the Centro de Estudios Sobre la Libertad.

In this chapter and in Chapters 7 and 8, I shall describe
the wide array of liberal proposals for reform and consider
their impact on practical politics.

PRIMARY AND SECONDARY EDUCATION

New liberals have been strong critics of government
schooling. The full-blooded libertarians, as Chapter 2
showed, oppose not only government schools, but also
compulsory schooling. To force every child to go through
an official school system during their most impressionable
years is to give the governing class a chance to control
and manipulate the minds of the young. And government
schooling is opposed because it may be used by the ruling
powers as an instrument to buttress their dominance.
Education is seen by anarcho-capitalists as 'learning'
rather than 'schooling'—a lifelong process whereby the
individual realises his or her potential. It should not
be looked upon merely as a mechanical process for the
acquisition of qualifications valued by employers.

Some of this thinking has made an impact on the academic debate in Britain and America, and in the early
1970s a 'free school' movement emerged and led to the
foundation of at least one free school in Britain in Scotland
Road, Liverpool, but it was short-lived. The libertarian

emphasis on self-realisation has had some effect on the teaching methods employed by some teachers, but its impact on government policy has been negligible.

More influential has been the new liberal advocacy of education vouchers, initiated by Milton Friedman. Friedman's idea was modelled on the veterans' programme which followed the Second World War. Each American veteran was entitled to receive a sum per year to spend on any educational institution of his choosing, provided it met mimumum standards. Friedman urges that the same principle be applied to education at school level. He does so because he believes that education has suffered from government involvement. Standards are widely believed to have declined; the atmosphere of schools is said not to be conducive to learning; some teachers are fearful of their personal safety; costs have risen without visible benefit; and many parents are denied control of their children's education as power is vested in professional educators (1980, pp. 151-2). According to Friedman, the Theory of Bureaucratic Displacement, formulated by Dr Max Gammon to account for the poor performance of the British National Health Service, applies with equal force to American public schooling. In 'a bureaucratic system', the theory says, '*increase in expenditure* will be matched by *fall in production*. ... Such systems will act rather like "black holes" in the economic universe, simultaneously sucking in resources, and shrinking in terms of "emitted" production' (p. 155).

Friedman is particularly critical of the poor education provided by government schools for black children from low-income families. It is, he says, 'undoubtedly the greatest disaster area in public education and its most devastating failure' (ibid., p. 151). His faith that a voucher scheme would assist the poor is reinforced by the experience of Harlem Prep. In the 1960s Harlem was devastated by riots and many teenagers dropped out of schools. Concerned parents and teachers took over empty shops and, using only private funds, founded 'storefront schools'. One of these was Harlem Prep. Its physical facilities were always unsatisfactory and many of its teachers formally unqualified, but it was successful. Many of its pupils, although they were regarded as misfits and dropouts, went to college, including some leading colleges. Unfortunately the school ran out of money and was taken over by the Board of Education, which radically altered its character (ibid., pp. 159-60). Under a voucher scheme it would have survived. Not surprisingly U.S. Gallup polls show that more non-whites favour vouchers than whites. In 1983 49 per cent of whites and 64 per cent of non-whites favoured vouchers. In 1985 the results were 43 per cent of whites and 59 per cent of non-whites.

The underlying reason for the failure of government schools is that parents have been stripped of the ability to care for their children as governments have increasingly shifted power from parents to officials and professional educators. The assumption that professionals will put the interests of children first is, says Friedman, mistaken. They have their own interests as officials, teachers and trade unionists. Indeed, they have an especially strong interest in diminishing parental power in order to provide greater professional leeway. The remedy, Friedman argues, is to reinstate parental power. Unless the balance of power between parents, on the one hand, and teachers and administrators, on the other, is altered standards will continue to fall. And only if parents have the purchasing power to take their children elsewhere, will their wishes be respected (1962, p. 91).

Friedman does not suggest that there is no case at all for a government role in education. In *Capitalism and Freedom*, he argues that there are two reasons for government to be involved. The first is that education has a considerable 'neighbourhood effect'; and the second is a paternalistic concern for the children of poor or irresponsible parents. A stable and democratic society could not be maintained, Friedman argues, without a degree of shared literacy, knowledge and values. To the extent that education contributes to the acquisition of such attributes, then others share in its advantages. This does not justify any amount or any type of government intervention, and it certainly does not legitimise the nationalisation of schools, but it does justify requiring all parents to educate their children (1962, pp. 86-7). The ideal answer would be private schooling for which parents would pay fees. However, Friedman cannot accept this because some parents would be unable to afford to meet the cost of adequate schooling. It is therefore necessary to offer financial help to the poor. Given present funding arrangements, the simplest way of achieving greater parental choice whilst also protecting the poor is to introduce a voucher scheme (1980, pp. 150-75). Instead of paying taxes and getting back from the government a place in a school for their children, parents would continue to pay taxes but receive back a voucher worth the cost of providing education for a child for one year. This voucher could be exchanged for a place in a school of the parents' choice. This would give back parents the power to control the education of their children (1980, pp. 158-75).

The idea of an education voucher made a considerable impact on political debate in Britain and the USA in the 1970s and 1980s, but to date its impact on official policy has been patchy. In Britain, after a short dalliance, the Conservative government officially abandoned interest in the idea in 1983, though at the time of writing (May 1986) Mrs Thatcher was reported to have retained an interest in the voucher concept.

In America there have been a handful of partial experiments with vouchers. The earliest was at Alum Rock in California, but it was not a full trial of a voucher scheme and produced rather inconclusive results (Levinson, 1976; Rand Corporation, 1981). From autumn 1985 Minnesota allowed government high school juniors and seniors to leave early in order to enrol at government or private colleges. State funds up to the average state expenditure per student ($3,100) follow the student to the chosen college. It is too early to evaluate the scheme, but to date it has proved popular with students and parents (*Educational Choice*, March 1986). In New York City parents of handicapped children may choose any public school at public expense. A recent review found that competition tended to improve programmes for the handicapped. The federal government is also promoting a voucher bill aimed at a disadvantaged minority. Under the proposed scheme any parent whose child is considered 'educationally deprived' by the local school district may opt to receive a voucher worth about $600. This could be used to purchase compensatory or remedial teaching from wherever the parent thinks best, whether a government school, a private school or a church school. At present remedial teaching must be provided by government school teachers.

In Britain in 1975 FEVER (Friends of the Education Voucher in Representative Regions) was founded to promote an experiment with education vouchers. Its chairman was Marjorie Seldon, who ten years earlier had advocated vouchers to give buying power to all 'irrespective of social class'. Without vouchers, she argued, the 'best bargains in schooling may go to those with the "know-how", the command of English, or of the political strings. ... There is a danger that ability to pay is being replaced by ability to persuade' (in Seldon, A., 1977, p. 193).

Kent County Council expressed a special interest and in February 1976 began a feasibility study. In 1981 Sir Keith Joseph became Secretary of State for Education and Science and declared himself to be 'intellectually attracted' by the voucher concept. The DES were asked to discuss the practicalities and presented Sir Keith with a list of around a dozen difficulties. In March 1982 FEVER responded to the DES paper, drawing on advice from 15 academics from Europe, North America and Australia. But there was no further response from the DES, and at the Conservative Conference in October 1983 Sir Keith declared the voucher to be 'dead'.

Two main arguments are advanced against education vouchers. The first is that topping up the voucher (which is allowed under Friedman's scheme, although not under some others) would enable the rich to use their wealth to buy superior education for their children, by, for instance, attracting the best teachers. The second argument is that diverse education would result and that some people would organise education in a manner of which some observers would disapprove. Schools might, for example, be founded on racial or religious lines, or the rich might keep to themselves, thus increasing social segregation (Seldon, 1986).

The new liberals have countered as follows. They point out that the present state system in Britain promotes residential segregation. Children largely go to the school designated for the area in which they reside. At present the outer city suburbs generally have schools which are arguably better according to criteria such as lack of crime, success in teaching children to read and write, or achievement in public examinations. Inner city areas are less well served. Under the present system the relatively well-off parent dissatisfied with his child's school can afford to buy a house within the right catchment area, whilst the poor parent cannot. New liberals argue that a voucher scheme would increase the power of just those parents whose children go to the worst inner city schools.

They would, for the first time, have real power to determine the direction of their children's education. The intellectual who, today, points out that such parents are too ill-informed to exercise choice could assist them by offering the information he believes them to lack. This would be preferable, the new liberals argue, to assuming that the answer is to subject such parents to the arbitrary power of the very same teachers and officials who are presently serving the inner city areas and manifestly providing a second-rate service.

The claim that the rich would offer higher salaries to attract all the best teachers is also, according to the new liberals, based on a misunderstanding. It assumes that teachers can be ranked in a single hierarchy according to competence. But teachers each have a variety of qualities in different proportions. The qualities which a wealthy school will pay extra to attract may not be the qualities which best fit a teacher to serve the children of low-income families. As long as the voucher was of a sufficient cash value to support a good standard of education—based as a starting-point, say, on the average cost per pupil of the education service today—and not, for instance, merely calculated to pay for some bare minimum, then there is little reason to suppose that the poor would end up in ghetto schools. On the contrary, it would be likely to spell the death sentence for today's government ghetto schools.

It is sometimes said that the state should lay down *minimum* standards. This is interpreted by critics of vouchers as meaning that the poor would only receive some minimum of education, whilst everyone else fortunate enough to have wealthier parents would enjoy a higher standard. But again, this supposes that what is valuable in education can be ranked in a single hierarchy. It also supposes that everything worth having in education costs more.

New liberals reply as follows. First, the state would enforce a standard, but it is misleading to look upon it as a minimum. The justification for the state's imposition of a standard is to ensure that everyone leaves school equipped for citizenship. It follows that this standard should lay down literacy and numeracy standards and require that all schools should offer access to public examinations, where parents require it. Whatever else schools may decide to do cannot be ranked in a single hierarchy. In particular a great deal will depend on the motivation and aptitude of individual teachers and these qualities do not vary with income, with the one proviso that teachers should be paid sufficient relative to other groups not to breed a sense of resentment. Far from meting out only a bare minimum for the poor, a voucher scheme would enable the parents of the poor, in combination with sympathetic teachers and activists, to work out and offer their own answers to the problems of city centre schools. It would only require a few teachers and activists of good will to transform radically the life-chances of low-income families. A voucher scheme would enable those individuals, who today champion the cause of the poor by means of street demonstrations demanding this or that government programme, to act directly to achieve their aims within individual schools. No longer would it be necessary to convince local bureaucrats and politicians of the merits of one's case. It would be enough to convince the relatively few parents and teachers involved in running the local school.

A variety of explanations for Sir Keith's change of mind about vouchers have been offered, but the most likely is that he was unwilling to take on the professional opposition. This also killed the Kent experiment. It was to embrace 26 local education authority schools, plus as many church schools as wished to join in. It was to have started in September 1984. The administrative problems were not seen as insuperable, and were indeed similar to those presented by the Kent open enrolment system introduced in December 1981, under which parental choice of school was permitted. The voucher scheme also required changes in the law to facilitate the new funding arrangements. These were not forthcoming.

The greatest obstacle to the introduction of vouchers anywhere has been the attitude of teachers, who oppose the alteration of the balance of power in favour of parents. Milton Friedman quotes the words of Dennis Gee, the headmaster of a school in Ashford, Kent, and secretary of a local teachers' trade union branch. Mr Gee said:

We see this as a barrier between us and the parent—this sticky little piece of paper ... in their hand—coming in and under duress—you will do this or else. We make our judgement because we believe it's in the best interest of every Willie and every little Johnny that we've got—and not because someone's going to say 'if you don't do it, we will do that'. It's this sort of philosophy of the marketplace that we object to. ...

We are answerable to parents through our governing bodies, through the inspectorate to the Kent County Council, and through Her Majesty's Inspectorate to the Secretary of State. These are people, professionals, who are able to make professional judgements. I'm not sure that parents know what is best educationally for their children. They know what's best for them to eat. They know the best environment they can provide at home. But we've been trained to ascertain the problems of children, to detect their weaknesses, to put right those things that need putting right, and we want to do this freely, with the cooperation of parents and not under undue strains.

Friedman comments that, 'In other words, Mr Gee objects to giving the customer, in this case, the parent, anything to say about the kind of schooling his child gets.

Instead, he wants the bureaucrats to decide' (1980, pp. 173–4). He refers to evidence from the last century which suggests that parents are very far from being incapable of choosing what is educationally best for their children. Professor E.G. West cites the findings of the Newcastle Commission, a government commission of inquiry which was set up in 1858 and which reported in 1861. The commission surveyed specimen districts containing one-eighth of the population of England and Wales. They found that in 1858 there were 2,535,462 scholars attending day schools. The average duration of schooling was 5.7 years. Most children seem to have been registered with a school from the age of six to the age of ten, although many went to school younger and many stayed until they were 12. The commission found that 95.4 per cent of children in the age group 6–10 were attending school.

Parents, including the very poorest families, were also paying fees for their children. An assistant commissioner reported the story of a school with 180 pupils in a coal mining district. A strike was called which reduced the miners to great distress, but 'such had become the desire of the children to remain at school, and of their parents to keep them there, that the greater number remained during a time when the provision of school fees must have encroached in most of the colliers' families on the very necessaries of life' (West, 1970, p. 165).

Thus, during the nineteenth century, the vast majority of parents were exercising precisely the sorts of choices that a voucher scheme would entail. Yet, in spite of the great success of voluntarism, greater state control was imposed by the 1870 Education Act. Professor West argues that the 1870 Act had three main effects. First, many private schools had to close down because less parents were willing to pay fees whilst the school boards were providing education funded by taxation. West estimates that the loss of school places caused by private school closures may have counterbalanced the growth in school places apparently produced by the building of board schools. Second, parents lost control of their children's education, and officials and teachers increased their power. Third, the standard of teaching may have declined because board schools put less stress on teachers' real competence and more on certification. Many experienced and competent teachers were lost to teaching due to their lack of paper qualifications.

The Adam Smith Institute has advocated an alternative to the voucher plan which would achieve many of the same ends. They advocate changes in the composition of school boards of governors. Boards would consist overwhelmingly of parents with children at the particular school and would be elected by postal ballot. The head and teachers would occupy non-voting places on the board. It would negotiate fixed term contracts with both the head teacher and his staff. Heads would be appointed for, say, five years.

The head would become the equivalent of a chief executive responsible to a board of directors. He would control the curriculum, timetable, discipline, and run the school generally. He would evaluate staff and be able to discipline, suspend or dismiss them in consultation with the governors. The local education authority would lose control of all these matters, but would continue to finance schools through a block grant calculated on a per capita basis. Salaries would no longer be negotiated nationally, but the local authority would retain responsibility for capital expenditure. New schools could also be opened. If a group of parents of around 25–30 wished to establish their own school they would be entitled to a per capita grant from the local council. This would also have the advantage of enabling local communities to prevent the enforced closure of village schools (Butler *et al.*, 1985, pp. 271–4). One advantage of the Adam Smith scheme is that it may not attract such widespread hostility from all the teachers' unions, in particular, the head teachers' unions might well recognise that the scheme would considerably enhance the status and freedom of manoeuvre of their members.

HIGHER EDUCATION

New liberals see great danger in central government control of the universities. Ultimately it could lead to the undermining of liberal democracy. Consequently they have long argued that higher education should be made more independent of central government by reducing its reliance on government funding. They have urged that this be accomplished by charging students higher fees and making higher payments to them to compensate. New liberals have often also recommended that payments to students should, at least partly, be made in the form of loans rather than straightforward grants. In 1962 Professor Prest (1966) gave evidence to this effect to the Robbins Committee. And Professors Peacock and Wiseman (1964) supported him in a paper published two years later. They doubted whether the Robbins Committee was correct in supposing that university independence was assured if fees comprised only 20 per cent of income, and questioned whether the University Grants Committee could shield the universities from political influence. They favoured a system of funding through student bursaries or vouchers and loans. The vouchers would be usable in colleges whether they were funded privately or by government, as long as each met minimum standards.

The same theme was pursued by Crew and Young (1977) over ten years later. They came out in favour of vouchers supplemented by loans to replace state grants. Vouchers, they argued, ought to be channelled through students and not paid to the universities direct. Colleges would fix fees as they believed best and governments would independently fix the value of the voucher. The difference, if any, could be met by private payments or loans. No other money would be forthcoming from government, other than research grants awarded on merit through the research councils. Faced for the first time with the possibility of bankruptcy, they argue that the universities would become more responsive to students and, through them, employers. In 1969 Professor Ferns urged that the University Grants Committee be abolished, a theme to which he returned in 1982. He recommended that each university should be given full control of its assets and curricula, and enjoy full discretion in charging fees to students and paying salaries to staff.

Also in an IEA paper, Lewis, Sandford and Thomson (1980) have urged the adoption of a loans scheme following their surveys of public attitudes towards the funding of student fees. In September 1978 they interviewed 1992 individuals throughout Great Britain. Respondents were asked whether they favoured the prevailing means-tested grant, an unconditional non-means-tested grant, a loan scheme, or a mixture of a loan and grant scheme. Excluding the 8 per cent don't knows, 25 per cent favoured the means-tested grant, 22 per cent unconditional grant, 39 per cent a loan scheme, and 14 per cent a mixed loan/grant system.

Separate surveys of student and parent opinion were also carried out. Students were found to resent the means-tested grant because, although they had reached the age of majority, they still found themselves dependent on their parents. Some parents shared this view and did not pay their assumed parental contribution. About half of the student respondents said they would prefer an unconditional grant, a view also taken by 36 per cent of parents. Lewis and his colleagues oppose the introduction of an unconditional grant as inequitable. Most students, they point out, will end up being among the top 10 per cent of earners, and most of their parents are already in higher earning catagories. There was not much support among parents and students for a loans scheme, with only around 10 per cent favouring it. However, about 34 per cent of parents and 24 per cent of students did favour either a loans scheme or a system combining loans and grants.

The advantages of a loans scheme are said to be these. First, it would end the subsidisation of the well-off by the less well-off. Families in which the head of the household is in a manual occupation comprise about 60 per cent of the population, but only about a quarter of university entrants come from such families. Second, it would give adult students independence from their parents. Third, no one would be deterred from entering higher education due to a lack of parental or personal income, since all who qualified academically would be entitled to a loan. Fourth, no one who, in the event, did not earn sufficient to pay back the loan would have to do so, since repayments could be adjusted to match liability for ordinary income tax.

One of the particular successes of the new liberals has been the foundation of the privately-funded University of Buckingham. But generally they have had little impact on the higher education policy pursued by the Thatcher government. University autonomy is as distant as ever, and neither student loans nor vouchers are any nearer. Ironically the political faintheartedness of the Thatcher government on student loans caused them acute political embarrassment during 1985 when well-off Conservative voters objected to paying higher fees for their student sons and daughters. A loans scheme would have overcome this difficulty.

SOCIAL SECURITY

Capitalism and Poverty

One of the targets of the new liberalism has been the version of history which taught that nineteenth-century capitalism made the lives of the workers worse than they had been in the eighteenth century. It had previously been taught by historians like Macaulay and economists like Alfred Marshall that the Industrial Revolution had improved the conditions of the great mass of the population. But from the late nineteenth century socialist historians like the Webbs, the Hammonds and G.D.H. Cole contended that conditions had worsened compared with the previous century. In the 1960s and 1970s this doctrine continued to be propounded by academics such as E.P. Thompson and Eric Hobsbawm.

This 'immiseration' thesis was criticised in the 1920s and 1930s by historians like John Clapham and Dorothy George, and a little later by T.S. Ashton, but nevertheless it continued to be the dominant orthodoxy during the post-war years. In 1954 Hayek, W.H. Hutt and others reopened the debate, pointing out that material standards had undeniably improved during the nineteenth century. According to Hayek, the new urban proletariat would not have come into being at all without the additional wealth industrialisation made possible. A smaller population would have continued to exist in a rural setting at a lower standard of life. More recently the IEA has published the *Long Debate on Poverty* (1974) in which the evidence is surveyed once again. Generally, the conclusion to which it points is that industrialisation brought growing prosperity for all and narrowed the gap between the wealthiest and the poorest citizens. Poverty is not a product of capitalism, in this view; on the contrary, the free market principles which brought about industrialisation also produced the prosperity which made it possible to eradicate extreme poverty for good.

Poverty and the Welfare State
The new liberals have also been severe critics of the modern welfare state. Social security systems in all western nations have been under criticism. In recent years Britain's arrangements have been particularly heavily criticised by commentators from all points of the political spectrum. The main criticisms advanced by new liberals (and many others besides) have been these.

1. National insurance contributions have been criticised as a regressive form of taxation. Since October 1985 this effect has been mitigated to some extent by the measures announced in the 1985 Budget. Up to October 1985 anyone earning between £35.50 and £265.00 a week had to pay 9 per cent of *all* earnings in national insurance contributions (not 9 per cent of earnings above the threshold, as applies to income tax) whilst a person earning less than £35.50 would pay no national insurance contributions. From October 1985 a person earning from £35.50 to £54.99 paid 5 per cent of all earnings, someone earning between £55.00 and £89.99 paid 7 per cent and the 9 per cent rate applied from £90 upwards.

2. It is expected that the state earnings-related pensions scheme (SERPS) introduced in 1975 and operational from 1978, will increasingly become too expensive. In 1985 there were 2.3 contributors to each pensioner. In 50 years time there will be only 1.6. It does not become fully operational until 1998, but not because a fund is building up in the interim. There is no fund. The scheme merely hands future generations a promissory note which is unlikely to be payable. Private provision is discouraged because employers are required to agree, not to pay acceptable premiums which can accumulate into a fund with which to buy an annuity, but to pay a future pension proportional to wages. They cannot therefore accurately predict the extent of their future liability.

3. Some intended beneficiaries of Family Income Supplement (FIS), housing benefit and supplementary benefit do not receive payment.

4. On the other hand, excessive payments are made to some people. This applies especially to FIS and housing benefit because entitlement is calculated over a short period, whilst payments are made over a longer time-scale. Family Income Supplement, for instance, is assessed on five weeks' earnings and paid for a year by means of a payment book. Child benefit goes to all, regardless of income.

5. The system, particularly supplementary benefit, has been criticised because it is organised in an excessively costly way. There is duplication of effort. Revenue is collected by the Inland Revenue and the Department of Health and Social Security (DHSS). Too many departments are involved: the DHSS, the Department of Employment, the Department of Education and Science (DES), the Department of the Environment, and the Treasury each has a hand. In addition, there are the local authorities, where responsibility is further subdivided between departments.

6. The complexity of the system has been heavily attacked. There are said to be too many benefits. Supplementary benefit has become so intricate as to defy comprehension by all but the full-time specialist. The manual

of guidance to officers is in two volumes with 16,000 paragraphs and 38,000 staff are employed on supplementary benefit cases alone.

7. The lack of integration between the tax and benefit systems causes the poverty and unemployment traps. Support for the working poor is particularly ill-coordinated.

What has been the new liberal approach to reform? The natural rights theorists, including anarchists like Rothbard and minimal staters like Nozick, dislike the welfare state in its entirety. They would have no national minimum maintained by government. All assistance to the poor would be voluntary. Such full-blooded voluntarism has not, however, been the mainstream new liberal view. The more pragmatic liberals like Friedman, Hayek and IEA authors have advocated a continued government role in the maintenance of a national minimum income. But there is no unanimous standpoint. Two quite different views about the relief of poverty by government may be distinguished: the 'incentives' and the 'stipulatory' approaches.

As Chapter 3 indicates, Milton Friedman has advocated a negative income tax (NIT) scheme to integrate the tax and benefit systems. A similar plan for implementation in Britain has been proposed by Professor Patrick Minford.

Professor Minford's proposal (1983; 1984) is based on two aims; to help the poor achieve an above-subsistence living standard without damaging incentives; and to privatise provision for health, education and pensions whilst ensuring that the poor spend adequately on these services.

For the poor in work Minford recommends two 'poverty lines'. The first is the subsistence income for each family. This must be, he says, a true minimum and must exclude all items not necessary for survival. Then there is a 'poverty threshold' income defined 'in relation to social views of the income *above* which help would *not* willingly be given by society' (1984, p. xiii). This is also the income tax threshold.

NIT achieves two aims. It never allows income to fall below subsistence level and for incomes below the poverty/income tax threshold a supplement of 70 per cent of the difference between actual income and the threshold is paid.

Minford uses FIS rates as a basis for his proposal. There are three stages. First, he tidies up existing means-tested benefits. FIS, housing benefit and the 'passport' benefits (such as free school meals) are all replaced by cash transfers.

Second, the personal national insurance contributions are abolished and tax thresholds raised. Child benefit is increased to offset the extra cost of buying health insurance and paying for education and pensions, and to overcome the poverty and unemployment traps.

Third, he dovetails benefits into the tax system by making cash transfers into NIT payments of 70 per cent of the difference between earnings and the new threshold.

NIT would be made conditional upon production of certificates stating that satisfactory arrangements had been made for health, education and pensions (1984, p. ix). National insurance benefits would continue. Unemployment benefit would be set at 70 per cent of previous net earnings. If taxes on the low-paid are cut, as Minford envisages, then wages will be relatively much higher, and thus the incentive to work much greater. Child benefit is fixed at £22.00 (at 1984 prices) per child per week.

Education would be privatised under Minford's plan, and fees are estimated at £700 a year. Health insurance premiums would be £147 for a single person and £473 for a married couple with two children. Pension provision is estimated to cost £93 a year. Child benefits are calculated to enable families to cover these costs. In the longer term Minford envisages that unemployment and other benefits would also be privatised.

Everyone would be covered by a minimum standard of comprehensive health insurance. The government would lay down a basic minimum of health cover which must be obtained. There would be additional payments to people who were unable to obtain standard insurance for the accepted premium, due to circumstances such as old age or chronic illness.

How would individual families fare under Minford's scheme? The poverty/income tax threshold for a couple would be £110, the FIS threshold. The basic rate of tax above the threshold would be 30 per cent; NIT below the threshold would be paid at 70 per cent. A married couple with two children would pay £38 a week for health, education and pensions. Taking this into account, such a couple earning £110 before tax would receive, after tax under present arrangements, £103. Under Minford's scheme they would receive £116, a £13 gain. A couple just above the threshold earning £120 receive £106 now, and under Minford's scheme would receive £123, a £17 gain. A couple with two children just below the threshold earning £100, receive £99 now, and under Minford's scheme would receive £113. They get their wage of £100, plus £7.00 NIT, plus £44 child benefit *less* payments for health, education and pensions of £38.00 (ibid., p. xiv).

Friedmanite 'incentives' plans have been criticised by another new liberal writer, Martin Anderson, a researcher at the Hoover Institution and one-time policy adviser to President Reagan. I shall call his approach 'stipulatory'. He argues that radical welfare reform is an impossibility. No radical plan can be devised that will simultaneously yield acceptable minimum levels of welfare benefits, financial incentives to work, and an acceptable overall cost to taxpayers (1978, p. 133). To overcome this dilemma he has enunciated seven principles which should underlie welfare reform.

1. Payment should be made according to need only. A welfare programme must conform with public opinion as it stands and American public opinion, he says, wants real need to be met by government action, but does not like welfare payments to be made to all and sundry.
2. Efforts to detect fraud should be increased.
3. Government should 'establish and enforce a fair, clear work requirement'. This is where he is most at odds with Friedman and Minford, who both advocate an incentives approach to the unemployment trap. In the view of Anderson, financial work incentives do not achieve their goal. To work effectively an intolerably low basic welfare payment would be necessary. The

high marginal rates of tax faced by welfare beneficiaries are also unavoidable without lowering welfare payments too far. The error in the financial incentives approach is, he asserts, that it attempts to 'persuade' people to work when they should be 'required' to do so (1978, p. 162). The principle should be that 'a person gets welfare only if he or she qualifies for it by the fact of being incapable of self-support'. If they don't qualify, he insists, 'they have no right to welfare'. If a person can earn part of what they need, they have an obligation to work to that extent (ibid., pp. 162–3).

It is not widely acknowledged that the Beveridge Report recommended a work test. 'The danger', thought Beveridge, 'of providing benefits, which are both adequate in amount and indefinite in duration, is that men, as creatures who adapt themselves to circumstances, may settle down to them.' He recommended that, after about six months, recipients of benefit should be required to attend a work or training centre. This would serve as 'a means of preventing habituation to idleness and as a means of improving capacity for earning' (1942, paras. 130–1). A scheme of this kind operates today in Germany, where recipients of state benefit must either work or re-train.

4. Inappropriate beneficiaries should be removed from the welfare rolls. Anderson believes there are two prime candidates in the American context: 'striking workers and college students who queue up for food stamps'.

5. A great many welfare recipients are one-parent families. He believes that absent parents should be required to contribute to the support of their offspring. In Britain there has been a sharp increase in the number of one-parent families relying on supplementary benefit. Between 1973 and 1983, the number doubled to 450,000.

6. The efficiency and effectiveness of welfare administration should be improved.

7. More responsibility for welfare should be shifted from the federal government to state and local governments and to private institutions. Generally, he says, the more decentralised the administration the better.

Impact on Policy

The new liberalism has had only a muted impact on the Thatcher government. The British social security system has been criticised from three main standpoints. First, a variety of modified Beveridge-style plans have been put forward. Under such schemes benefits continue to be financed out of taxation (whether earmarked in the form of national insurance contributions or not) whilst benefits are paid as of right, irrespective of income. Second, there have been a number of proposals for integrating the tax and benefit systems. These fall into two groups: (a) Friedmanite negative income tax plans based on means testing through the taxation system; and (b) the social dividend type of scheme, under which everyone receives payments equivalent to the national minimum regardless of their income. Third, the privatisation of welfare provision has been strongly recommended, and especially the privatisation of pensions.

The Thatcher government's proposals for reform in its 1985 White Paper were essentially in the modified Beveridge tradition. The contributory principle was retained. 'People', said the earlier Green Paper, 'do not regard their contributions as just another tax' (DHSS 1985, p. 40). The complete alignment of the tax and benefit systems was rejected as not necessary and, in any event, unrealistic under present conditions. But there would be an investigation into bringing PAYE and national insurance contributions more into line (ibid., p. 41). At the time of writing, the supplementary benefits system was to be replaced by a simple income support scheme entailing less discretion. Unemployment and sickness benefits would continue to be provided by government, and child benefit would continue to be paid regardless of income.

Under the Green Paper, basic pensions were to remain a government responsibility, whilst *additional* pension provision would become private and compulsory. However, the privatisation of pensions to permit the market to function more flexibly has been abandoned. Sickness benefit was partially privatised during the first Thatcher government, but this was more an administrative manoeuvre than an attempt to release pent-up private initiative. The government merely mandated employers to pay out sick pay for the first few weeks of illness, a move which brought with it none of the potential of a free market for innovation.

The government's answer to the poverty and unemployment traps does, however, derive from new liberal thinking. The government favours a Friedmanite incentives approach. Tax and national insurance thresholds will be adjusted to increase work incentives and a new 'family credit' will be introduced to replace Family Income Supplement. To overcome the inefficiency of FIS and partially to integrate taxes and benefits, family credit payments to poor working families with children will be paid through the pay packet and not by means of a payment book. Benefits will be set against tax and national insurance contributions so that beneficiaries know exactly where they stand.

GUIDE TO READING

The classic case for education vouchers is made in Chapter 6 of *Free to Choose* by Milton and Rose Friedman. Also invaluable are two books by E.G. West, *Education and the State* (1970) and *Education and the Industrial Revolution* (1975). A useful review of the arguments against education vouchers, though now a little dated, is Mark Blaug's essay in the IEA paper, *Education: a Framework for Choice*, Beales (ed.) (1970). See also his discussion of both student loans and education vouchers in *An Introduction to the Economics of Education* (1970). More recently Blaug have produced an updated survey (1984). Peston (1984), in the same volume, provides a strongly critical view. A still useful review of the various types of voucher, including variants supported by egalitarians, can be found in Alan Maynard's *Experiment With Choice in Education* (1975). Also valuable is the Open University reader, *Economics and Education Policy*, Baxter *et al.* (eds)

(1977). The most recent discussion of the voucher story is Seldon (1986). To keep up to date with US voucher experiments contact the Clearinghouse on Educational Choice, 1611 North Kent St, Arlington, Virginia.

A useful analysis of poverty policies can be found in Le Grand and Robinson (1984a), Chapters 10 and 11. See also Parker (1982; 1984).

7 Political Impact: Health, Housing and the Environment

HEALTH

The National Health Service has been severely criticised by the new liberals. In the early 1960s the lead was taken by Dennis Lees. Generally, he asserted, the market is superior to the ballot box as a means of registering consumer preferences. He rejected the view that medicine differed from other consumer goods to such a degree that it could not be supplied in the market. Health care was like the generality of goods purchased by consumers, and therefore if the aim was to satisfy the consumer, health care should be supplied in the market. But under the NHS, political decisions replaced personal choices. Expenditure on the NHS was not considered on its merits, but instead a sum was allocated which depended in the main on the wider economic policies of the government of the day. Though governments have repeatedly expressed concern about the rising cost of the NHS, expenditure has been less than consumers would probably have chosen to spend in a free market. When Lees was writing, spending on hospital building had been particularly inadequate.

Because the NHS had a virtual monopoly of medical care, there were no strong external forces making for improvements in quality and efficiency as there would be in a competitive market. Insistence on a single standard stifled the internal forces that could promote improvement. If medical knowledge is to advance this requires freedom to experiment and adapt to change. Central ministerial control was, therefore, said to be inimical to progress. In addition, the NHS had created discontented professions. Successive Ministers of Health had used their 'extraordinary power to exploit doctors and dentists in the interests of general financial stability'.

Reform, urged Lees, should be based on at least six principles.

1. It should aim to diminish the role of political decisions and to enlarge the influence of consumer choice. Central government should confine itself to ensuring the maintenance of minimum standards and providing subsidies, where necessary.
2. Governments should move away from taxation and free services to private insurance and fees. They should allow tax concessions to those who can provide for themselves, and give direct assistance to the 'dwindling minority' who cannot.
3. The control of hospital services should be dispersed by transferring ownership from central government to local authorities and private institutions.
4. Professional incomes should be determined by markets not Ministers. Fees should be freely settled between doctors and their patients (who may reclaim part from public funds).
5. The pricing system should be reintroduced in the drugs market by requiring patients to pay a percentage of the cost of each prescription, with special provision for costly life-saving drugs.
6. The capacity of the medical and dental schools should be freed from state control by financing student fees by loans rather than grants (Lees, 1965, pp. 76–9).

By the 1970s the new liberal critique of the NHS was being led by Arthur Seldon. Much of the rhetoric in favour of the NHS emphasises protection of the poor, or the elimination of price 'barriers'. But, according to Arthur Seldon, these are not the real reasons why impatient reformers support the NHS. It is rather that they wish to establish 'instant equality'. They dislike any plan to give cash to the poor to pay for health care because they believe it is 'obscene' to pay for it (1977, p. 85).

Arthur Seldon attacks the tendency to look upon a price as a 'barrier'. This has led to a policy of removing the 'barrier' standing between the citizen and health care. He agrees that at any moment a price may be more than a poor person can afford, and that the abolition of prices is one way of solving their problem. But it has other effects too. In particular it removes the other functions of prices in measuring and disciplining demand and either discouraging or generating supply. Moreover, the poor can be helped in more effective ways.

The removal of price has depressed the supply of funds for medical care and inflated the demand for it. It has created 'an unreal world in which resources that are scarce and should be husbanded have been made to appear plentiful because they are supplied "free"'. Nor has price abolished rationing, but merely changed it from an economic process to an administrative one: appointment systems, waiting-lists, queueing and 'political wire-pulling' (Seldon, 1968, pp. 2–3). This makes 'politicians important and creates jobs for bureaucrats'. The principle 'first come, first served' sounds fair, says Seldon, but it 'favours the fleet of foot, the loud in voice'. Better treatment may result if you know your doctor personally, or if you are a professional and 'speak his language', or if you are 'cunning' and able to 'work the system'. The supreme irony of NHS rationing is that favouritism is widespread. The NHS has not abolished inequality: 'it has driven inequality underground and made it more difficult to correct' (1977, pp. 85–6).

Seldon does not argue for a wholly unfettered market, but favours the 'mixed' systems of private and government finance evolved in America and Australia: 'These mixed systems create no false hopes and no myths. They show what the vast range of medical services cost, and they allow people to pay in the ways they prefer. They have created no Nirvana, or mirage of "the best medical care for everyone"...' (p. 90). His preferred scheme is to issue health vouchers to each person to cover the cost of insurance premiums. This would ensure that everyone was covered and provide for each person once again to acquire the skills needed to exercise choice.

As Chapter 4 indicated, the IEA has measured support for health vouchers in a series of surveys carried out between 1963 and 1978. In 1978 the cost of a year's health insurance per person was then £60, through organisations such as BUPA, Private Patients Plan, and Western Provident Association, and the average annual cost of the NHS was £140 per head. Respondents were given two priced alternatives: a £30 voucher per person conditional upon adding a further £30; or a £40 voucher to be topped up by £20. A remarkable 51 per cent said they would accept a £30 voucher, and 57 per cent thought they would accept a £40 voucher (Harris and Seldon, 1979, p. 106).

In Britain intellectual opinion remains predominantly socialistic and this is especially true of thinking about the NHS. The new liberal criticism of the NHS has aroused much passionate denunciation and has resulted in defenders of the NHS coming up with new arguments in its support, but few minds have been changed. The chief reason is that support for the NHS is rooted more in emotion than in reason. Some are attached to it because of their commitment to compulsory equalisation, but more are devoted to it because they associate the NHS with elementary decency or fair play.

At one stage, this view that the NHS represented the very utmost in altruism was the main argument used in support of it. Against this demand-side case that the NHS was necessary to ensure that the poor received adequate health care, the new liberals successfully argued that this could be accomplished in more than one way—by subsidies, or by vouchers. Such alternatives could protect the poor whilst also enhancing their ability to direct their own affairs by increasing the power of the patient *vis-à-vis* professionals and administrators.

Against this argument supporters of the NHS countered with a supply-side case for the NHS. The consumer, they said, could not exercise the choices that are essential to the market process. This was partly because the consumer was too ignorant, and partly because of professional monopoly power. In addition, the health market is distorted by the insurance mechanism which means that, unlike a normal market, competition promotes neither efficiency nor effectiveness. The choice on the demand side, writes Mr Nick Bosanquet in his critique of the new liberalism, 'is not between a market system and a government monopoly free at the point of consumption', it is between 'a national system of health care and a system of third party payment with quite extensive subsidies to those who cannot get coverage' (1983, p. 151). He then makes the extraordinary claim that 'in reality there are only two possible budgetary contexts for medicine'. One is a cost-plus system in which 'doctors decide what is best for the patient...then simply send in the bill for the best treatment to the third party'. The other is 'to set an overall budget within which individual decisions have to be contained'. This, he says, could be done through the NHS or a national health insurance scheme like Canada's. But the 'essential choice is between a cost plus system or one that introduces budget constraint' (ibid., pp. 151–2).

His error is to assume that a market cannot provide pressures for cost-containment. But developments in the American health markct in recent years show this claim to be wholly false. During the late 1970s and early 1980s there has been a great flowering of competition in the US health marketplace (Green, 1985a; 1986b). Government programmes to promote cost-containment have played their part. Both Medicare and Medicaid have frequently been restructured to encourage cost-consciousness.

More important still have been the developments in the private sector. Cost-effective alternatives to hospital inpatient care have developed rapidly, especially ambulatory (or day) surgery centres. Home care backed by specialist nursing agencies also competes with hospital inpatient care, not only because it is cheaper but also because patients often prefer a less institutionalised environment. Hospital outpatient departments face equally strong competition from emergency centres as well as from group practices. Health maintenance organisations (HMOs) have a long history, but have begun to expand rapidly in recent years. Instead of charging for every visit to the doctor, the HMO receives a fixed payment per month in return for which the patient receives all necessary medical services without further payment. In 1972 there were 142 HMOs with 5.3 million members. Ten years later membership had doubled to 10.8 million. Since then membership had been increasing at rates in excess of 15 per cent a year. Between June 1984 and June 1985 HMO enrolment increased by 24.9 per cent with total membership reaching an all-time high of 18.9 million members in 393 HMOs (Interstudy, 1985).

More recently, preferred provider organisation (PPOs) have emerged, largely as a reaction to the success of HMOs. The PPO is an effort to secure the advantages of the HMO without the necessity for the subscriber to confine his choice of doctor to a fixed panel. When an individual joins an HMO he or she pays a monthly premium and the HMO is fully at risk for any health care required by the subscriber. The HMO also 'locks-in' its subscribers, that is, if they go to a doctor outside the HMO panel they have no insurance cover. The PPO is different in two main respects. First the PPO itself bears no financial risk for the medical expenses incurred by subscribers. These are borne by the insurer, whether an insurance company or a self-insured employer. The providers are paid on a fee-for-service basis, at negotiated discounts, not by the individual patient, but by the insurer. Second, the PPO does not lock-in subscribers. If consumers choose to use the services of a PPO doctor they are of course covered, but if they use an outside hospital or doctor they still enjoy cover, though at a lower level (perhaps 80% or less).

In 1975 there were no PPOs. They emerged in the late 1970s. In 1982 the American Hospital Association identified 33 PPOs in its first survey. A more recent study claimed that during the first half of 1985 PPO membership grew by a phenomenal 346 per cent from 1.3m to 5.8m (*Health Care Competition Week*, 7 October 1985).

The implication of these developments is this. Health

economists have been quick to interpret evidence from America about skyrocketing costs (during a period when governments were pumping millions of dollars into the demand side) as evidence that the insurance mechanism generated perverse incentives, and particulary an incentive to over-consume. Recent developments suggest that this conclusion has been arrived at too hastily. The market in the last few years has shown a tendency to adjust over time. And in the last few years there has been a great flowering of inventive mechanisms for cost-containment without cutting corners at the patient's expense.

These developments contradict the supply-side case for the NHS, a view which rests on the belief that competition—which ordinarily puts the consumer in the driving seat—cannot work in health care. The producer is said to be too powerful due to professional monopoly power and due to the unavoidable ignorance of consumers about medical matters. Events in the US market show this conclusion to be false. The producer's monopoly power has been undermined by government action to eliminate legal barriers to competition. Today the US market is no longer dominated by the producer. One of the main reasons is that federal and state governments no longer reinforce professional power to the extent they once did. The Federal Trade Commission (FTC) has been particularly effective in outlawing the restrictive practices of the American Medical Association, such as its advertising ban. A turning-point came in 1982 when the Supreme Court ruled in the FTC's favour. Advertising by American doctors is now growing.

The consumer's lack of knowledge has been overcome in a variety of ways, by third-party endorsements, by counselling and by the emergency of approved panels of doctors. Such panels simplify the consumer's choice, because he or she knows that every doctor on the panel acts in accordance with the rules of the organisation, whether it is an HMO or a PPO. These rules lay down fees, and provide for the review of each doctor's performance by professional colleagues as well as by administrators acting on the consumer's behalf.

Thus, the 'inevitable monopoly' thesis which lies at the root of the supply-side case for the NHS fails to find support in the US market. Historical evidence from Australia (Green and Cromwell, 1984) and Britain also refutes it (Green, 1985b). It cannot therefore be argued that the market is unavoidably incapable of supplying health care.

Impact on policy
It is not only privately-insured Americans who are benefiting from competition. Under the influence of new-liberal thought, Medicare beneficiaries have also been given greater freedom of choice. Under 1982 legislation they are free to enrol in health maintenance organisations (HMO). When they choose to do so the HMO receives 95 per cent of the average per capita cost for the locality. This is a voucher in all but name, and subsequently the Department of Health and Human Services has been promoting a Voucher bill to widen the alternatives beyond HMOs. Under this scheme, a wide array of alternative health plans will be able to register with Medicare and advertise their wares. Medicare beneficiaries will be free to select their insurer during annual open-enrolment periods.

In Britain, however, the main thrust of the new liberal case has made little impact on the Thatcher government. There has been no move in the direction of consumer sovereignty, and new liberals continue to urge more forthright government action. Vouchers remain the most commonly advocated alternative (a recent variant is a 'refundable health voucher' advocated by Green, 1984). More recently still, a period of experimentation has been urged to throw up new information about the relative merits of the three main alternatives on offer: central direction, managerial decentralisation and consumer sovereignty (Green, 1986a). The government has also been urged to eliminate those barriers to competition in the health market which are the result of government interference (Green, 1985c).

The government has privatised some NHS services, like cleaning, catering and laundry, and the introduction of competitive tendering has sharpened up the cost-effectiveness of these services. According to a survey carried out by York University, savings due to privatisation made by local authorities as well as health authorities averaged 26 per cent (Hartley and Huby, 1985, p. 23). The government is also actively considering the privatisation of the management of some NHS hospitals.

However, a great many obstacles remain in the path of the private sector. The Health Services Board was abolished in 1980, but its power to ban the building of new private hospitals was given to district health authorities, which have a clear vested interest in stifling competition. There has been some encouragement to the private sector, however. Advice from the DHSS to regional and district health authorities encouraged them to see the private sector as an ally. The private sector could make a 'valuable contribution' to the development of health services (DHSS, 1983), possibly helping to relieve pressure on hard-pressed NHS services. In the financial year 1982–83 a tax concession was introduced for subscribers to group private health insurance plans who earned less than £8500 a year.

But generally, there is no sign that the Thatcher government plans to rectify the main defects of the NHS as seen by new liberals. In September 1982 the Central Policy Review Staff recommended a shift to private health insurance. But the report was unequivocally rejected. In early 1986 consumer sovereignty in health was off the political agenda.

HOUSING

The general principles of a new liberal housing policy have been described in the Adam Smith Institute's *Omega File*, a major 'micro-political' investigation of policy options across a wide range of issues, published in 1985. Government housing policies pursued since 1915, says the report, have had a 'major and adverse' effect: 'Far too much of what is wrong with housing today can be directly attributed to political intervention overriding individual choice and initiative' (Butler *et al.*, 1985, p. 336). What is needed most of all

is a new philosophy, an outlook which recognizes that the imposition of a preconceived order of housing will not meet actual needs. In place of that centralized order, the new philosophy will seek to foster the conditions in which a spontaneous response is possible to a variety of changing housing needs. If the conditions are there, then buyers and sellers can, by their interactions, meet those needs far more adequately, and with greater flexibility, than can any group of planners with notions of what people ought to receive. (p. 343)

Yet, in practice, the measures recommended by the Adam Smith Institute remain highly interventionist, due in great measure to their awareness of short-run political realities. The ASI report envisages the continuation of mortgage interest relief. It heavily criticises the distortions produced by other government subsidies but is silent about mortgage interest tax relief. Indeed, their proposal to abolish stamp duty on house purchase would reinforce the existing tendency of mortgage subsidies to channel resources disproportionately in the direction of the relatively rich.

The council housing sector is criticised because it ignores demand and supply. In the private sector, prices inform builders what types of property are wanted and which locations sought after. But in the public sector no such price information is available, because housing has been provided for rent at less than the economic cost. Consequently demand has outstripped supply and rationing by queueing has followed. Divorced from real measures of demand, councils have built many hundreds of thousands of houses and flats which are now 'difficult to let'. The Adam Smith Institute keenly advocates the stepping-up of the sale of council houses, even at an historic loss (p. 338). For properties remaining in the council sector they propose the introduction of economic rent structures which reflect the relative demand for different types of housing and different localities and not the historic cost (p. 339).

The ending of rent control on privately rented property

has long been sought by new liberals. They oppose the rent-freezing first introduced in Britain in 1915 and the rent regulation introduced from 1965 onwards. The chief argument used to support government control of rents is that they would rise 'too high' and impose hardship on some tenants. Against this, new liberals have argued that (a) generally no such hardship occurs; and (b) rent control may protect sitting tenants but it only does so at a cost to prospective tenants. In particular the supply of housing for rent tends to dry up severely as rents are forced below the level at which landlords can make renting pay, and the physical condition of the remaining rented stock tends to deteriorate as rent income becomes insufficient to cover maintenance costs.

Academics and policy-makers across the political spectrum recognise these defects of rent restriction, but little action is ever taken due to a fear that rents would initially rise rapidly and that controlling politicians would be blamed—at great political cost. In recognition of this fear the Adam Smith Institute contends that decontrol should only be done slowly. They recommend that all new tenancies should be decontrolled but that sitting tenants continue to enjoy protection (p. 342). Other new liberals urge the immediate ending of rent control and point out that we already have evidence of what happens when rent control is terminated, and that the effects are not alarming. The US Department of Labor conducted surveys in some American cities before and after decontrol in 1949. By then there had been control for eight years. Until 1946 there has also been general wage and price control, but in that year it was abandoned. The general price level rose by 32.4 per cent from 1946 to 1949. Against this background, aggregate rents rose by 14.5 per cent from 1946–49 (when some increases were permitted by the government's Housing Expediter), and in the year after decontrol they rose by 3.5 per cent. It was not until 1954 that rents caught up with other prices. As for the particular effects of deregulation, in cities where it occurred the average rent increase which followed deregulation was 11.6 per cent (Walker, 1975, pp. 193–4).

New liberals concede that in a market there would be hardship for families on low incomes. But, they argue that rent restrictions and 'bricks and mortar' subsidies are a wasteful way to help the poor and advocate instead 'mobile' housing allowances. Rent rebates (now housing benefit) are mobile in this sense, but an alternative preferred by some new liberals, including Milton Friedman, is a reverse income tax scheme which incorporates a sum 'sufficient to allow households to purchase housing of a suitable quality'. Housing vouchers are rejected because they would be unnecessarily restrictive (Gray, 1968, pp. 48–9; McKie, 1971, p. 62).

The new liberalism has had a considerable impact on the housing policy of the Thatcher government, except in one field where change was arguably most justified—the private rented sector. The government has decided not to deregulate private rents, despite the huge distortions it generates, not least the reduced mobility of labour which results. Some landlords, approved by the Department of the Environment, can build for rent outside the Rent Acts, but this applies to very few properties.

Other measures have encouraged a shift away from the public sector. New public sector house completions in the UK were reduced from 108,000 in 1979 to 54,000 in 1984, whilst private sector completions increased from 144,000 to 158,000. Council house subsidies have been cut and rents increased sharply. The 1980 Housing Act gave council tenants the right to buy council housing at up to 50 per cent discounts (increased to 60 per cent in 1984). Between 1979 and 1984 around 750,000 houses have been sold. Around 61 per cent of housing in the UK is now owner-occupied, compared with 55 per cent when the government came to power.

ROADS

Roads are frequently taken for granted as one of those goods that ought to be provided by governments from taxation. Some advocates of the new liberalism, however, have urged that prices can play a vital role here too. Mr Gabriel Roth, for instance, proposes that the present method of paying for roads and road use indirectly—by the road fund licence, petrol and purchase taxes—should be replaced by an arrangement which varies charges with road use. He places the costs which arise out of a journey into four categories: private costs, such as petrol; road use costs, such as wear and tear on the roads and the capital cost of providing them; congestion costs, measured in time lost and additional petrol consumed; and community costs, such as noise, fumes and the creation of danger. Over twenty years ago he proposed a method by which road use, congestion and community costs could be subjected to pricing. In 1964 a similar scheme had been recommended by the Smeed Committee, set up by the Ministry of Transport.

Each car would carry a meter which would be activated as it passed over cables in the roads. Charges could be made higher for using congested areas or for using certain areas at busy times of the day. Some parts of central London, for instance, could be declared high-priced 'red' zones at all times, and others at peak times only. In this way road users could adjust their conduct to reduce their own costs, and if mileage charges were properly fixed, the pursuit of self-interest could lead them to serve others (Roth, 1966).

The Adam Smith Institute also recommends that government should be stripped of its responsibility for road building and maintenance. They advocate the establishment of a National Highways Trust, with sole responsibility for the road network. It would be wholly independent of government and would have four main duties: (a) to survey the whole road system and determine an order of priority for the application of a pricing system; (b) to maintain the present roads on a self-financing basis; (c) to arrange contracts for the building of new roads; (d) to act as a planning body for new roads. Its main income would be from the proposed road meter charges and a much lower road licence. It would be able to borrow in the capital markets. A National Highways Trust is necessary, they believe, in order to take roads and road funding out of politics, in an effort to link road building and maintenance to the willingness of users to pay. The aim would be to ensure that road-use pricing was extended as widely as possible and that the total cost of any section of road should be met by road users (Butler *et al.*, 1985, pp. 185–7).

PUBLIC TRANSPORT

Gabriel Roth and his colleague Anthony Shephard (1984) also argue that public transport in cities need not be provided by government-owned or franchised monopolies. They cite several examples of transport networks for use by the public in foreign cities which function at a profit, and provide a fast, regular and reliable service. Examples of informal public transport (IPT) are the minibus services of Hong Kong and Kuala Lumpur, which are so successful that their numbers are limited by the authorities to protect franchised services. The matatu of Nairobi are similar. 'Route associations' have developed in Buenos Aires and Calcutta. These are like bus-driver cooperatives in which individual owners join an association which bears responsibility for serving a regular route. The associations compete with each other. In Buenos Aires bus services have been wholly returned to the private sector, with considerable success.

In Manila the 28,000 licensed jeepneys (named after surplus US wartime jeeps) provide regular services and compete with the big bus companies. The dolmus of Istanbul and minibuses of Cairo are similar. In Puerto Rico publicos (shared taxes and minibuses) have been functioning for many years. They charge higher fares than normal buses, but are faster.

The common characteristics of these successful alternatives are private ownership, small size of firm, small vehicles, voluntary banding together in route associations, profitable operation, and a greater willingness to please passengers reflected in a more flexible response to special requirements. IPT, the authors say, 'is not an instantly effective panacea' but they do believe that deregulation in Britain would provide a better service than existing government networks.

One of the chief reasons for maintaining conventional systems is cross-subsidisation, the practice of charging high fares on profitable routes to support loss-making routes, particularly in rural areas. Against this, the authors answer that it is 'impossible to predict what human ingenuity might come up with, if allowed, to solve the need for cheap rural transport'. Cheap minibus services offering a staging service might emerge, or computer-controlled despatching of custom buses could develop, or post-buses might flourish. No one knows for sure. But it is certain that the present large subsidised undertakings are ill-equipped to provide for rural areas. Cross-subsidisation prevents the full and rational development of services that earn surpluses and discourages operators from assessing the costs and revenues of individual services. Moreover, they argue, it is an inefficient way of helping those in need because it is indiscriminate.

How much influence have these ideas had on government policy? New liberal proposals to charge road users by means of meters according to their mileage or time spent in congested areas have won few converts anywhere, let alone in the Thatcher government. However, new liberals have had an impact on the government's public transport policy. Between 1930 and 1980 bus services were subject to a restrictive licensing system. But as a result of the 1980 Transport Act bus deregulation experiments have been conducted in three localities, and long-distance coaches have been opened up to competition with highly beneficial results. Long-distance coach travel is now fast and cheap. Some operators show films en route and on-board catering services have also emerged. Competition from express coach services also compelled British Rail to offer cheap saver tickets. Experimental deregulation of local services has been carried out in parts of Norfolk, Hereford and Worcester, and Devon. In these areas little improvement resulted in rural services, but urban services have become cheaper and more frequent. Above all, the National Bus Company's local monopolies have been forced to introduce very considerable improvements. As a result of these trials, all local bus services (with the exception of London) have now been deregulated, though provision for local authorities to subsidise rural routes will remain (Department of Transport, 1984; 1985).

GUIDE TO READING

For a discussion of the issues surrounding road use and public transport, consult Le Grand and Robinson (1984a), Chapter 8. Their chapters on health and housing are also instructive. David Heald's *Public Expenditure* (1983) discusses the privatisation of health and housing from what he calls a 'left-Keynesian' standpoint. And for some alternative views about privatisation generally, see Steel, D. and Heald, D. (eds) (1984). Health, housing and public transport are also discussed in *Privatisation*, edited by Le Grand and Robinson (1984b). Hibbs (1982) offers a good review of the arguments for competitive markets in road, rail and air transport.

8 Political Impact: the Economy, Industry and Agriculture

ECONOMIC POLICY

The new liberalism is best known for its impact on the economic policies of western governments, and especially for its contribution to the understanding of inflation. Indeed, for many people 'monetarism' is synonymous with the new liberalism. However, as we have already seen, not all the new liberals see eye to eye about the causes of inflation, nor about the cure for it.

New liberals agree that inflation is a great scourge, but beyond this there are considerable differences of emphasis and interpretation. Hayek, as Chapter 5 revealed, is so frustrated by the repeated failure of governments to maintain sound money that he believes it should be taken out of their hands altogether. He recommends the promotion of competition between several international currencies in the belief that sound money is more likely to emerge from mutual adjustment in the market. There are also considerable differences in the political impact enjoyed by new liberal thinkers. Elements of Milton Friedman's thinking about inflation have been widely accepted, but Hayek's preferred solution is a long way from implementation. As a former Governor of the Bank of England commented when Hayek's plan for competing currencies was put to him: 'That may be for the day after tomorrow' (Hayek, 1978a, p. 12).

An issue about which economists have sharply differed is the importance of trade unions in causing inflation. The 'cost-push' theory of inflation holds that in a seller's market trade unions are able to push up wages, and in so doing create inflation. Some economists conclude from this that full employment can therefore only be maintained without inflation if government enforces an incomes policy. New liberals have generally strongly opposed incomes policies, although there is a difference of opinion about the importance of trade unions in causing inflation, a question which, according to Arthur Seldon, once caused division at the IEA 'almost to the point of splitting the atom' (Minford *et al.*, 1980, p. 101). The alternative to cost-push theory is usually called the 'demand-pull' theory of inflation. It holds that inflation results when governments increase the money supply faster than output. Many new liberals combine elements of both the cost-push and demand-pull theories.

John Burton of the IEA, for instance, argues that the rate of growth of the money supply is only a *proximate* cause of inflation and it is therefore necessary to ask a deeper question: what causes the money supply to grow quickly? He does not argue that trade unions are the chief cause of inflation. Indeed, he says that neither trade unions nor any other private institution are a fundamental source of inflation. But they are the '"bellows" heating the monetary furnace' (1980, p. 103). Trade unions, particularly in the public sector, can make financial gains by using their monopoly and lobbying power. Public sector pay rises are conceded by governments which then aspire to avoid facing the true impact of their decisions by counting on inflation to erode trade union gains. The unions, on the other hand, may develop a vested interest in the 'fiscal illusion' produced by inflation. Their real gains are concealed by purely inflationary changes in money values (ibid., p. 105). Thus, trade unions do not cause inflation, but they do generate some of the pressures which lead governments to increase the money supply, which, in turn, causes inflation.

Closely related to the control of the money supply is the problem of controlling public expenditure. New liberals are not unanimous in the importance they attach to budget deficits in determining inflation. Friedman, for instance, has argued that inflation can be defeated without limiting the budget deficit—as long as interest rates are not interfered with. However, he accepts that in recent years governments have debased their currencies largely as a means of funding their deficits, and he therefore agrees that any effort to control inflation could not ignore fiscal policy for long. Along with other new liberals, he therefore favours the reduction of the huge deficits which have been a feature of the post-war years. But he insists that inflation is a wholly monetary phenomenon, and his main reason for favouring budget retrenchment is because it enhances individual freedom, and not because it is the key to controlling inflation. The contrary view has been most strongly advocated in Britain by Professor Patrick Minford. He and his colleagues at Liverpool do not disagree that inflation is a largely monetary phenomenon, but they insist that it will never be brought under control unless budget deficits are significantly reduced.

The media often speak of Thatcherism and monetarism as if they were interchangeable terms, and it is commonly supposed that the policies of the Thatcher government have closely followed new liberal prescriptions, with Friedman the leading guru. The Medium-Term Financial Strategy, announced in March 1980, owed much to Friedman's thinking. The rate of growth in the money supply was to be gradually reduced over the years 1980/81 to 1983/84. However, contrary to Friedman's view it was accepted that the budget deficit must also be reduced steadily, as part of the anti-inflation strategy. The exchange rate was to be allowed to continue floating, to avoid 'importing' inflation. The government also departed from a strict Friedmanite position by initially opting to control the money supply as measured by Sterling M3, a wide monetary aggregate. Friedman prefers policy to be based on a much narrower measure. Moreover, the initial strategy of reducing the rate of monetary growth according to a clear rule was abandoned within a year or so in favour of a more discretionary, though no less counter-inflationary, policy.

Just as Hayek has become frustrated with the failed
efforts of governments to tackle inflation, so Friedman
and other new liberals have increasingly given up hope
that governments will control budget deficits. They have
increasingly turned to the advocacy of constitutional reform to force governments to balance budgets. The constant pressure for legislative action to limit budget deficits
paid off in December 1985, when the President finally
signed into law the Gramm–Rudman-Hollings Act, which
requires the budget deficit to be eliminated in stages by
1991.

A balanced budget rule has also been proposed for
Britain. Buchanan *et al.* believe that the fundamental
weakness of the British system of government is its open-
ness to abuse by vote-buying politicians. To prevent economic manipulation for short-term political profit they
recommend that a balanced-budget rule should be phased
in over five years. This would require the adoption of a
new House of Commons standing order: 'This House requires that total government expenditure does not exceed
total government revenue from taxation and charges'
(1978a, p. 82). They recognise that revenues are particularly difficult to predict, and propose that as the financial
year progresses an automatic adjustment rule should be
followed—also enforced by means of a House of Commons
standing order—to cut expenditure if it overshoots budget
projections. They suggest that if a projected deficit 'accidentally' emerges expenditure must be adjusted to restore
balance within three months. If a surplus is projected then
the excess must be used to diminish the national debt
(Ibid., pp. 82–3).

More recently John Burton has advocated a still more
radical change. He sees the present position as one of
'fiscal anarchy' and recommends that an Economic Bill of
Rights with two main elements should be put before the
British people in a referendum. As well as laying down a
balanced-budget rule it should also limit government
spending to 25 per cent of GNP (with provision for this
figure to be overridden in national emergencies) (1985, p.
99). Other new liberals have also advocated constitutional

changes. Professor Alan Peacock (1985) favours macro-economic controls on government spending, and more detailed proposals have been advocated by Brian Crozier.

Crozier advocates the introduction of a written constitution backed up by a constitutional court to interpret and enforce it. The constitution should lay down basic rights, of which Crozier lists eighteen. These include the traditional liberal rights, including the right to own, buy and sell property, to travel freely, to equal treatment under the laws, and to sound money; as well as some which prescribe a certain standard of life, such as the right to a minimum of education and to protection from poverty (1979, pp. 45–6).

The Thatcher government has come under increasing new liberal attack for focusing too narrowly on controlling inflation and too readily putting up with the unemployment that follows. New liberals accept that lower unemployment in the years before 1979 was achieved only at the cost of accelerating inflation, and that inflation should be controlled in order to permit the market to function. But many find the fatalism of the Thatcher government in the face of rising unemployment to be misguided. True, there is no escape from the 'natural rate' of unemployment (p. 66 above), but the natural rate is not fixed in perpetuity. It depends on a number of other factors, some of which are susceptible to influence by the government. For instance, high taxation is said to discourage enterprise; labour market distortions caused, *inter alia*, by trade unions and wage councils create unemployment; and the tax-benefit system causes the unemployment trap. In this view, the government should combine its anti-inflation strategy with a vigorous campaign to eliminate supply-side obstacles to fuller employment.

INDUSTRIAL POLICY: CLEARING THE WAY FOR THE ENTREPRENEUR

New liberals have also been very critical of the general direction of industrial policy since the 1930s. John Burton points out that the market offers an evolutionary process which encourages the emergence of new ideas, products and organisations. Only products which over the long run can attract money from consumers will remain available, and only organisations which remain financially viable over a period will remain in being. In his view there are two key elements in the market process. The first is the profit motive, which encourages persons to search out ways of making a return, either by satisfying a demand or by cutting costs in some existing enterprise. The second is the price mechanism, which coordinates the activities of the many market participants. Government subsidies, grants, loans, and the like interfere with the evolutionary process of the market whereby consumers' interests are served. In particular, government interference eradicates or distorts the price mechanism.

He distinguishes between two kinds of government intervention: accelerative policies designed to 'pick winners'; and decelerative policies, usually aimed at restoring a lame duck to good health. Government, he argues, is ill-equipped to perform either role. Decelerative policies to save poorly performing industries invariably tend to discourage the making of the adjustments required to serve the consumer and thus survive in the market. And accelerative policies are no better. In common with many new liberals, Burton criticises the strategy adopted by the Conservative government soon after coming to power in 1979. Ministers described their policy as one of 'constructive intervention'. Expenditure on industrial policy was not reduced, but the focus of intervention was shifted from subsidising lame duck enterprises towards assisting the *sunrise* industries, particularly electronics. For Burton and many other new liberals, it remains unsatisfactory because it does not represent a restoration of 'economic evolution'.

Regional policy has been particularly heavily attacked as highly ineffective and wasteful. It has been estimated that between 1960 and 1982 only 250,000 jobs were diverted to the regions. The Adam Smith Institute regards this as a 'feeble benefit' compared to the expense incurred.

Nevertheless the Thatcher government has continued with regional policy, although the ASI concedes that there has been some curtailment of past extravagances. The number of assisted areas under regional policy has been reduced. In 1979 an incredible 44 per cent of the working population was covered. By 1983 this had been reduced to about 27 per cent.

New liberals recommend a more cost-effective approach based on the removal of barriers to entrepreneurship and labour mobility. This would require measures to free the housing market and the easing of planning restrictions and central regulations. The Adam Smith Institute, for instance, argues that the building of advance factories is no longer justified. The English Industrial Estates Corporation should, therefore, be abolished and its assets sold, together with the assets of the Scottish Development Agency, the Highlands and Islands Development Board, the Welsh Development Agency, and the regional development agencies. Regional Selective Assistance allows the improper 'political distribution' of money into favoured private hands. It should be abolished. Regional Development Grants should also be phased out (Butler *et al.*, 1985, pp. 90–1).

New liberals have proposed a variety of other measures to restore consumer service through 'economic evolution'. Generally, they favour a 'supply-side' strategy under which the government seeks to make a vigorous private sector possible, instead of trying to interfere with demand by macro-economic manipulation of the economy. John Burton urges the government to deregulate the product and labour markets, eliminate government-imposed entry barriers and cut taxation. He recognises that there would be considerable resistance from the business lobby which benefits greatly from government subsidies. To overcome this resistance he suggests a 'big-bang' approach, like Ludwig Erhard's 'bonfire of controls' in Germany in 1950.

The 'enterprise zone' initiative taken by the Thatcher government was in great measure inspired by the new liberalism. But, in the view of the Adam Smith Institute, enterprise zones have ceased to be an instrument of 'econ-

omic liberalism and have become instead a further refine-
ment of economic interventionism'. Enterprise zones, they
say, should not have become 'subsidy islands'. Enterprise
ought to be promoted by the removal of regulations.

John Burton recommends that all small businesses (with
less than 100 employees) should be treated as a 'general
experimental zone' of the economy. The Adam Smith
Institute supports this strategy, although it favours a restriction to organisations with up to 20 or 25 employees.
Such companies should be relieved of their obligations
under employment and other onerous legislation, and
the VAT limit should be raised from around £19,000 to
£100,000 (Butler *et al.*, 1985, pp. 109, 376).

To assist further the small business sector, Gorman and
Lewis propose the establishment of a deregulation unit of
the Law Commission. Under the Law Commissions Act of
1965 the Law Commissioners are required to 'reduce,
simplify and modernise' the laws. A simple amendment to
the Act would enable a special deregulation unit to be
established to focus on small business (1983, pp. 19–21).
They and the Adam Smith Institute also urge that the
Inland Revenue should stop harassing the self-employed.
On the contrary, they say, self-employment should be
encouraged, defined possibly by a willingness to be excluded from the protection afforded by the Employment
Acts.

Unlike full-blooded libertarians (see Chapter 2), the
new liberalism of the IEA or the Adam Smith Institute is
not opposed as a matter of principle to all government
interference. Sometimes their prescriptions carry them
well away from classical liberalism. For instance, in
an IEA paper, Binks and Coyne, who describe their
approach as Austrian, advocate government subsidisation
of loan finance for small firms. They argue that the chief
problems faced by small businessmen are (a) that suitable
premises are frequently not available, and (b) that finance
is difficult to obtain. They recommend that government
help should take the form of interest rate 'holidays' or
subsidies, with a built-in mechanism for realignment with
prevailing market interest rates over time (1983, p. 78).

One of the major difficulties is how to handle loss-making nationalised industries. Generally the Adam Smith Institute favours the privatisation of nationalised industries, though as its President, Madsen Pirie (1985), insists, this does not mean that the institute demands a single blanket prescription for all industries. Privatisation is a broad *approach*. Each nationalised industry has its own special problems and circumstances which must be taken into account in seeking to make it more responsible to consumers through market evolution.

The Landrover and Rangerover division of BL (now Rover), they say, should be sold off and would undoubtedly survive in the market. The same applies to the spares division. The Leyland truck and bus division should be separated from the rest of BL and given its own board and accounts. Then it should be sold, or failing this, given to its work-force. Ultimately the Austin Morris car division should also be sold (1985, p. 93).

British Shipbuilders should continue to be disposed of. If parts of it can command a price in the market they should be sold, if not, they should be given to the work-force, with the debt written off. The success of the Redhead Shipyard on Tyneside shows that self-management can work. Eighty of the workforce used their redundancy money to buy the yard. Now the workforce is over 100. Care should be taken to ensure that no loss-making rump remains in government hands. Parts of the company that cannot be sold or given away should be closed (1985, pp. 94–5). The British Technology Group (National Enterprise Board) should also be sold, over a three-year period. 'The best form of government assistance to the economy', says the *Omega File*, 'is to allow the market to decide on its own destination' (p. 106).

New liberals have also been keen advocates of freeports. There are around 400 elsewhere in the world. The pattern varies, but the essential characteristic is that each is treated as foreign territory for customs purposes. No tax is levied on incoming goods. This idea was taken up by the Thatcher government and six freeports have been established. But, in the view of the Adam Smith Institute, 'bureaucratic caution and compromise has made them ineffective shadows of the real thing'. They urge the government to establish additional freeports with far less taxation and much less industrial regulation than the existing ones. There should be less planning restrictions, and much industrial and labour legislation should be suspended (Butler and Pirie (eds.) 1983; Butler *et al.*, 1985, p. 376).

It is sometimes said that the new liberalism is a philosophy which, contrary to new liberal claims, does not enhance the freedom of *individuals* so much as facilitate wealth-making opportunities for large institutions. A common retort is that institutions comprise people and that wherever you find wealthy corporations you also find prosperous individuals. But regardless of the validity of this claim, a great many new liberals are also hostile to corporate wealth, whenever it rests on unmerited legal privileges. An important contribution by Philip Chappell and Nigel Vinson argues that private ownership is the vital underpinning of a free society, but stresses that private ownership must be personal. The authors note that ownership in Britain is concentrated in institutional hands and becoming more so, due chiefly to tax privileges enjoyed, by corporations. 'Ownership at second hand', they say, 'whether through institutions or the state is a sorry substitute' for personal control (1985, pp. 1–2). They therefore advocate the establishment of personal investment pools (PIPs), based on the principle that the individual and the institution should enjoy equal tax status. Every person would be free to pay a proportion of their income into their PIP, which would embrace a wide variety of assets, including property, bank and building society deposits and equities. In this manner, ownership would be diffused and every person would have the opportunity to hold a direct and tangible stake in the prosperity a free society can offer. A very small step in the direction urged by Chappell and Vinson was taken by Chancellor of the Exchequer, Nigel Lawson, when he introduced personal equity plans in his 1986 Budget.

Political Impact
Increasingly the Thatcher government has come to accept the supply-side approach. In July 1985 the White Paper, *Lifting the Burden*, was published, setting out what the government had done and planned to do to ease the regulative burden on businessmen. To date, however, the government has fallen far short of the aspirations of its supply-side critics. Consider town planning.

Town Planning: Since 1909 British local authorities have had powers to control land uses within urban areas, and since 1947 they have had extensive arbitrary powers to control land use. The new liberals have been constant critics of these powers, a view which found popular support during the 1960s and 1970s as the perverse effects of planning policies, particularly in respect of housing and roads, made 'planners' a dirty word. But the new liberals have not argued for the total abandonment of all planning powers. Instead they have urged only that the market ought not to be wholly supplanted by official regulation. With suitable controls, the market, guided by the price mechanism and private agreements, can accomplish many planning goals more effectively. Hayek, for instance, writes that, 'The general formulas of private property or freedom of contract' do not provide an immediate answer to the complex problems of city life (1960, p. 34). And, he says, 'the price mechanism operates only imperfectly and does not take into account many things we would wish to see taken into account' (p. 356).

In a more recent discussion the Adam Smith Institute explores the possibility of developing a liberal planning system in Britain. They point out that, contrary to the arguments of the planning lobby, the evidence does not support the view that the market produces chaos or a multiplication of nuisances like noise, air and water pollution. They cite evidence from a number of American cities which have no formal planning, such as Houston, with its population of 2 million, and Pasadena, Beaumont and Wichita Falls, each with a population of around 100,000. Without controls or imposed land-use zones, development in Houston has followed a largely acceptable pattern. Zoning has tended to occur 'naturally'. There is control, but it is exercised, not arbitrarily by officials, but by means of restrictive covenants, which cover around two thirds of the city (Butler *et al.*, 1985, p. 368).

In Britain planning powers have significant side-effects. Planning produces very considerable development delays. In Belgium in 1979, for instance, it took about six weeks on average to get planning permission for a 50,000 sq.ft factory, whilst in Britain a similar scheme took on average eight months (ibid., p. 366). Such delays cost money and added to the other restrictions, often discourage development altogether, resulting in widespread dereliction and the diminution of employment opportunities. Planning has also, they say, been ineffective, and often counter-productive. Certainly, while claiming to promote beauty and good taste in architecture many local authorites have produced ugly and poor quality housing and shopping developments. And in spite of declared policies of employment promotion, planning restrictions have seriously impeded the emergence of new small businesses. It has been ill-recognised that a great many new businesses start at home, and if that option is not available many new firms will not get started at all.

The Adam Smith Institute has suggested how planning might be reformed. Their general approach is to replace prevailing planning powers by a system which retains protection for historic and rural areas, but which otherwise generally assumes planning consent, and which provides protection for neighbours against nuisances—like air, noise and water pollution—without subjecting all citizens to the arbitrary power of planners.

To protect neighbours against nuisances like pollution and congestion they suggest the replacement of present planning control by low-cost, easy-to-use, land-use tribunals which could hear complaints between parties and issue directives. The use of restrictive covenants should be officially encouraged and more reliance could be placed on private building and insurance codes in place of official regulation. If insurance companies, for instance, linked premiums for their public liability policies to the safety of buildings this would be likely to have a considerable effect on building standards. The ASI favours limited zoning, with possibly three basic categories: (a) restricted zones policed nationally to cover conservation areas, green belts and the like; (b) general zones—which would cover most areas—in which the only regulation would be to eliminate nuisances; and (c) a few industrial zones, where even less restrictions would apply to encourage the vigorous tackling of dereliction (pp. 369–70).

The Thatcher government has accepted these arguments up to a point. It plans to introduce Simplified Planning Zones, in which planning permission procedures will be less burdensome; to extend the General Development Order, to permit more types of development to take place without requiring planning permission at all; and it is reviewing the Use Classes Order, to enable the uses of existing buildings to be changed without requiring permission. Controls on advertising are also to be relaxed (*Lifting the Burden*, 1985, pp. 10–13). Generally, new liberals regard these changes as too limited in scope. Without significant further deregulation they fear that unemployment levels will remain high for very much longer.

Trade Union Reform

New liberals have been severe critics of trade union privileges. Hayek believes that trade unions have contributed to Britain's decline, but he stops short of outright hostility to them. 'I believe', he says, 'that everybody, unless he has voluntarily renounced it, ought to have the right to join a trade union.' But, he goes on, no one ought to have the right to force others to join. And on the right to strike he says: 'I am even prepared to agree that *everybody* ought to have the *right* to strike, so far as he does not thereby break a contract or the law has not conferred a monopoly on the enterprise in which he is engaged. But I am convinced that nobody ought to have the right to *force* others to strike' (1984, p. 51; emphasis in original).

Hayek attributes the unwarranted power of trade unions to legal privileges. The privileged immunity from civil liability, initially granted by the 1906 Trade Disputes Act, is the chief culprit:

These legalised powers of the unions have become the biggest obstacle to raising the living standards of the working class as a whole. They are the chief cause of the unnecessarily big differences between the best- and worst-paid workers. They are the prime source of unemployment. They are the main reason for the decline of the British economy in general. (Ibid., p. 52)

The present ability of any trade union to obtain better terms for its members rests, writes Hayek, on its 'legalised power to *prevent other workers from earning as good an income as they otherwise might*. It is thus maintained, literally, by the exploitation of those not permitted to do work that they would like to do' (ibid., pp. 52–3; emphasis in original). Trade unions, Hayek says, have now become the 'open enemies of the ideal of freedom of association by which they once gained the sympathy of true liberals. Freedom of association means the freedom to decide whether one wants to join an association or not' (ibid., p. 61).

Hayek criticises Keynes for giving the impression that the *general* level of wages was more important than *relative* wages:

His erroneous conception that employment could be directly controlled by regulating aggregate demand through monetary policy shifted responsibility for employment from the trade unions to government. This error relieved trade unions of the responsibility to adjust their wage demands so as to sell as much work as possible, and misrepresented full employment entirely as a function of government monetary policy. (Ibid., p. 57)

But it is not possible to keep a market economy functioning at 'full speed ... without *some* wages occasionally falling while others rise'. Full employment can only be maintained by adjusting wages in each sector to changing demands. And this means raising some wages and lowering others (ibid., p. 56).

Hayek attaches great importance to trade union reform. He goes so far as to say, 'that there can be no salvation

for Britain until the special privileges granted to the trade
unions three-quarters of a century ago are revoked'. It is
not the skill of her entrepreneurs or workers that has
become ossified in Britain, but the price structure and the
'indispensable discipline it imposes' by signalling what has
to be done to meet the demands of consumers, rewarding
those who do it and penalising those who fail' (ibid., p.
58).

Since Hayek was writing in the late 1970s the Thatcher
government has introduced a number of measures to remove some of the most damaging trade union privileges.
The Employment Acts of 1980 and 1982 (which eliminated
some of the privileges enjoyed by pickets and closed shop
agreements) and the Trade Union Act of 1984 (which
attempted to restore control of trade unions to rank-and-
file members by requiring secret ballots) have achieved a
good deal. But for many new liberals the most serious
omission in the government's programme to date is the
failure to tackle the coercive power of public sector trade
unions. As the next stage in trade union reform Charles
Hanson urges the introduction of no-strike contracts for
workers in essential services, especially those where withdrawal threatens the health and safety of the population at
large. All trade unions in such services should also lose
the remaining immunities from legal action which apply to
other citizens. To ensure fair play, a 'last-resort' method
of settling disputes should be introduced, such as the
arrangements already made for the police and the army
(1984, pp. 76–7).

Preserving Market Signals, but Sharing the Burden
As well as being associated with 'monetarism' the new
liberalism is especially noted for its hard-headed 'economic realism'. There is no escaping, new liberals will
insist, the harsh realities of economic life. Hayek, for
instance, says that when people find themselves unemployed, or having to move house to a new job, or getting
paid less than they would like, these are all necessary
hardships because they represent signals that we are failing to serve our fellows. And similarly, if we find our pay

rising, or our company expanding, then this is a signal that we are serving fellow citizens well.

Some of Hayek's critics cannot turn their minds past the hardship of unemployment or the frustration of low pay. And as a consequence they denounce him as callous, and they write off the market as inhumane. This is a mistake. The signals sent by the market are one thing, but some of the hardship that goes with the signal may be avoidable. Hayek is correct in pointing out that we ignore market signals at our peril and that we should not encourage governments to intervene to eliminate hardship if it also eliminates the signal, as when badly organised and declining industries are subsidised. But this does not mean that the costs of making the adjustments necessary to provide better service have to be borne by individuals alone and unaided. Some new liberals have increasingly shown interest in devising mechanisms to ease the burden on those who are the immediate losers as industries adjust to consumer demands.

New liberals emphasise that market adjustments must be made if we are to put consumers first. But how much, they ask, can the cost to individuals of economic evolution be cushioned or mitigated without obliterating the vital signalling role of the market? For instance, according to John Burton, instead of subsidising defunct enterprises which are failing to serve the consumer, industrial policy should subsidise individuals adversely affected by industrial change. To this end he recommends the introduction of vouchers or tax credits for retraining. Economic change produces losers as well as gainers, and it is right that workers in obsolescent industries should be helped to adapt. Anyone who lost their job would be given a voucher entitling them to be retrained at the taxpayer's expense. If individuals preferred the cash in order to start their own business, this should be permitted. Such thinking has had a considerable impact on the Thatcher government, which has followed a policy of making quite generous compensation payments to redundant workers in steel, coal and shipbuilding. Such measures modify relative prices, and they have an opportunity cost, but they do not eradicate market signals, and are therefore acceptable.

AGRICULTURE

Farmers, too, are not immune from new liberal efforts to end sectional abuse of the state. In an IEA book, Richard Howarth (1985) criticises the agricultural support policies pursued since the Second World War. He argues that during and just after the war agricultural policy succeeded in its aim of expanding the supply of home produce. But, he contends that since the mid-1950s agricultural support policies have been wholly unsuitable.

The usual justification for price support is that farm prices are peculiarly unstable, but whilst prices may have been stabilised the side-effect has been a massive over-supply of produce. This has been severely exacerbated by the Common Agricultural Policy. The cost has been borne by the taxpayer and the consumer. The Institute for Fiscal Studies has estimated the cost to consumers as the equivalent of a 4.5 per cent tax on gross incomes (Howarth, 1985, p. 121).

According to Howarth, farmers have not benefited financially. As a group, their income relative to other groups has been stable. A high proportion of the gross benefits received in price and output support has been dissipated in higher land values, rents and interest payments. These have created barriers to new entrants. Howarth agrees that agricultural support policies have 'fed the people plentifully', but argues that a free market could have done so equally well and at lower prices. He recommends the phasing out of support over a 5–10-year period, backed up by compensation payments to farmers to ease the transition. The underlying object is a freely competitive agriculture, without internal subsidies and without external protection. He would, however, retain protection against dumping and favours the maintenance of 'food security' in case of national crisis (ibid., pp. 122, 127).

The Potato Marketing Board should disappear along

with the Wool Marketing Board. The Milk Marketing Boards should be disbanded. If farmers wish, they could be reformed as cooperatives. The promotional and advisory services of the boards could continue, but the manipulation of the market to the benefit of suppliers should end. The Agricultural and Horticultural Development Scheme and the Agricultural and Horticultural Grant Scheme encourage 'wasteful' investment and promote environmental damage. They should be abolished. Hill livestock allowances under the EC should be replaced, and headage payments, which only encourage over-grazing, should also be abolished (ibid., pp. 127–8). The wool and potato price guarantees should be phased out over five years, and there should be no government expenditure on research and development. The privatisation of Forestry Commission land, begun by an Act of 1981, should be accelerated (pp. 128–9).

The greatest obstacle, however, is the Common Agricultural Policy. Even so, Howarth does not believe that Britain should run the risk of unilaterally leaving the CAP. Instead he recommends that the government should do everything within its means to speed the eventual demise of the scheme. Howarth believes it to be such an abomination that, in time, it is bound to collapse or wither away (ibid., p. 135). Due chiefly to the virtual impossibility of reforming the Common Market, new liberal thinking has had little or no impact on the agricultural policy of the Thatcher government.

GUIDE TO READING

Le Grand and Robinson (1984a) has a useful discussion of regional policy. Public sector industrial relations are considered in Heald (1983), Chapter 9. Minford (1983) sets out a contemporary new liberal view of the unemployment problem, whilst Burton (1983) provides an accessible account of the wider supply-side standpoint. An up to date discussion of the right to strike can be found in Shenfield (1986).

9 Conclusions

The label 'new right' has become attached to a variety of standpoints critical of the statism which has dominated political thought and action in the West since the 1930s. The common theme is that individuals should be able to direct their own lives to a far greater extent than is now possible, and that one of the chief obstacles to greater self-direction is the over-mighty state. But this still leaves considerable room for disagreement about the proper scope of government.

THE ROLE OF GOVERNMENT

One group, the anarcho-libertarians, would wholly dismantle the state. This, pure, unadulterated liberalism reverts to one of the methods of thinking about the state adopted during the seventeenth century, when modern liberalism originated. In their efforts to decide how (if at all) nations should be governed, men like Hobbes and Locke (though they drew fundamentally different conclusions) asked themselves what society was like before there was any government. They postulated a 'state of nature', and from this condition inferred how men should be ruled. Rothbard and other anarcho-libertarians look back to Locke for their inspiration, though they find it impossible even to support his preference for a minimal state devoted only to the maintenance of law and order and protection against foreign enemies.

Nozick follows the same line of inquiry and re-opens the questions asked by Locke, but then proceeds by an ingenious argument to show that a minimal state could be justified by inference from the state of nature. But he draws the line at a minimal state. No one, he says, should be coerced by the state for their own good, and nor should they be forced to help others.

The mainstream new liberals, Friedman, Hayek and the public choice school—in Britain the tradition represented by the Institute of Economic Affairs—take a different path to their conclusions. They do not ask what life would be like without a state. They accept that it is there and, like their classical liberal forbears, they believe it should be. But they believe its present scope to be harmful. They firmly reject the view which has been dominant for most of this century, that state power is a relatively unproblematic force for good. But to question this assumption is not the same as believing that 'small' government is always good and 'big' government always bad. The size of government as such, is not their central concern. For mainstream new liberals, government has four main objects. The first is to protect its citizens from potential or actual foreign enemies. The second is to maintain liberty. That is, they hold that every person should be as self-directing as possible, and the potential of each person for self-development as unimpaired as possible. This is the task of law. It should eliminate private restraint by maintaining rules which tell each person what the state regards as just conduct by one person towards another, thus helping to settle in advance the frequent collisions and clashes of interest that are bound to occur. Equally important, the law should set limits on what the state may do to its citizens, thus preventing the state from transforming itself from a protector into a predator.

The third object of government is to maintain a framework within which men and women can cooperate efficiently. This is the aspect of liberalism on which economists tend to focus. As far as possible competition should prevail, or at least, every supplier should be open to competition. Neither private nor government contrivances should

be allowed to obliterate or blur the crucial signalling role
of the free market. This does not mean that a wholly
unfettered market is believed desirable. On the contrary, the government may need to be vigilant, not only
to detect and outlaw private efforts in restraint of competition, but also to prevent its own ostensibly pro-
competitive endeavours from being twisted to serve
contrary ends.

The fourth aim of government, according to the new
liberal mainstream, is to underwrite the material security
of its people. This is the 'safety net' philosophy. The free
play of competitive forces is vital if the high and mighty
are to be knocked off their pedestals when they fail to
serve their fellows as well as competitors. But at any given
moment not everyone will be able to enter the contest and
the state may quite properly prevent such citizens from
falling below a certain decent minimum standard of life.
But, again, the new liberal warns that it is all too easy for
well-intentioned uses of state power to produce perverse
results. A clear line must be drawn, for if every person's
material holdings are put at the disposal of whoever can
seize the reigns of power then there will soon be little
liberty left. This is why Hayek is so against progressive
taxation. Taxes, he says, should be proportional, with
each paying the same percentage. Thus, the mainstream
new liberal seeks material *security* for fellow citizens,
but not material *equality*. The state may also provide
certain services which the market may not supply—
'public goods', as economists call them. Mainstream
new liberals do not, therefore, advocate a minimal state:
'Far from advocating such a 'minimal state''', says Hayek,
'we find it unquestionable that in an advanced society
government ought to use its power of raising funds by
taxation to provide a number of services which for various
reasons cannot be provided, or cannot be provided adequately, by the market' (1979a, p. 41) But here too,
there is a danger that 'public goods' will be too widely
interpreted, and new liberals urge constant vigilance
against abuse.

THE IMPACT OF THE NEW LIBERTARIANISM

To date, notwithstanding the rhetoric of the Thatcher government, the new liberals' impact on practical politics has been patchy. The Reagan government has been more receptive, though if Milton Friedman is representative of new-liberal opinion, it too has fallen well short of expectations. The most fundamental defects of collectivism have been barely touched by governments anywhere.

The mechanism which deeply corrupts western politics, the buying of votes by political parties, remains unaltered. It is the root cause of inflation, and whilst some governments have brought inflation under control the government monopoly of money remains open to abuse by future incumbents. Governments continue to be seen as instruments for the redistribution of income. Mainstream new liberals do not advocate the total withdrawal of government from redistribution, but do insist that a clear line should be drawn between the elimination of poverty and the pursuit of egalitarian levelling in the name of 'social justice'. This line of demarcation has nowhere been satisfactorily drawn, though in America it has been more nearly approached than elsewhere. The failure to draw a clear line explains why the welfare state is so often said to benefit, not the poor, but the rich, or at any rate the middle class. But this unexpected result is inevitable, for if material holdings are placed at the disposal of the government of the day, and if the government of the day has to win support by making promises to winning coalitions of electors, then it is very likely that already well-off people will take the opportunity to turn the state machine to their own advantage. The poor are not the only ones capable of political organisation. This new liberal insight that majoritarian democracy is inherently likely to serve the interests of the already powerful remains ill-recognised.

The new liberals have, however, changed the agenda, in some cases irrevocably, in the academic as well as the political world. As Chapters 6–8 revealed, new liberal ideas have made their mark on practical politics, if not always in determining the details of government programmes, then certainly in framing many of the issues. During the 1970s, when the new liberalism was beginning to make its mark on the political scene many academics, especially social scientists, continued to ignore and denounce it. Today the denunciation is no less vigorous, but many leftist academics concede that the terms of the debate have altered.

Sociology and social policy continue to be dominated on the one hand by Marxists, who utterly condemn the 'capitalist' or 'state capitalist' status quo, and on the other by pragmatic socialists who accept the narrow conceptions of today's problems favoured by professionals and administrators. But neither of these groups can wholly ignore the new liberalism, as they could ten years ago. A recent essay by Professor David Donnison reveals the extent of the steady, rising, influence of the new liberalism. He warns against unthinking rejection of privatisation in favour of the former centralised prescriptions, with their 'unsolved problems' and urges socialists to support self-management, decentralisation, and 'enterprise'. Yet, he variously describes Tory privatisation as 'reactionary', 'brutal' and 'barbaric'. In general he gives the impression of trying to adjust socialist thinking to the evidence of post-war government failure, and in reality is turning to the new liberalism for alternative ideas, but he cannot bring himself to give the 'new right' any credit (1984, pp. 45-57).

In an article in *Marxism Today*, Professor Stuart Hall of the Open University, more openly discusses the impact of the new liberalism on the political left. 'Realignment' is the order of the day, he argues, and by realignment he means a conscious, sometimes painful, questioning of what those who identify themselves with the left now stand for. Two pressures, he says, have brought about this re-examination. First, there have been a number of 'strategic reversals', of which the defeat of Scargillism is the most significant. The second factor is 'Thatcherism', by which he means the new liberalism. The new right, he argues, has taken the initiative from the left, and the left has yet to come to terms with the confidence and vitality of the liberal revival (1985, pp. 14-15).

Political science remains dominated by analysts of election results, but the public choice school has begun to undermine the assumptions underlying traditional psephology. In particular public choice has cast doubt on the theory of the electoral mandate: the assumption that majority voting can be seen as the passing of a rational judgement on a political programme. For the public choice school, the scholar seeking to understand the roots of any government's programme should first examine the motives and interests of politicians and administrators, not the electoral preferences of voters. Also under the influence of the public choice school, political science has become more concerned with the 'science' of liberal-democratic constitution making.

Nor will political theory be the same again. The social contract method of reasoning has taken firm root, though due as much to the influence of the social-democratic John Rawls as to the new liberals. Hayek's exposition of evolutionary liberalism has sharpened the terms of a debate that has lain dormant since the days of Hume and Burke.

Of all the social sciences, economics has been the most fundamentally challenged. The domination of macroeconomic manipulation of national economies by governments has been strongly criticised. Macro-aggregates are not real acting phenomena, the new liberals have successfully argued, and so if we wish to change the world we must understand human action at the micro-level: the individual, the factory, the company, the cartel, the trade union. The manipulation of macro-aggregates must produce largely unintended consequences, because aggregates do not act, have goals, motives or interests, and nor do they adjust to or find themselves impelled by circumstances.

More fundamentally still, the inclination of economists to see their subject as the study of 'efficient allocation' has been challenged. This applies especially to the traditional treatment of competition, the cornerstone of much market analysis. Conventional discussions stress the importance of possessing perfect information about alternatives, whilst the Austrian view emphasises that competition is necessary *because* we do not have perfect information. If we did, competition would indeed be very difficult to justify. In their efforts to turn economics into a technique for use as an impartial policy-making tool, economists have over-emphasised the knowledge that lies at the disposal of policy makers. But the Austrian school has unanswerably shown that we must be aware of the *limits* of our knowledge, and argued that consequently we should be more modest in our uses of the state's powers of coercion. In this view, a great deal of today's fashionable econometrics is futile mumbo-jumbo.

To date it is the public choice school that has made the most impact on economics, whilst the Austrian tradition is only very slowly being absorbed. Some evidence of the impact of the public choice school is suggested by its influence on the authors of the widely used textbook by Julian Le Grand and Ray Robinson, *The Economics of Social Problems*. In the first edition (1976) any demonstration of 'market failure' inclined them to favour state intervention, with only slight reservations. The second edition (1984) reveals a more thorough awareness of the dangers of assuming that a 'market failure' automatically justifies government intervention. 'Government failure' is also a distinct possibility. But they have yet to absorb the thinking of the Austrian school. Austrian thinking, and especially Hayek's thought, is still not widely appreciated.

The impact on the academic world highlights one of the chief characteristics of the new liberalism. It is a movement of ideas. It is not predominantly a class movement, based on some vested interest—big business, trade unions, the working class, the middle class. For this reason the new liberalism is not reflected in party political organisation.

There are libertarian parties in the USA and Australia, but they attract relatively few votes. The US Libertarian Party points out that it is America's third largest party in voting terms, but it is very far behind the two major parties. In Australia the libertarian Workers' Party fought elections throughout much of Australia, receiving only five per cent of the votes in its most successful constituency. In 1977 it became the Progress Party, and achieved 18.6 per cent of the votes in its best seat. Since then its influence has waned. In Britain there is no political party devoted to libertarian principles, although the Libertarian Alliance, the Adam Smith Club and the Carl Menger Society each perform an educational and propagandist, but not electoral role. The main impact of the new liberalism has been felt on the existing political parties through the power of ideas.

MARKETS AND MORALITY

It is frequently said that markets promote selfishness. For instance, Le Grand and Robinson assert that there 'can be little doubt that the market fosters personal attributes, such as greed and a lack of concern for one's neighbour' (1984a, p. 267). What truth is there in such claims? The new liberals have typically argued, not that selfishness is a good thing, but that selfishness exists whether we like it or not, and they have urged that we must therefore strive towards institutions which prevent selfishness from doing too much harm. Competition is said to be the chief safeguard available, preventing any producer whose principal aim is to make money from doing so except by serving the consumer. It is conceded that competition may produce perverse results, and that in these circumstances the government may step in, but if it does so then it should reinforce rather than replace competition. But it is a mistake to regard profit seeking as the only approved motivation. The case for liberty rests only in part on the value of competition in channelling the efforts of possibly selfish individuals into the service of their fellows. It also rests on the belief that there are any number of alternative ways of meeting human wants—some like charity and mutual aid the very antithesis of profit seeking—and that only in a free society can such alternatives flourish.

Thus, the claim that the new liberalism either promotes

selfishness or turns a blind eye to it, is unjustified. But it
is true that the new liberalism lacks a solid association
with any particular moral stance, and to that extent its
roots in popular culture may be rather shallow. The new
liberalism gained in popularity in the 1970s because collectivism had failed to deliver the expected benefits, and
consequently the advantages of competition came to be
understood afresh. Its popular support still largely rests on
the recognition that collectivist prescriptions have failed
and that economic 'realities' must be faced. In January
1985 Sir Geoffrey Howe made this claim:

> We have staked out the new common ground on which the political
> debate is taking place. It matters little whether it is called a Conserva-
> tive consensus, or a new radicalism, or economic realism. What matters
> is that we have established a post-nationalization, post-trade union
> monopoly era, an era in which there is no longer a world-weary accep-
> tance of national decline and a dependent relationship between the
> individual and the state. (Speech in Cambridge, quoted in Riddell,
> 1985, p. 247.)

He was almost certainly correct in summarising the political impact of the new liberalism. A few months later, Roy
Hattersley, the deputy leader of the Labour Party, chose
as his subject for the annual Fabian Lecture, 'Socialism
and Markets', urging that markets had a role within socialism. Much earlier, David Owen had emphasised that
markets should play a central role in social democracy.

Thus, after a long absence from the political agenda,
markets are back in the political arena, but whether the
new liberalism takes firmer root depends on whether or
not its supporters can inspire, not only mere 'economic
realism', but also a more deep-seated moral regeneration.
A free society is only supportable if its adherents advocate
a moral code which among other things constrains the
pursuit of selfish gain and requires the successful to help
the less fortunate. It is no historical accident that when
liberty was most respected in Britain, liberty and conscience went hand in hand. As respect for individual freedom declined in the latter part of the nineteenth century,
so it became necessary to proselytise in favour of duty.

And it was during the years from 1859 to 1880 that Samuel Smiles was writing books entitled *Self-Help*, *Character*, *Thrift* and *Duty*. Indeed, to a degree, one of the chief spokesmen, for the new liberalism, Hayek, has appeared to undermine one of its principal potential moral foundations. He has done so by emphasising that outcomes in a free market may not be deserved. Far from it, he says, they may depend on luck as much as effort. Hitherto, one of the moral bases of liberalism was that it promised a social order in which honesty, ability and hard work would reap their reward. Hayek has, I suggest, overstated the accidental nature of material outcomes. No social order can guarantee that hard work will bring success, but, compared with any known alternative, a new liberal social order makes it more likely that diligence will pay off. But more important still, in his efforts to show that an 'extended order' cannot be made to conform to some pre-ordained end-result, Hayek tends to understate what is arguably the paramount attraction of a market: that it is the best method known to us for channelling the efforts of all into the service of others.

This is a very powerful argument for a free society. Market signals, like falling wages, factory closures and loss of job, are messages, says Hayek, which tell us whether or not our actions are well adapted to the service of others. If no one wants to buy the product you make, you can only insist that you have a right to go on making it if you believe that the wishes of other citizens should be overridden. What Hayek is saying is that in a properly functioning market, the only people who will make money will be those who perform good service for their fellows. The mechanism, he concedes, is imperfect. Some people will enjoy riches through sheer chance, and others will try their best and fail. But in an extended order the free market principles he enunciates enable us to get as close as we can to linking reward with service. It is imperfect, but there is no better way.

We cannot know on a face-to-face basis everyone with whom we deal. Thus we cannot imbue all our dealings with the emotional qualities that typify relationships with family and friends at their best. But though we cannot love all our fellow members of the human race, we can, through compliance with the abstract signals of the market, be of service to them. This claim that the market promotes universal service has as strong an appeal as the socialist aspiration of international brotherhood.

References

Acton, J. (1907) *The History of Freedom & Other Essays*, London: Macmillan.

Acton, J. (1930) *Lectures on Modern History*, London: Macmillan.

Alchian, A. (1977) *Economic Forces at Work*, Indianapolis: Liberty Press.

Alchian, A. and Demsetz, H. (1973), 'The property rights paradigm', *Journal of Economic History*, vol. XXXIII, pp. 16–27.

Anderson, M. (1978) *Welfare*, Stanford: Hoover Institution.

Arblaster, A. (1984) *The Rise and Decline of Western Liberalism*, Oxford: Blackwell.

Ashford, N. (1981) 'The neo-conservatives', *Government and Opposition*, vol. 16, pp. 353–69.

Barry, B. (1978) *Sociologists, Economists and Democracy*, London & Chicago: University of Chicago Press.

Barry, N.P. (1979) *Hayek's Social and Economic Philosophy*, London: Macmillan.

Barry, N.P. (1981) 'Re-stating the liberal order: Hayek's philosophical economics', in Shackleton and Locksley (1981), pp. 87–107.

Barry, N.P. (1983) 'The new liberalism', *British Journal of Political Science*, vol. 13, pp. 93–123.

Baxter, C., O'Leary, P.J. and Westoby, A. (eds) (1977) *Economics and Education Policy: A Reader*, London: Longman/Open University.

Beales, A.C.F. *et al.* (1970) *Education: A Framework for Choice*, London: IEA.

Becker, G. (1976) *The Economic Approach to Human Behaviour*, Chicago: University of Chicago Press.

222 *References*

Benn, A. (1982) *Parliament, People & Power*, London: Verso.
Beveridge, W. (1942) *Social Insurance and Allied Services*, Cmd. 6404, London: HMSO.
Beveridge, W. (1944) *Full Employment in a Free Society*, London: Allen & Unwin.
Binks, M. and Coyne, J. (1983) *The Birth of Enterprise*, Hobart Paper 98, London: IEA.
Black, D. (1958) *The Theory of Committees & Elections*, London: Cambridge University Press.
Blaug, M. (1970) *An Introduction to the Economics of Education*, Harmondsworth: Penguin.
Blaug, M. (1984) 'Education vouchers—it all depends on what you mean', in Le Grand and Robinson (1984b), pp. 160–76.
Bosanquet, N. (1983) *After the New Right*, London: Heinemann.
Brennan, H.G. and Buchanan, J.M. (1981) *Monopoly in Money & Inflation*, Hobart Paper 88, London: IEA.
Brittan, S. (1982) *How To End the Monetarist Controversy*, Hobart Paper 90, 2nd edn, London: IEA.
Buchanan, J.M. (1975) *The Limits of Liberty*, Chicago/London: University of Chicago Press.
Buchanan, J.M. (1986) *Liberty, Market and State*, Brighton: Wheatsheaf.
Buchanan, J.M. and Wagner, R.E. (1977) *Democracy in Deficit*, New York: Academic Press.
Buchanan, J.M., Burton, J. and Wagner, R.E. (1978a) *The Consequences of Mr. Keynes*, Hobart Paper 78, London: IEA.
Buchanan, J.M. *et al.* (1978b) *The Economics of Politics*, IEA Readings 18, London: IEA.
Buchanan, J.M. and Tullock, G. (1981) 'An American perspective: from "markets work" to public choice', in Seldon, A. (ed.) (1981).
Burton, J. (1978) 'Epilogue' in Cheung (1978).
Burton, J. (1980) 'Trade unions' role in the British disease: "an interest in inflation"?', in Minford *et al.* (1980).
Burton, J. (1981) 'Positively Milton Friedman', in Shackleton and Locksley (1981), pp. 53–71.
Burton, J. (1983) *Picking Losers...?*, Hobart Paper 99, London: IEA.
Burton, J. (1985) *Why No Cuts?*, Hobart Paper 104, London: IEA.
Butler, E. (1983) *Hayek*, London: Temple Smith.
Butler, E. (1985) *Milton Friedman*, Aldershot: Gower/Maurice Temple.

Butler, E. and Pirie, M. (1983) *Freeports*, London: Adam Smith Institute.

Butler, E., Pirie, M. and Young, P. (1985) *The Omega File*, London: Adam Smith Institute.

Chappell, P. and Vinson, N. (1985) *Owners All*, London: Centre for Policy Studies.

Cheung, S.N.S. (1978) *The Myth of Social Cost*, Hobart Paper 82, London: IEA.

Coase, R. (1960) 'The problem of social cost', *Journal of Law and Economics*, vol. III, October, pp. 1–44.

Cole, G.D.H. (1947) *A Guide to the Elements of Socialism*, London: Labour Party.

Collard, D. (1968) *The New Right: A Critique*, Fabian Tract 387, London: Fabian Society.

Crew, M.A. and Young, A. (1977) *Paying by Degrees*, Hobart Paper 75, London: IEA.

Crozier, B. (1979) *The Minimum State*, London: Hamish Hamilton.

DHSS (1985) *Reform of Social Security*, Vol. 1, Cmnd. 9517, London: HMSO.

Denman, D.R. (1984) *Markets Under the Sea?*, London: IEA.

Department of Transport (1984) *Buses*, Cmnd. 9300, London: HMSO.

Department of Transport (1985) *Buses: The Government's Response to the Second Report from the House of Commons' Transport Committee*, Cmnd. 9561, London: HMSO.

Descartes, R. (1637) *Discourse on Method* (Everyman edn, 1912), London: Dent.

Dicey, A.V. (1905) *Lectures on the Relation Between Law and Public Opinion in England During the Nineteenth Century*, London: Macmillan.

Donnison, D. (1985) 'The Progressive Potential of Privatisation', in Le Grand and Robinson (eds) (1984b).

Downs, A. (1957) *The Economic Theory of Democracy*, New York: Harper and Brothers.

Ferns, H.S. (1982) *How Much Freedom For Universities?*, Occasional Paper 65, London: IEA.

Forte, F. and Peacock, A. (eds) (1985) *Public Expenditure and Government Growth*, Oxford: Blackwell.

Friedman, D. (1978) *The Machinery of Freedom*, 2nd edn, New York: Arlington House.

Friedman, M. (1953) *Essays in Positive Economics*, Chicago: University of Chicago Press.

Friedman, M. (1962) *Capitalism and Freedom*, Chicago: University of Chicago Press.

Friedman, M. (1970) *The Counter-Revolution in Monetary Theory*, Occasional Paper 33, London: IEA.

Friedman, M. (1974a) 'A Theoretical Framework for Monetary Analysis', in Gordon, R.J. (ed.) (1974).

Friedman, M. (1974b) *Monetary Correction*, Occasional Paper 41, London: IEA.

Friedman, M. (1974c) 'Inflation, Taxation, Indexation', in Robbins *et al.* (1974).

Friedman, M. (1975) *Unemployment Versus Inflation?*, Occasional Paper 44, London: IEA.

Friedman, M. (1977a) *From Galbraith to Economic Freedom*, Occasional Paper 49, London: IEA.

Friedman, M. (1977b) *Inflation & Unemployment* (The 1976 Alfred Nobel Memorial Lecture), Occasional Paper 51, London: IEA.

Friedman, M. (ed.) (1956) *Studies in the Quantity Theory of Money*, Chicago: University of Chicago Press.

Friedman, M. and R. (1980) *Free to Choose*, London: Secker & Warburg.

Friedman, M. and R. (1985) *The Tyranny of the Status Quo* (revised edn). Harmondsworth: Penguin Books.

Friedman, M. and Schwartz, A.J. (1963) *A Monetary History of the United States 1867–1960*, Princeton: Princeton University Press, 1971.

Friedman, M. and Schwartz, A.J. (1982) *Monetary Trends in the United States and the United Kingdom*, Chicago & London: University of Chicago Press.

Godley, W. and Cripps, F. (1983) *Macroeconomics*, London: Oxford University Press.

Gordon, R.J. (ed.) (1974) *Milton Friedman's Monetary Framework: A Debate with his Critics*, Chicago: University of Chicago Press.

Gorman, T. and Lewis, R. (1983) *Worried To Death*, London: Centre for Policy Studies.

Gough, T.J. and Taylor, T.W. (1979) *The Building Society Price Cartel*, Hobart Paper 83, London: IEA.

Gray, H. (1968) *The Cost of Council Housing*, London: IEA.

Gray, J. (1983) *Mill on Liberty: A Defence*, London: Routledge and Kegan Paul.

Gray, J. (1984) *Hayek on Liberty*, Oxford: Blackwell.

Green, D.G. (1984) 'How to save the nation's health: the libertarian left view', *Economic Affairs*, vol. 4, no. 3, pp. 51–5.

Green, D.G. (1985a) 'American health care: the re-awakening of competition', *Economic Affairs*, vol. 6, no. 2, pp. 22–3.

Green, D.G. (1985b) *Working-Class Patients and the Medical Establishment*, Aldershot: Gower/Temple Smith.

Green, D.G. (1985c) *Which Doctor?*, London: IEA.

Green, D.G. (1986a) 'Awakening Market Suppressed by NHS', *Economic Affairs*, vol. 6, no. 3, pp. 28–9.

Green, D.G. (1986b) *Challenge to the NHS: A Study of Competition in American Health Care and the Lessons For Britain*, London: IEA.

Green, D.G. and Cromwell, L. (1984) *Mutual Aid or Welfare State*, Sydney: Allen & Unwin.

Hall, S. (1985) 'Realignment—for what?', *Marxism Today*, December, pp. 12–17.

Harris, R. (ed.) (1965) *Freedom or Free-For-All?*, London: IEA.

Harris, R. and Seldon, A. (1971) *Choice in Welfare 1970*, London: IEA.

Harris, R. and Seldon, A. (1977) *Not From Benevolence...*, London: IEA.

Harris, R. and Seldon, A. (1979) *Over-Ruled on Welfare*, London: IEA.

Hartley, K. and Huby, M. (1985) 'Contracting-out in Health and Local Authorities: Prospects, Progress and Pitfalls', *Public Money*, September, pp. 23–26.

Hartwell, R.M. *et al.* (1974) *The Long Debate on Poverty*, 2nd edn, London: IEA.

Hayek, F.A. (1931) *Prices and Production*, London: Routledge.

Hayek, F.A. (1949) *Individualism and Economic Order*, London: Routledge and Kegan Paul.

Hayek, F.A. (1952) *The Sensory Order*, London: Routledge and Kegan Paul.

Hayek, F.A. (ed.) (1954) *Capitalism and the Historians*, Chicago: University of Chicago Press.

Hayek, F.A. (1960) *The Constitution of Liberty*, London: Routledge and Kegan Paul.

Hayek, F.A. (1967) *Studies in Philosophy, Politics & Economics*, London: Routledge and Kegan Paul.

Hayek, F.A. (1968) *The Confusion of Language in Political Thought*, Occasional Paper 20, London: IEA.

Hayek, F.A. (1973) *Law, Legislation & Liberty*, vol. 1, *Rules and Order*.

Hayek, F.A. *et al.* (1975a) *Rent Control: A Popular Paradox*, Vancouver: The Fraser Institute.

Hayek, F.A. (1975b) *Full Employment at Any Price?*, Occasional Paper 45, London: IEA.

Hayek, F.A. (1976a) *The Road to Serfdom*, London: Routledge and Kegan Paul.

Hayek, F.A. (1976b) *Law, Legislation & Liberty*, vol. 2, *The Mirage of Social Justice*.

Hayek, F.A. (1978a) *Denationalisation of Money—The Argument Refined*, Hobart Paper 70, 2nd edn, London: IEA.

Hayek, F.A. (1978b) *New Studies in Philosophy, Politics, Economics & the History of Ideas*, London: Routledge and Kegan Paul.

Hayek, F.A. (1979a) *Law, Legislation & Liberty*, vol. 3, *The Political Order of a Free People*, London: Routledge and Kegan Paul.

Hayek, F.A. (1979b) *The Counter-Revolution of Science*, 2nd edn, Indianapolis: Liberty Press.

Hayek, F.A. (1984) *1980s Unemployment & the Unions*, Hobart Paper 87, 2nd edn, London: IEA.

Hayek, F.A. (forthcoming) *The Fatal Conceit*.

Heald, D. (1983) *Public Expenditure*, Oxford: Martin Robertson.

Hibbs, J. (1982) *Transport Without Politics*, Hobart Paper 95, London: IEA.

Hill, C. (1978) *The Century of Revolution 1603–1714*, London: Abacus.

Hobhouse, L.T. (1964) *Liberalism*, London: Oxford University Press.

Horowitz, I.L. and Lipset, S.M. (1978) *Dialogues on American Politics*, New York: Oxford University Press.

Hoskins, W.G. (1965) *The Midland Peasant*, London: Macmillan.

Hospers, J. (1967) *An Introduction to Philosophical Analysis*, 2nd edn, London: Routledge.

Hospers, J. (1971) *Libertarianism: A Political Philosophy for Tomorrow*, Los Angeles: Nash Publishing.

Howarth, R.W. (1985) *Farming For Farmers?*, London: IEA.

Hume, D. (1911) *A Treatise of Human Nature* (2 vols), Everyman edn, London: Dent.

Hume, D. (1906) *Essays, Literary, Moral & Political* (1906 reprint), London: Ward, Lock & Tyler.

Illich, I. (1973) *Deschooling Society*, Harmondsworth: Penguin Books.

Interstudy (1985) *HMO Summary, June 1985*, Excelsior, Minnesota: Interstudy.

Kaldor, N. (1982) *The Scourge of Monetarism*, London: Oxford University Press.

Kaldor, N. (1983) *The Economic Consequences of Mrs Thatcher*, Fabian Tract 486, London: Fabian Society.

Kant, I. (1787) *The Critique of Pure Reason*, 2nd edn, trans. Norman Kemp Smith, London: Macmillan.

Keynes, J.M. (1936) *The General Theory of Employment, Interest and Money*, London: Macmillan.

Kirzner, I. *et al.* (1980) *Prime Mover of Progress*, IEA Readings 23, London: IEA.

Kristol, I. (1978) *Two Cheers For Capitalism*, New York: Basic Books.

Kristol, I. (1983) *Reflections of a Neo-Conservative*, New York: Basic Books.

Jacoby, N.H. and Pennance, F.G. (1972) *The Polluters: Industry or Government?*, London: IEA.

Lachmann, L.M. (1973) *Macro-Economic Thinking and the Market Economy*, Hobart Paper 56, London: IEA.

Laslett, P. (1965) *The World We Have Lost*, London: Methuen.

Lees, D.S. (1965) 'Health Through Choice', in Harris, R. (ed) (1965), pp. 21–94.

Le Grand, J. and Robinson, R. (1976) *The Economics of Social Problems*, 1st edn, London: Macmillan.

Le Grand, J. and Robinson, R. (1984a) *The Economics of Social Problems*, 2nd edn, London: Macmillan.

Le Grand, J. and Robinson, R. (eds) (1984b) *Privatisation and the Welfare State*, London: Allen & Unwin.

Levinson, E. (1976) *The Alum Rock Voucher Demonstration: Three Years of Implementation*, Santa Monica, Calif.: Rand Corporation, P.5631.

Lewis, A., Sandford C., and Thomson, N. (1980) *Grants or Loans?*, IEA Research Monograph 34, London: IEA.

Lipsey, R.G. (1983) *An Introduction to Positive Economics*, 6th edn, London: Weidenfeld & Nicolson.

Lipsey, D. and Leonard, D. (1981) *The Socialist Agenda: Crosland's Legacy*, London: Cape.

Littlechild, S.C. *et al.* (1979) *The Taming of Government*, London: IEA.

Locke, J. (1924) *An Essay Concerning Human Understanding*, ed. A.S. Pringle-Pattison, Oxford: OUP.

Locke, J. (1963) *Two Treatises of Government*, New York: New American Library (Mentor).

Locksley, G. (1981) 'Individuals, Contracts and Constitutions: the political economy of James M. Buchanan', in Shackleton and Locksley, 1981, pp. 33–52.

228 *References*

Lucas, J.R. (1980) *On Justice*, Oxford: Clarendon Press.
Lukes, S. (1973) *Individualism*, Oxford: Blackwell.
Macaulay, T.B. (1967) *History of England* (4 vols), London: Heron Books.
Machan, T. (ed.) (1974) *The Libertarian Alternative*, Chicago: Nelson-Hall.
Machan, T. (ed.) (1982) *The Libertarian Reader*, Totowa, New Jersey: Rowan and Littlefield.
Macpherson, C.B. (1973) *Democratic Theory: Essays in Retrieval*, London: Oxford University Press.
Maynard, A. (1975) *Experiment with Choice in Education*, Hobart Paper 64, London: IEA.
McIlwain, C.H. (ed.) (1918) *The Political Works of James I*, Cambridge, Mass: Harvard University Press.
McKie, R. (1971) *Housing and the Whitehall Bulldozer*, London: IEA.
Meade, J.E. (1985) *Wage-Fixing Revisited*, Occasional Paper 72, London: IEA.
Menger, C. (1950) *Principles of Economics*, New York: Free Press.
Mill, J.S. (1972) *On Liberty* (with *Utilitarianism & On Representative Government*), Everyman edn, London: Dent.
Minford, P. (1983) *Unemployment: Cause and Cure*, Oxford: Martin Robertson.
Minford, P. (1984) 'State expenditure: a study in waste', *Economic Affairs*, supplement, vol. 4, no. 3, pp. i–xix.
Minford, P. *et al.* (1980) *Is Monetarism Enough?*, IEA Readings No. 24, London: IEA.
Minister without Portfolio (1985) *Lifting the Burden*, Cmnd. 9571, London: HMSO.
Mises, L. von (1981) *Socialism*, Indianapolis: Liberty Classics.
Mueller, D.C. (1979) *Public Choice*, London: Cambridge University Press.
Neale, J.E. (1953) *Elizabeth I and Her Parliaments 1559–81*, London: Jonathan Cape.
Niskanen, W.A. (1971) *Bureaucracy and Representative Government*, New York: Aldine Atherton.
Niskanen, W.A. (1973) *Bureaucracy: Servant or Master?*, London: IEA.
Niskanen, W.A. (1975) 'Bureaucrats and Politicians', *Journal of Law and Economics*, vol. XVIII(3), pp. 617–43.
Niskanen, W.A. (1978) 'Competition among Government Bureaus', in Buchanan, *et al.* (1978).

Nozick, R. (1974) *Anarchy, State and Utopia*, London: Blackwell.
Nozick, R. (1982) 'On the Randian Argument', in Paul J. (1982), pp. 206–31.
Olson, M. (1971) *The Logic of Collective Action* (reprinted with additional appendix), Cambridge: Harvard University Press.
Olson, M. (1982) *The Rise and Decline of Nations*, New Haven & London: Yale University Press.
Parker, H. (1982) *The Moral Hazard of Social Benefits*, London: IEA.
Parker, H. (1984) *Action on Welfare*, London: Social Affairs Unit.
Paul, J. (ed.) (1982) *Reading Nozick*, Oxford: Blackwell.
Peacock, A. (1985) ' "Macro-economic" Controls of Spending as a Device for Improving Efficiency in Government', in Forte and Peacock (eds), pp. 143–56.
Peacock, A. and Wiseman, J. (1964) *Education For Democrats*, Hobart Paper 25, London: IEA.
Pennance, F.G. and Gray, H. (1968) *Choice in Housing*, London: IEA.
Pennance, F.G. and West, W.A. (1969) *Housing Market Analysis and Policy*, Hobart Paper 48, London: IEA.
Peston, M. (1984) 'Privatisation of Education', in Le · Grand and Robinson (1984b), pp. 146–59.
Pigou, A.C. (1929) *The Economics of Welfare*, 3rd edn, London: Macmillan.
Pirie, M. (1985) *Privatisation in Theory and Practice*. London: Adam Smith Institute.
Plant, R. 'Democratic Socialism and Equality', in Lipsey and Leonard (eds) (1981), pp. 135–55.
Plant, R. (1984) *Equality, Markets and the State*, Fabian Tract 494, London: Fabian Society.
Popper, K. (1966) *The Open Society and Its Enemies*, 5th edn (2 vols), London: Routledge and Kegan Paul.
Popper, K. (1972) *Conjectures and Refutations*, 4th edn, London: Routledge and Kegan Paul.
Popper, K. (1975) *Objective Knowledge* (reprinted with corrections), Oxford: Clarendon Press.
Posner, R. (1973) *Economic Analysis of Law*, Boston: Little, Brown and Co.
Posner, R. (1981) *The Economics of Justice*, Cambridge, Mass: Harvard University Press.
Prest, A.R. (1966) *Financing University Education*, Occasional Paper 12, London: IEA.
Rand, A. (1961) *For the New Intellectual*, New York: Signet.

Rand, A. (1964) *The Virtue of Selfishness*, New York: Signet.

Rand Corporation (1981) *A Study of Alternatives in American Education*, vols I–VII, esp. vol. VII, *Conclusions and Policy Implications*, Santa Monica, Calif.: Rand Corporation R–2170/7–NIE.

Rawls, J. (1973) *A Theory of Justice*, London: Oxford University Press.

Ray, J. (1984) 'Governments do compete for citizens—in Australia', *Economic Affairs*. vol. 5, no. 1, p. 60.

Reekie, W. Duncan (1984) *Markets, Entrepreneurs and Liberty*, Brighton: Wheatsheaf.

Reimer, E. (1971) *School is Dead*, Harmondsworth: Penguin Books.

Riddell, P. (1985) *The Thatcher Government*, Oxford: Blackwell.

Riker, W. (1962) *The Theory of Political Coalitions*, New Haven & London: Yale University Press.

Robbins, L. *et al.* (1974) *Inflation: Causes, Consequences, Cures*, IEA Readings 14, London: IEA.

Roth, G. (1966) *A Self-Financing Road System*, Research Monograph 3, London: IEA.

Roth, G. and Shephard, A. (1984) *Wheels Within Cities*, London: Adam Smith Institute.

Rothbard, M. (1977) *Power and Market*, 2nd edn, Kansas: Sheed Andrews & McMeel.

Rothbard, M. (1978) *For a New Liberty: The Libertarian Manifesto*, 2nd edn, London & New York: Collier-Macmillan.

Rowley, C.K. (1983) 'The post-war Failure of British Government: a public choice perspective', in Seldon (ed.) (1983).

Ruggiero, G. de (1927) *The History of European Liberalism*, London: Oxford University Press.

Russell, B. (1979) *History of Western Philosophy*, London: Allen & Unwin/Book Club Associates.

Sampson, G. (1984) *An End to Allegiance*, London: Temple Smith.

Scruton, R. (1984) *The Meaning of Conservatism*, 2nd edn, London: Macmillan.

Seldon, A. (1968) *After the NHS*, Occasional Paper 21, London: IEA.

Seldon, A. (1977) *Charge*, London: Temple Smith.

Seldon, A. (1981) *The Emerging Consensus?*, London: IEA.

Seldon, A. (ed.) (1983) *Agenda For Social Democracy*, London: IEA.

Seldon, A. (ed.) (1985) *The 'New Right' Enlightenment*, Sevenoaks: E & L Books.

Seldon, A. (1986) *The Riddle of the Voucher*, London: IEA.
Shackleton, J.R. (1981) 'Gary S. Becker: the economist as empire-builder', Shackleton and Locksley (1981), pp. 12–32.
Shackleton, J.R. and Locksley, G. (eds) (1981) *Twelve Contemporary Economists*, London: Macmillan.
Shand, A. (1984) *The Capitalist Alternative*, Brighton: Wheatsheaf.
Shenfield, A. (1986) *What Right to Strike?*, London: IEA.
Smith, A. (1776) *The Wealth of Nations*, Everyman edn, London: Dent, 1977.
Smith, A. (1976) *The Theory of Moral Sentiments*, Indianapolis: Liberty Classics.
Sowell, T. (1980) *Knowledge and Decisions*, New York: Basic Books.
Sowell, T. (1981) *Markets & Minorities*, New York: Basic Books.
Steel, D. and Heald, D. (eds) (1984) *Privatising Public Enterprises: Options and Dilemmas*, London: Royal Institute of Public Administration.
Stigler, G. (1949) *Five Lectures on Economic Problems*, London: Longmans.
Stigler, G. (1963) *Capital and the Rate of Return in Manufacturing Industries*, Princeton: Princeton University Press.
Stigler, G. (1975) *The Citizen and the State: Essays on Regulation*, Chicago: University of Chicago Press.
Stigler, G. (1982) *The Pleasures and Pains of Modern Capitalism*, Occasional Paper 64, London: IEA.
Taylor, T. (1980) *The Fundamentals of Austrian Economics*, London: Adam Smith Institute.
Taylor-Gooby, P. (1985) *Public Opinion, Ideology and State Welfare*, London: Routledge and Kegan Paul.
Thompson, E.P. (1977) *Whigs and Hunters*, Harmondsworth: Penguin.
Toye, J.F.J. (1976) 'Economic theories of politics and public finance', *British Journal of Political Science*, vol. 6, part 4, pp. 433–47.
Tuccille, J. (1971) *Radical Libertarianism: A New Political Alternative*, 2nd edn, New York: Harper & Row.
Tullock, G. (1970) *Private Wants, Public Means*, New York: Basic Books.
Tullock, G. (1976) *The Vote Motive*, London: IEA.
Tullock, G. (1979) 'Bureaucracy and the Growth of Government', in Littlechild, *et al.* (1979).

US Government (1984) *A Competitive Assessment of the US Pharmaceutical Industry*, Washington: US Department of Commerce.

Walker, M.A. (1975) 'Decontrol', in Hayek *et al.* (1975).

Webb, S. (1890) *Socialism in England*, London: Swan Sonnenschein.

West, E.G. (1970) *Education and the State*, 2nd edn, London: IEA.

West, E.G. (1975) *Education and the Industrial Revolution*, London: Batsford.

Index